IN LIGHT OF AFRICA

Globalizing Blackness in Northeast Brazil

In Light of Africa explores how the idea of Africa as a real place, an imagined homeland, and a metaphor for Black identity is used in the cultural politics of the Brazilian state of Bahia. In the book, Allan Charles Dawson argues that Africa, as both a symbol and a geographical and historical place, is vital to understanding the wide range of identities and forms of racial consciousness that exist in Bahia's Afro-Brazilian communities.

Dawson's ethnographic journey extends from the city of Salvador to the West African coast and back to the hinterlands of the Bahian interior. Along the way, Dawson encounters West African entrepreneurs, Afrobeat musicians, devotees of the Afro-Brazilian religion *Candomblé*, professors of the Yoruba language, and hardscrabble farmers and ranchers, each of whom engages with the idea of Africa in their own personal way.

(Anthropological Horizons)

ALLAN CHARLES DAWSON in an assistant professor in the Department of Anthropology at Drew University.

Anthropological Horizons

Editor: Michael Lambek, University of Toronto

This series, begun in 1991, focuses on theoretically informed ethnographic works addressing issues of mind and body, knowledge and power, equality and inequality, the individual and the collective. Interdisciplinary in its perspective, the series makes a unique contribution in several other academic disciplines: women's studies, history, philosophy, psychology, political science, and sociology.

For a list of the books published in this series, see page 192.

ALLAN CHARLES DAWSON

In Light of Africa

Globalizing Blackness in Northeast Brazil

UNIVERSITY OF TORONTO PRESS
Toronto Buffalo London

© University of Toronto Press 2014
Toronto Buffalo London
www.utppublishing.com
Printed in the U.S.A.

ISBN 978-1-4426-4931-6 (cloth)
ISBN 978-1-4426-2669-0 (paper)

Printed on acid-free, 100% post-consumer recycled paper with vegetable-based inks.

Library and Archives Canada Cataloguing in Publication

Dawson, Allan Charles, 1973–, author
In light of Africa : globalizing blackness in northeast Brazil / Allan Charles
Dawson.

(Anthropological horizons).
Includes bibliographical references and index.
ISBN 978-1-4426-4931-6 (bound). – ISBN 978-1-4426-2669-0 (pbk.)

1. Blacks – Brazil – Bahia (State) – Ethnic identity.   2. Blacks – Race identity-
-Brazil – Bahia (State).   3. Blacks – Brazil – Bahia (State) – Social conditions.   I. Title.   II. Series: Anthropological horizons

F2551.D39 2014   981'.5100496   C2014-903669-8

University of Toronto Press acknowledges the financial assistance to its
publishing program of the Canada Council for the Arts and the Ontario
Arts Council, an agency of the Government of Ontario.

 Canada Council **Conseil des Arts**
for the Arts **du Canada**

ONTARIO ARTS COUNCIL
CONSEIL DES ARTS DE L'ONTARIO
an Ontario government agency
un organisme du gouvernement de l'Ontario

University of Toronto Press acknowledges the financial support of the
Government of Canada through the Canada Book Fund for its publishing
activities.

For the communities in Brazil and West Africa where I worked and lived, and for Amie.

Contents

Figures and Table

Figures

Table

IN LIGHT OF AFRICA

Globalizing Blackness in Northeast Brazil

Chapter One

Blackness and Africanity in Brazil and Elsewhere

What is Africa to me?
Copper sun or scarlet sea
Jungle star or jungle track
Strong Black men or regal Black
Women from whose loins I sprang
When the birds of Eden sang?
One three centuries removed
From the scenes his father told
Spring grove, cinnamon tree
What is Africa to me?   Countee Cullen, "Heritage" (1925, 36)

In this stirring verse, Countee Cullen, one of the luminaries of the Harlem Renaissance, evokes the image of a wild, sensuous and verdant Africa, a place of fertility and life where the African American could perhaps find succour. In almost all of his work about race and colour, Cullen seeks to remind that, ultimately, all descendants of enslaved Africans are forever strangers in the New World, exiles from Africa, both geographically and spiritually. For Cullen, Africa was a place where Black men and women were kings and queens – proud and free. More importantly, Cullen provided African Americans – long considered a people without history – with the powerful image of a beautiful past in a mythical, "remembered" Africa. Cullen had no first-hand knowledge of Africa (Davis 1953, 390) and perhaps it was not required to express the connection with this "homeland." But if he, as part of the cosmopolitan Harlem literati in the 1920s, had no first-hand knowledge of Africa as a place, how much less do the populations of the Recôncavo, the rural interior of Bahia, or the urban neighbourhoods of Salvador, Bahia's bustling state capital, know of Africa as an actual place?

However, many individuals in Salvador and other towns throughout Bahia can quickly respond with words such as "Yoruba," "Nigeria," "Angola," "*Orixá*," "Biko," "Mandela," or "Selassie" when asked what they know about Africa. Moreover, there is the sense that for some, these words carry important meanings for those who are Black. Why? For many it is because these places and names and the societies they denote are important parts of their religious practice. For others it is because they are actively involved in political movements that seek equality and opportunity for the Black people of Brazil, especially in the less industrialized and underdeveloped Northeast. Finally, for many it is because the "Africanness" of Afro-Brazilian culture and of Brazilian culture in general is now so ubiquitous, processed, sold, commodified, and represented in so many different ways – from soap-operas or *telenovelas* to beer advertising, from popular musical artists such as Caetano Veloso and Gilberto Gil to the ultimate stereotyped expression of Brazilian life, *carnaval* – that "Africanismo," if you will, has become as Brazilian as *bossa nova* and football. One such contemporary interlocutor of Africa and Africanity in Bahia – though, as we shall encounter here, there are many others – is Georgia.

Georgia is in his late thirties and was born in the Ghanaian port city of Cape Coast, capital of the country's Central Region, and the traditional centre of the Fante people. Cape Coast is a UNESCO World Heritage Site as it is home to both Cape Coast Castle and Elmina Castle – two important points of embarkation for the transatlantic slave trade. In his youth, Georgia left Cape Coast for the Ghanaian port of Tema, just outside of Accra, where he signed on as a deckhand on one of the many transoceanic container vessels that regularly ply the sea-lanes between the Atlantic ports of West Africa and Asia. For almost five years he worked these ships, learning German, French, and a smattering of other West African languages, and working a variety of on-board trades including kitchen boy, cook, crane operator, captain's valet, and mechanic. After five years, with no real port to call home, Georgia found himself washed ashore in the Nigerian metropolis of Lagos where he lived for another three years, learning Yoruba, taking a Yoruba name, and gaining familiarity with Yoruba traditional religion.

Georgia is a raconteur whose facility for language and canny nose for opportunity has led him to many an open port and forms of employment. His current home is now the city of Salvador, Bahia. Georgia

Figure 1.1 Georgia or "DJ Sankofa" as he is known in Salvador. Photo courtesy of Kweku Aidoo.

works as an Afrobeat musician and DJ at Sankofa bar in Pelourinho, and frequently as a tour guide for those individuals interested in exploring the African and slave history of the state of Bahia. As part of his repertoire of tours, he occasionally provides tours of the slave fort in Salvador's harbour – a twist of fate not lost on Georgia. He tells his clients, many of whom have already visited Ghana prior to their tour of Brazil:

> I come from Cape Coast, you know. So, it's right that I give you this tour, you know. Slaves left for Brazil from my hometown and we have two forts like this back home. In the past I could have been one of those slaves! Oh, so now, instead of showing you the fort in Ghana, I show you the fort in Brazil! Ironical, no?[1]

Another important component of Georgia's tours is a visit to so-called authentic houses of Afro-Brazilian religious practice or *Candomblé*.

Here, travellers witness the religious forms which have made Bahia famous – both in the literature of Brazilian authors such as Jorge Amado and in the anthropology of scholars such as Melville Herskovits, Ruth Landes, J. Lorand Matory, and others. Invariably, conversation between tourists and Georgia turns to his opinions about Afro-Brazilian culture: "Do they get it right? Is this really similar to what you saw growing up in *Africa*? Georgia, you speak Yoruba, can you understand the Yoruba phrases used in the rituals?" Just as invariably, Georgia responds, "Yes! This is just like what I would see when I lived in Lagos. In fact, I think the rituals here are more accurate because Brazil wasn't colonized by the British who tried to stamp out these kind of witchcraft practices!"

He is a consummate master of his craft. He has a quick wit and charm to spare and is able to spin a wonderfully convincing web of legitimacy around stories about his "African" homeland. To be sure, sometimes his tales get a little tall, especially when he tries to go for a little bit of added colour by highlighting the place of "sacrifice" in "African" societies. Ultimately however, the clients of this transnational *griot* are almost always convinced by his performance and are ever eager to hear more about the "true" Africa. Why should they not be? Georgia's story is compelling and one which rings true; indeed, it seems much like a contemporary concatenation of the ongoing back and forth, flux and reflux, the call-and-response dialogue across the Atlantic that Africans and residents of the Americas have participated in for centuries, always making, remaking, and integrating narratives of homeland, diaspora, the sacred, the seemingly exotic, and the banal into the quotidian culture of their new home. When I first encountered Georgia, he was extremely pleased to know someone who had spent time in Ghana. The vast majority of Africans living in Salvador are from Nigeria. Georgia knows most of the Nigerians in town and often works with them, but seemed extremely happy to talk about a place other than Lagos. I know most of Georgia's boyhood haunts and we talked through the night about Ghana on the evening of our introduction and on many nights after. After taking some time to get to know Georgia better, I asked him if I might accompany him on one of his tours to a house of *Candomblé* worship, a *terreiro*, in his home neighbourhood. He was very reluctant at first, informing me that "this was his business, and we wouldn't have time for me." I explained that I would not say a word during the tour and would be there solely to unobtrusively observe, listen, and help out if needed. Now, I had seen Georgia working a number of times prior to accompanying him on a tour. During the weeks since our introduction I had gotten to know the group of young Nigerian men, primarily Yoruba from Lagos but also some Igbo from the Niger Delta area, with whom he associated and worked. Whenever we met for evening drinks or to talk, there was usually a large number of Brazilians present who were members of a *terreiro* or who were enrolled in Yoruba classes at the local university. These were individuals eager to learn about Africa and all things African, and Georgia was often at the centre of this group, weaving tales of African chiefs, leopard hunts, tribal warfare, and rites of initiation.

After the tour Georgia told me he was glad that I came along, but equally glad that I didn't contradict him in any way. Georgia was quite familiar with what anthropologists do and it appears as though he was reticent at first to include a member of that peculiar tribe in his work. At one point in our discussions he even remarked to me that he had read some of "Rattray"[2] in school in Cape Coast. Georgia:

> The reason is that many people don't want to hear about the traffic problems in Lagos or Accra, or the problems with the politicians in Nigeria. My best contacts are with the Brazilians. Yes, I work with the American tourists, but I keep those Brazilians who want to know Africa close because through them I can get work playing "African" music at carnaval; I can have a market for selling African arts and crafts that I help import from Lagos. Listen my friend, Afro-Brazilians want to know more about Africa than African Americans and for many of them Africa means Yoruba – and it's like many want to be African![3]

Georgia is a cultural entrepreneur through and through. He is actively engaged in helping to define what counts as "African" in the urban context of contemporary Salvador, Bahia, a city steeped in layers of African heritage and with a population whose vast majority is descended – to some extent or another – from enslaved Africans. Race and ethnic identity in Salvador and in much of Bahia is about Blackness, about how the place of Africa and the past of slavery help to construct exactly what "Black" means. His stories, and the others presented in this ethnographic account, are ultimately intended to help us better understand how "Africa," as both a discursive concept and as a real place, is used by Brazilians in Bahia in mobilizing various forms of Blackness and ethnic identity.

Blackness in Bahia

In Salvador and, more broadly, in the state of Bahia, what it means to be Black is continuously being redefined. For much of Brazil's history Blackness meant, for many, little more than a skin colour. To be sure, this phenotypic category typically meant a life of poverty, menial work, and exclusion from decision-making and political office, but it was not a category that necessarily implied a different cultural or symbolic universe from the rest of Brazilian society – simply a more impoverished and disadvantaged perspective on that universe. However, in the predominantly Afro-Brazilian cultural milieu of contemporary Bahia, Blackness has now come to be frequently equated with an array of beliefs and ideas, many of which are distinct from what might be called mainstream "Brazilian" culture. For members of the Afro-Brazilian religious congregations, Blackness, they assert, must come to mean more than just an awareness of African descent. For these groups it implies the practice of what they believe are "African" religious rituals, "African" values, and the learning of an African language – in other words, the Africanization of their Black identity. Concomitantly, this form of Blackness also encourages, for some, the rejection of Christianity and European ideas, such as syncretism and belief in Catholic saints. This approach to Blackness is one that has become dominant in popular depictions of Salvador and of Bahia, but it is not one that is articulated by all Brazilians. The Africanization of Black identity is highly contested and differing points of view on how and indeed whether Africa should be incorporated into definitions of Afro-Brazilian Blackness abound. The present work is concerned with precisely this diversity of voices. It seeks to explore the ways in which Brazilians of African descent in the northeastern state of Bahia employ the concept of a "remembered" Africa as a homeland and source of identity, how Africa symbolizes the past, present, and future for many Afro-Brazilians, and how entrepreneurs of identity – anthropologists included – have used and continue to use the "African" past of Black communities in Brazil and elsewhere in the Americas as the symbolic mainstay of Black identity.

So, like Cullen, I begin then with a question. How do contemporary intersections, engagements, and exchanges between Africa and Brazil continue to influence the extent to which elements of real and imagined African cultures are included in constructions of Blackness in Bahia? Well, to begin, these interactions take the form not only of nebulous exchanges of popular culture, but of direct person-to-person interchange between Africans and Black Brazilians both in Bahia and in the African "homeland." Ethnographically speaking then, this work will trace the patterns of dialogue between Africa and Northeast Brazil in a variety of contexts. These include the practice of cultural tourism or pilgrimages to West Africa conducted by the devotees of Afro-Brazilian religious centres; the discourse of cultural, religious, and intellectual elites in the Africanizing of Brazilian Blackness; the lives of West African cultural brokers who now work and reside in the city of Salvador and who are actively engaged in negotiating ideas of Africa for a Brazilian audience; and the attitudes and beliefs of people who are not part of the process of Africanization, such as devout Black Catholics, evangelicals, and residents of the impoverished interior country of Bahia.

Further, the present work seeks to scrutinize the construction of Black identity in both urban and rural contexts within the state of Bahia – and more generally in Brazil – and shifts away from attempts to recreate and verify the "authentic pasts" of enslaved Africans and focuses instead on the rhetorical and ideological labour that discourses on Africa and both African and slave origins are made to perform in the domain of Brazilian ethnic identity and Black identity in Brazil. This largest of South American nations and home to the largest community of people descended from enslaved Africans is, it would seem, at an important point in the history of race relations in the African diaspora. To be sure, Brazil is still a country where racism towards those perceived to have African or indigenous heritage is palpable. It can be felt, as it is felt throughout the Americas, in city neighbourhoods, in the rural agricultural regions, in business, religion, indeed in every aspect of daily life. As R.L. Segato (1998) writes, "there is no way to speak of the participation of Africa wherever it has flourished after slavery without contemplating the variety of cognitive operations of discrimination and exclusion we blend under the common term racism" (130). However, Brazil has made important strides in this area. From the appointment of the first Afro-Brazilian president of the Brazilian Supreme Court in 2012, to changes in the constitution that afford the descendants of maroon communities a title, to their land to the celebration of Afro-Brazilian culture in many domains of Brazilian society, the country has made huge strides in this area. Despite enormous challenges ahead, Brazil is starting to come to terms with a history of slavery and racism in a way that seeks to celebrate Blackness and Africanity. Indeed, Luiza Bairros has called Afro-Brazilian society "a community of destiny" (2008, 50), celebrating both the advances that Brazil has made in race

relations and emphasizing the challenges that the country's Black community still faces. However, she asserts that this "destiny" can only be
achieved through a concerted and unified effort on the part of all members of the Black community to come together to continue to fight racism and, once and for all, "collapse the myth of racial democracy"
(Bairros 2008, 51). But, herein lies the dilemma. If, indeed, race relations in Brazil are at a crucially important nexus, how then to proceed?
For example, similar attempts to homogenize and "totalize" (Hanchard
1993) the experiences of Black communities have been tried elsewhere,
including Garvey's Pan-African Nationalism (Bair 1994) or the Black
Power movements in the United States in the 1960s. However, these
programs, while being forced to combat institutionalized and endemic
racism, also had to deal with the problem of unifying an array of voices
and ideals within the Black community. Such movements often have to
presume that Black people are the same in their world view and in their
experience of oppression not just in one country but also across the diaspora. This, according to Hanchard (1993, 91), is the paradox of totalizing discourses within the Afro-American experience – a unifying
message, though vital for social mobilization is politically and, I might
add, culturally inoperable. Ultimately, though, I demonstrate here that
a coherence and unity of message is as illusory in Brazil as in the United
States, for the Brazilian Afro-diaspora community here is one that con-
founds the notion of a unitary history with a single point of origin as
much as it does in the U.S.

Now, anthropology has helped to demonstrate convincingly that
race and ethnic identity are categories best understood as the situational construction of self in relation to other individuals, other collectives,
and the broader society as a whole. As Barth (1969) demonstrated so
insightfully, identity is never just a boolean or binary choice – accept an
identity of oppressed, "muzzled" mute or accept an identity of proud
son or daughter of Africa. All individuals, all communities, all societies
employ and negotiate multiple identities – ethnic, racial, and otherwise
– in daily interactions with other individuals and other collectives. For
many Black communities in Bahia, Africanized notions of Blackness
have relevance, but they are not always the most important identity or
the only identity in their cultural repertoire. As such, one constantly
defines and redefines his or her identity based on context, history, environment, interaction, and circumstance. Although the process of ethnic
identity construction often entails considerable external ascription and

definition, groups that are on the margins of society, historically oppressed groups, , enslaved groups, –and those without power or control over their lives do not always have to accept the label or category that the broader society imposes upon them. They can and do forge their own sense of self and identity. Through the process of identity creation, individuals and collectivities imagine and create themselves. Collective identity emerges at both the psychological and social levels out of the efforts of individuals to organize their senses of self, based on perceived commonalities with each other and difference from "others." Consequently, identity must be fluid and dynamic: evolving, disappearing, changing, and reforming in response to changing social contexts.

Throughout the present work I emphasize Blackness as a generative ethnic category and a form of racial consciousness and not as a social boundary defined by phenotypic characteristics. Consequently, "Black" and "Blackness" are presented in a capitalized form to distinguish them from mere descriptions of skin colour. "Black" identity represents an idea of collectivity and group membership that goes beyond forms of racial classification and shared ancestry implied in the use of "black" to describe the pigmentation of an individual's skin. Black ethnic identity means different things to different people. Indeed, much of this work deals with the contestation of what should count as Black identity – what Barth (1969) refers to as the "cultural stuff" within an ethnic boundary (15). For members of communities that reckon and present themselves as Black in Brazil, this term means more than just a skin colour or a "Black culture," per se, that is defined by notions of class, racism, and colonial history. In Brazil, Black as an ethnic category increasingly means an array of cultural practices, religious beliefs, and contested ideas about the importance of Africa in the construction of Black identity. Blackness and the multiplex tactical options available for expressing it must also be seen as a form of racial consciousness that is rooted in how different communities in the diaspora understand, evaluate, and respond to the asymmetries of racism. Race in Brazil, as it is everywhere, is about power and a conscious recognition of these disparities between socially defined ethnic groups. Racial consciousness, then, is an awareness of the structural, political, and economic processes that, as Hanchard puts it, "correlate and distribute meanings and practices of racial difference" (1993, 86). Furthermore, in any exploration of the multiple strategies employed by a community that has lived under the hegemony of another class, race, or ethnic group and is now engaged in both a practical and ideological debate on how to counter such oppression one must inevitably, as Hanchard (1993) exhorts, turn to the work of Gramsci.

Bahia continues to be thought of by Brazilians and travellers alike as the most "African" part of Brazil and there is good reason for this. Not, though, for the reasons explored by Landes (1947), Carneiro (1948), Reis (2003), and others – though they all make compelling arguments for why Bahia is steeped in African heritage. Rather, in the twenty-first century, as Bairros' community of destiny employs African symbols, exalts an oft-unheralded African past, and rightly lionizes heroes of resistance from Zumbí to Abdias do Nascimento, a once marginalized African past – both real and imagined – has taken centre stage as a symbolic mainstay of modern Black resistance in Bahia. Indeed, the different ways in which Africa is used – discursively, ideologically, and practically, both by Brazilians and Africans like Georgia and others, in Brazil – is at the heart of this ethnographic project. Additonally, those engaged in negotiating the idea of Africa in Bahia must contemplate the key theoretical question posed by Gramsci (1971): How do revolutionary and emancipatory movements find space – ritual, political, identarian – for differences in ideology, in expressions of resistance, and for divergent symbolic repertoires that express counterhegemonic thought when victory in such a struggle is often premised upon a unified and unfragmented voice?

Blackness in Bahia has become – perhaps has always been – a cultural and social trope that includes, for those with whom the concept resonates, aspects of ancestry, religious practice, economic condition, and community. This work seeks to place these ideas of Blackness, ethnic identity, and racial consciousness – as manufactured through interaction with Africans and ideas of Africa – within a frame where the multiple faces and voices of Blackness are considered in dynamic tension with the dominant tropes and manifestations of this identity that emanate from the key interlocutors and stakeholders of the Black and anti-racism movements in Bahia. Moreover, I endeavour to show that even in settings where historically marginalized communities – be they religious, ethnic, racial, gendered, or sexual – gravitate towards identities and forms of consciousness that represent a tactic of complete opposition and reversal of all forms of oppression, there still remains a heterogeneity of voices and limitations on the degree of cohesion and solidarity in social action. Georgia and his cohorts in the Bahian West African community are keyed-in directly to overtly Africanized forms of Black identity, racial consciousness, and expression. But other forms, often found in the very bodies and food of those seen to be the epitome of Africanity in Bahia, also exist and seek to present their own approach to Bahian Blackness – this book is about that contestation.

I argue in this work that the African-oriented approach of many of Bahia's Black movements have created an explicit symbolic "retcon" of a Brazilian history filled with misery and sadness in which Africanity was diminished, ignored, or scorned. This approach has now come to constrict and curtail the space available – ideologically and literally – for innovation, flexibility, alternative identities, and different approaches that speak to multiplex ideas about Blackness. It should be noted that a true heteroglossia of consciousness is, in many ways, more representative of an African philosophy and aesthetic – cosmologies *and* ideologies that are very much *in the making*. However, Bairros (2008), Nascimento (1980), and others in Bahia maintain that a fractured or fragmented response to racism – different ideas about what it means to be Black in Brazil and the varied roles of Africa, religion, and popular cultural movements – prevents consensus and, consequently, the ability to mobilize action and ideology in terms of what Blackness means to all Afro-Brazilians. But, therein lies the rub. There is great diversity in the Black communities of Bahia and of Brazil and not all of them are interested in articulating an African-oriented identity. Indeed, many Black women and men in Bahia and in Brazil do not want to conceive of Blackness in the same terms as those laid down by the Black movements, by a *terreiro*, by scholars, or by carnaval *blocos*. It is in this diversity, in this heteroglossia, that we see the urgency of incorporating a Gramscian approach to understanding Blackness in Bahia and indeed to understanding the diversity of perspectives on Blackness and the importance of Africa in Black identity discourses across the African diaspora.

Important for any study that seeks to understand multiple interpretations and representations of a subaltern culture – here, historically enslaved and oppressed Black societies of Brazil, indeed of the African diaspora – is Gramsci's understanding that such cultures are never homogenous and that they often contain within divergent ideas about how to combat racism and subjugation. Moreover, it cannot ever be assumed that all members of such a culture would subscribe to the same philosophies and tactics of opposition. For a counter-hegemony to successfully challenge the nigh global presence of racism in former plantation societies, such movements must come to terms with the truths of the day-to-day lives of oppressed people (Gramsci 1985). These quotidian realities are at the core of what my diverse array of informants throughout Bahia related to me about how the philosophy, strategy, and *telos* of a Black identity project rooted in the Africanity of religion, food, and memory means for them as Afro-Brazilians. From historically Black neighbourhoods in the city of Salvador to Bahian tourist locales to the dry and hardscrabble interior of the *sertão*, I seek – within the framework of a Barthian approach to identity and a Gramscian model for understanding the oft-heterogonous social movements of oppressed peoples – to interrogate how African-oriented identities and ideas about racial consciousness permeate the often radically different economic and political worlds of people who are broadly constructed by some actors, certainly from a social perspective, to inhabit the same identity.

In the chapters that follow, I attempt to demonstrate that a broad array of different expressions of Blackness – and by extension, Africanity – are being manufactured, presented, supported, and championed by different stakeholders, including intellectuals, across the spectrum of Bahian society. These – to use West's (1990) term – "Black cultural workers" are actively engaged in producing the kinds of alternative identities and manifestations of Blackness that "deconstruct earlier modern Black strategies for identity formation, demystify power relations that incorporate class and construct more multivalent and multidimensional responses that articulate the complexity and diversity of Black practices" (90). How then is this space created and maintained? Through what channels must these alternative forms of Blackness flow in order to be integrated into a truly holistic form of Black identity for Bahia and Brazil? There can, of course, be little debate as to the relative importance of Africa as a site of origin and source of ineffable idioms *à la* Geertz (1973) for Blackness throughout the diaspora – this is and must be a truism for all peoples descended from enslaved Africans. But even this common point of origin in the past of all Afro-American peoples must be seen as something that was made out of the encounter between the West and the peoples of Africa and so is thus a memory left open to the vagaries of interpretation and deployment in constructions of consciousness – racial and otherwise.

Now, as Hanchard (1993) has noted, Gramsci does suggest that Black intellectuals – in this case, in the United States – could be engaged in the organization and ongoing preservation of Africa as a symbolic homeland in social constructions of Black identity. Gramsci speculates whether such a class of intellectuals could "have sufficient assimilating and organizing capacity to give a 'national' character to the present primitive sentiment of being a despised race, thus giving the African continent a mythic function as the common fatherland of the negro peoples?" (1971, 21). But if such unity of message and of consciousness is, as noted earlier, illusory, why do such messages and movements persist? For Gramsci, the histories of oppressed, marginalized, and dominated peoples must necessarily be fragmented, but they are also not immune from the ideological domination of a particular message, of a particular fragment of the past; crucially, a past that, in the case of plantation societies like Brazil, sought to always diminish heterogeneity and diverse ideas about self and collective – slavery. In a system of political, economic, bodily, and psychological subjugation that created binaries such as slave–master, Black–white, chattel–owner, pagan–Christian, and savage–civilized, totalizing and monolithic constructions of opposition find purchase. Consequently, an emphasis on what Foucault (1978) has called "tactical reversals" in strategies of opposition and resistance persist even after a subaltern group has become unchained.

Over the past few decades, anthropology has become increasingly focused on processes such as resistance and identity formation within the context of transnationalism, globalization, migration, commodity exchange, diaspora, translocality, and hybridity. These concepts have all become important tropes and figures within which anthropological work is inscribed and given analytical freshness. Often, however, these approaches can only be celebrated as new paradigms if much foundational intellectual inquiry is either rejected out-of-hand as being too much entangled with colonial enterprise or other equally distasteful associations, or simply wrong-headed, or is just ignored altogether. Trouillot (1991) has warned, most profoundly, of the dangers of an overly narrow and hazy understanding of the history of anthropology and the role of anthropology in making history. Rather than focusing on the metaphors of text and postmodernity, as the Writing Culture (1986) school has done, anthropology must ultimately be more concerned with coming to terms with its historical place in the making of "other" cultures.

In the area of Afro-American anthropology, this warning has particular resonance, as anthropologists have been instrumental in guiding the in situ construction of identity and discourse about ethnicity in Black communities throughout the Americas. Yelvington (2001) rightly notes that much of this "older" anthropology has been drawn on – witness Georgia's reticence – by "disempowered communities of Black men and women in the New World to justify their place within nationalizing processes" (250). Consequently, regardless of how out-of-date such ideas as survivals, retentions, purity, or even that old saw, syncretism, might seem, it is vital to understand the impact these ideas have had on the communities we study. In discussing Afro-Cuban *Santería* or *regla ocha*, Palmié (1995) notes that "'natives' are well aware of the conceptual and narrative constructions scholarly producers of knowledge about their religion have foisted upon their religion" and that locally produced non-scholarly histories inevitably must address conceptions created by academics and propagated within popular culture (82–3). I would argue that the form these rejoinders to scholarly constructions take, certainly in the case of Brazil, invariably reframes the same ideas about the purity of African tradition laid out and inculcated into popular culture by an earlier generation of anthropologists. As David Scott (1991) writes:

> What is noteworthy is that even in non-anthropological discourse, anthropology, taken as the (self-described) "science of culture," is often seen as crucial in providing the authoritative vocabulary in terms of which the claims of difference are established. Anthropology – and for quite definite historical reasons, American cultural anthropology more specifically – has often taken as providing what we might call the foundational discourse for the cultural politics of identity among peoples of African descent in the New World. (262)

In his *The Invention of Africa*, V.Y. Mudimbe (1988) illustrates how the concept of Africa was invented and used – or abused – in the European imperial enterprise and also explores how a discourse of Africa was pervasive not only in colonialism, but also formed the basis of African nationalist movements, Pan-Africanism, African scholarship, and development. This discourse about Africa is manifested at three levels: a primary or popular level where founders and founding events are mythologized; a second-level or academic discourse about Africa where the first level is inscribed into a rational field; and a third-level or meta-discourse – a history of histories. It is at this third level where Cullen inquires "What is Africa to me?" and at which this present research seeks to answer the question poised earlier in this introduction. I invoke Mudimbe here, but also Hobsbawm and Ranger (1983), since this research and the work of Mintz and Price (1976) implies the active in-tentionality and agency not only of those enslaved communities out of which grew Afro-American society, but also of the academics in the 1920s and 1930s who were responsible, certainly in Brazil, with redefin-ing much of what the concept of Africa means to Afro-Brazilians in Bahia. This work acts as a meta-discourse on the ways in which stake-holders have told and continued to suffuse "Africa" into collective identities. More importantly, it seeks to combine this approach with an exploration of how Afro-Brazilians have continued to self-consciously construct traditions which they label as "Black," "African," "Yoruba," or "*Afrodescendente.*"

I would also like to follow, as others such as Capone (Capone 2004) and Parés (2001, 2004) have, David Scott's (1991) proposal that anthro-pology should attempt to shift the *problématique* of Africans and their descendants in the Americas away from a "sustained preoccupation with the corroboration or verification of authentic pasts" (280). Scott's proposal that anthropology relocate away from narrative constructions of history to the discursive field of "tradition" and how it is transacted in the politics of identity has obvious relevance for a project that seeks to understand how a concept such as "Africa" has been invented and reinvented in the Brazilian context. Scott suggests that anthropological work on Afro-America should be concerned primarily with interpret-ing the varying ways in which "Africa and slavery are employed by New World peoples of African descent in the narrative construction of relations among pasts, presents and futures" (280–1). However, I, like R. Price (2006, 134), am not enough of a postmodernist to be willing to ignore the past in the plantation, or the history of transatlantic interac-tion, or the evidence left from the brutalities of the Middle Passage. Taken together, these fragments of the past help us to understand how the discourses of the present are formed.

An approach to Afro-Brazilian identity and contemporary social pro-cesses that focus on how the "Africa" concept is used is not incompati-ble with accepting that Black societies in Brazil are largely a product of creolization. Indeed, this approach almost requires that creolization be accepted as a historical baseline or starting point. Understanding how the "Africa-concept" is used in identity discourse is about the creation of ethnic categories and social boundaries with meaning and resonance for constituent members. The formation of new African American com-munities in the context of the plantation through the use of shared grammatical principles and ideas about the universe – brought from

Africa – was similarly about the creation of meaning and about defining what aspects of an African identity were, moving forward, important for collective representation and, ultimately, ideas about Blackness. Finally, Trouillot's (1998) warning that "as social theory becomes more discourse oriented ... historical circumstances fall further into a hazy background of ideological preferences" is well taken (15). Both "event" and "discourse" have their place and it is the job of the anthropologist to find the theoretical middle ground that bridges the two, much like M.G. Smith did in his 1957 evaluation of the state of Caribbean anthropology. For at stake, ultimately, in this debate is who is empowered to define what it means to be Black in Brazil, to be an *Afrodescendente*, the extent to which being Black in Brazil means having an engagement or interaction with the idea-symbol-construct of Africa, and to whom these definitions of Blackness do or do not apply.

Now, Gramsci (1971) argues that cultural elites can and do control the ideological sectors of society and that these elites are frequently traditional intellectuals – writers, academics, novelists, photographers, *anthropologists*. In Bahia, this elite has sought to clearly define the counter-image and counter-narrative to centuries of racism, enslavement, and oppression as a praise song not merely to Blackness, but rather towards Africanized and African-oriented manifestations of Blackness. Many writers and intellectuals in Bahia, as eloquent champions of equality, justice, and acceptance, are, I might suggest, not limiting insomuch as they are tactically circumscribing the opportunities for the development of new forms of expression and minimizing competing discourses of Blackness within the vibrant setting that is Bahia. This ultimately does serve to place limits on the extent to which emancipatory ideas and truly revolutionary thought can help to alleviate the poverty and racism suffered by Black people in Bahia, throughout Brazil, and the diaspora.

Black Movements

In this work I speak of "Black" social movements in Brazil and of "Black" peoples in Brazil. I refer to these as "Black" in order to distinguish them as more than just the fruits of thought and action committed by people with a particular skin colour – but as the product of the ideas and labour of culturally distinct Black communities, that, as a result of the slave trade and of life on the plantation, had no other term to describe their collectivities and their identities other than a colour. In

Brazil, "Afro-Brazilian" is the term that is largely used to describe Black communities and the Portuguese word, *preto*, to describe Black skin colour. Increasingly, however, another word for Black – *negro* – is used to describe not only the colour of people's skins, but also as an appellation to describe a discrete ethnic identity. I say *ethnic* identity, precisely because those involved in manufacturing, negotiating, and presenting the markers and criteria for membership in this group look to symbols and ideas that they believe are *ethnically* distinct from mainstream Brazilian society. I make no proclamations or assertions that one appellation or label is better than another. I use "Black" as an identity category because some people in Brazil who have black skin colour do not identify with an African-oriented representation of ethnicity, and because I seek to stress the diverse aspects of Black Brazilian "culture," rather than ideas about nationality or purported origin. Put simply, I propose that the way in which "Black" is defined as an ethnic category differs greatly throughout the Americas and that "Black," therefore, must be understood as more than just a skin colour. Ideas such as "Black" power and "Black" identity draw on more than just a word that describes the higher presence of melanin or certain hair forms or facial features. These concepts speak directly to emic perceptions that Black communities possess and retain cultural resources that are *ethnically* vibrant, complete, and different from those within other communities.

Other scholars have attempted to demonstrate that Blackness, as an identity category, needs to be understood in the context of shifting and diverse ideas of Black culture, the history of Black communities, and the relevance of an idea of Africa. Peter Wade (1986, 1993, 1995, 1999, 2006), who has conducted extensive ethnographic research with Black communities in Colombia, has shown that multiplex and diverse definitions of Blackness in that country are often at odds with each other. Wade (1995) asserts that dominant definitions of who is Black often lead to the reification of Blackness and the perpetuation of "essentialist notions of race" (351). Thomas et al. (2006, 2007), in a series of recorded conversations, have demonstrated how certain key symbols, many of them oriented towards Africa, have dominated globalized ideas of Blackness. However, they also demonstrate that within the context of what they term "Diasporic Hegemonies" (Thomas et al. 2006, 163), there exists a plurality of ideas about what Blackness should mean. Andrews (2004), in his survey of Afro-Latin America, describes a process that he calls the "Blackening" of social movements in Latin America during the 1970s (183–90). This form of mobilization, in countries such as Brazil,

Colombia, Costa Rica, Panama, and Peru, took the form of increased emphasis on elements of Black culture – primarily expressions of Africanity in the Latin American context – as a way to unify and concretize an identity for Black people. Often these Africanized ideas of Blackness failed to resonate with many poorer Black men and women, but all of the "Blackening" movements discussed by Andrews focused on a construction of Blackness that transcended phenotype and skin colour and emphasized the "cultural" aspects of Black identity. Stefania Capone's (2004) work on what she calls the "search" for Africa in Brazil emphasizes the different ways in which the "Africa-concept" is used and reified with the sacred space of the *terreiro* to create multiple ideas about African-inspired religious practice rooted in different African cultures. However, these distinct cultural voices within and across different *terreiros*, though often engaged in debates about purity, originality, and authenticity, are still deployed by others towards what might be seen – in the context of this study – as a similarly African-oriented form of Afro-Brazilian identity. She writes, "Today when we observe the panorama of Afro-Brazilian religions ... each *terreiro* has its own ritual specificity, which is the fruit of the tradition to which it belongs" (Capone 2010, 8). However, for Capone these traditions do not necessarily equate with a unified voice about Blackness or, for that matter, Africanity – rather, such formulations are often constructed by intellectuals and other key identity stakeholders in Bahia's Black movements.

Ultimately, all of these studies demonstrate that locally invented notions of Blackness draw on diverse cultural sources and an array of symbols that go beyond the colour of one's skin or ideas about the source and origin of such Blackness. In this work, similar processes of reification are explored in how Blackness is constructed in the state of Bahia. So, while African-oriented constructions of Blackness have dominated, these ideas look not to notions of skin colour, but to the mobilization of what the leaders of such movements define as Black culture and Black history. Indeed, this form of Black Brazilian identity seeks to emphatically reject membership based on the vagaries of skin colour and accentuates the importance of Black cultural praxis and the reorientation of Black identity towards Africa. This study then follows the path that Black identity wends within two major domains: first, it seeks to interpret the impact that a *contemporary* flow of ideas and peoples between Bahia and the coast of West Africa has on how Afro-Brazilian construct popular Blackness in Brazil; second, the work explores how Bahians, both rural and urban, use or employ a discourse about "Africa" and the slave past in conceptions of personal and collective ethnic identity. In emphasizing concepts and ideas, however, I do not wish in this work to ignore the actual brutality of life on the plantation or the inhumanity of the Middle Passage. Pasts *are* important to how contemporary identities are constructed. However, I emphasize that an exploration of contemporary identity processes is more important than determining the "true" ethnic composition of the slave plantation, and I assert that attempting to authenticate the past is, ultimately, of little utility to an understanding of how Africa is incorporated into contemporary identity processes. Moreover, I largely approach this material with the understanding that Brazilian society is very much a product of rapid creolization that began within the milieu of the plantation. Consequently, the search by enslaved Africans to find commonality in the diverse symbolic and cultural repertoire that different African groups brought to their existence in the plantation necessitated that the *idea* of Africa become an important signifier of group identity. Indeed, any study that seeks to understand how Africa – as a concept and symbol – is mediated and negotiated in the process of making culture must necessarily, I believe, begin with the assumption that the creolization of slave communities was the norm and that within this context "Africa" rapidly became more of a symbolic resource than an actual or historical place. This is largely because Africa is, and remains, a *contested* symbol of Black identity in Brazil, and throughout Afro-America, as opposed to an assumed, ineffable, or essential connection with precise areas in the African motherland.

Rather, I suggest that the futility lies in continued attempts by many scholars (see Gomez 1998, 2005, 2006; Hall 2005) to divine and uncover the precise ethnic composition of the enslaved population in American societies and to make assertions about present-day ethnic conditions from this data. Certainly, there is little doubt that particular regions of Africa contributed far more to the slave population of the Americas and specifically to Brazil than other parts of the continent, that certain regions were over-represented in the seventeenth century, others in the eighteenth century, and so on. Further, ideas about where one's ancestors originated have always, will always, fascinate and stir the fragmented descendants of enslaved, displaced, or migrant peoples. However, cultural practice in Black communities in Brazil and, I believe, in much of the Americas which evokes and "remembers" an African past or an idea of Africa is about identity today, not about the nature of the past. It is constructed in a world in which racism, prejudice, and marginalization abound and is, in almost every way, a response to these societal patterns. The past is important, but when it proves difficult to unearth, it is not unsafe to assume that much contemporary discourse about the past is just that – discourse – and that the consequences of history are more and more about how the past is viewed rather than what *really* happened. Fragments of these pasts, then, help us to understand the formation and structure of discourse in the present. Indeed, by accepting the process of creolization in the context of the plantation as a baseline for our study of situational identity formation, one avoids much of the critique that such approaches to identity are flawed by an inherent ahistoricism.

Black activists in Bahia now present, to those they assert as their constituents, a set or, following Goffman (1974), frame of ideas about what experiences they deem important for membership within a particular group. In the context of identarian social movements, Goffman used frames to describe the process through which bodies of symbols and ideas pertaining to an ideology are communicated to constituents or participants of a particular community and to those opposed to the ideology. Social movements gain traction and are successful when there is resonance between the goals of organizers and elites, those involved in mobilizing a community, and the quotidian beliefs and ideas of the community – this, Goffman (1974) termed "frame alignment." Essentially, this means that social movements, such as the redefinition of group identity, can only work when there is more or less some degree of compatibility between the new frame offered by the leaders and the frame of beliefs that define the daily life of community members. Burdick (1998a) similarly invokes Goffman's frame concept to demonstrate how a social movement, such as Brazil's *Movimento Negro Unificado* (MNU), can use a set of ideas about African heritage and culture to construct identity claims:

> The Brazilian black consciousness movement ... expects nonwhites to pay special attention to their descent from slaves and African forebears, and to set aside their other ancestries; it calls upon them to reinterpret experiences once understood as having been shaped by personal idiosyncrasy or class prejudice as having been shaped by racism; it asks them to place a special value on their bodily response to drumming; while marginalizing their bodily response to, say, violins; it urges them to be especially appreciative of Afro-religious practices ... while distancing themselves from the practice, say, of wearing the suit acquired in a baptist church. (8–9)

Burdick's study reveals how Black forms of popular Christianity deal with the realities of racism in Rio de Janeiro and suggests that the MNU are only able to see proud and liberating forms of Black expression in the African-oriented space or *terreiros* of Afro-Brazilian religious practices, neglecting other Black cultural traditions. Many Black leaders in Salvador similarly assert that any Black man or woman who truly wishes to combat racism, to subvert the myth of "racial democracy," and to empower his or her own community, *must* begin by embracing the African elements of Afro-Brazilian culture. Specifically, this implies membership in a *Candomblé terreiro*, the principal form of Afro-Brazilian religious centre found in Bahia, involvement with an Afro carnaval association, and an expectation that Black Brazilians will work towards public recognition of their descent from African forebears. For these movements, Black identity and Black community becomes much the same thing. Black movements of this kind have been explored in detail by British sociologist Paul Gilroy. In *There Ain't no Black in the Union Jack*, Gilroy (1987) suggests that for Black social movements in Britain, the principal context in which these kinds of ideas and demands are articulated is that of "community." He writes:

> Though it reflects the concentration of Black people, the term refers to far more than mere place or population. It has a moral dimension and its use evokes a rich complex of symbols surrounded by a wider complex of meanings ... Community, therefore, signifies not just a distinctive political ideology but a particular set of values and norms in everyday life. (234)

Black movements in Bahia similarly assert that the boundaries of the Black community must be defined by the common experience of subjugation and a need to escape from racism and the categorization of Black people as a population that requires assimilation into the broader society. They argue that the elements that define Black communities in Salvador and in much of Brazil – the same elements that compose their social "frame" – are about antagonism between ethnic boundaries and about reconciling, internally, competing definitions of the Black movement and of community.

However, a frame can often fail to resonate with constituents and in some ways the present work is directed at uncovering the extent to which these new identity claims actually permeate the Black community in Salvador and beyond, into the rural area of Bahia. Elites and cultural entrepreneurs can often fail to understand that the quotidian and mundane aspects of "real life" are generally far more important to an individual's existence than manifestations of religious performance or the nuances of identity. Many Black Brazilians are untouched or uninterested in the identity-oriented discourses of Africanity offered by many of Brazil's Black movements. They see little in these ideologies that speak to their daily lives as impoverished and marginalized peoples. Hanchard (1994) puts it another way, asserting that "many of the working poor [in Brazil] do *not* have a 'hidden transcript,' that is to say, a strategic agenda of private, ideological interests that contradict public articulations of ether consent of material compliance with dominant actors in a given society" (71).

Even if participants of a particular social identity or members of a "community" participate in some aspects of a social "frame" that speaks to an ideology of change and resistance, they may openly reject others. Indeed, discourses that seek to activate ethnic identity are often extremely difficult to mobilize. As Gilroy (1987) writes, "The political rhetoric of leaders is, after all, not a complete guide to the motivations of those who play a less prominent role" (234–6). Interpretations of public manifestations, rituals, political rhetoric, and, yes, even identity discourse, can run the gamut from excited and wholehearted support to unveiled indifference. Although we, as anthropologists, may be swayed by the inspiring speech of activists exhorting their "people" to "rediscover" their Blackness and their African heritage, it is our job to determine to what extent individuals, as lone actors and as members of a collective, embrace these ideas.

Globalizing Blackness or Ongoing Creolization

In the ethnographic context of Northeast Brazil, I use the metaphors of dialogue and an at times discordant polyphony to frame the process of identity-making as part of an ongoing process of globalizing Blackness. This process has much in common with the creolization that took place in the plantation societies of the Caribbean and Latin America. As others have explored in detail (see Howard 1999; Matory 2005, 2006; Mintz and Price 1976; Palmié 2006; R. Price 2006; S. Price 2006; Singleton 2006; Yelvington 2001, 2006b), the *problématique* of Afro-American society – that is, how do we understand and analyse the role of enslaved Africans in making the societies of the Americas – has been heavily guided by the debate over the degree of creolization that took place in the plantations. In the Mintz and Price (1976) formulation, plantation society was primarily composed of heterogeneous groups of Africans – some over-represented, such as the Yoruba in certain areas, the Akan in other areas, and some groups very much under-represented – who created new Afro-American cultures in the context of the plantation through the use of certain common features of social organization and world view as a cultural resource.

The *locus classicus* for this American ethnogenesis can be found in the remarkable creativity and resilience of Maroon societies such as the Saramaka (R. Price 1975, 1983). I assert here that globalizing Blackness, as a concept, draws upon a similar baseline grammar or symbol bank that Mintz and Price (1976) assert served to facilitate coherent Black community formation in and around the plantation, but functions, instead, at a translocal, transregional, and dialogic level. These key symbols are now dominated by a common belief in what counts as "African" for Black communities – among these are ideas or concepts such as "ancestor," "drum," "earth," "nature," "possession," "return," "rhythm," "roots," "slave," "spirit," "trance," and others. Much like Sylvanus' (2007) idea of a "fabric of Africanity," such symbols are then mediated, processed, and reinterpreted by leaders and communities in locales like Salvador and throughout the Afro-American world in an imaginary that seeks to articulate Black identity with reference to the African. It is part of an ongoing process that serves to increasingly bring together, and in some quarters harmonize, disparate and quite distinct notions of Blackness in different locales of the Americas.

I see the development of globalizing Blackness not as a new form of creolization, but certainly as something of a creolizing-like process or an extension of creolization – but with a distinctly political character; borne certainly out of the kind of cultural, linguistic, and religious hybridization typified by creolization, but now actualized and made manifest by distinct forms of resistance and political counter-hegemony organized by leaders, luminaries, and intellectuals in Salvador. I make this distinction – and it is an important one – primarily because the concept of creolization has, of late, come to encompass far too much theoretical and ethnographic terrain. As Hannerz (1987) writes:

A macro-anthropology of culture which takes into account the world system and its center-periphery relation appears to be well served by a creolist point of view. It could even be the most distinctive contribution anthropology can make to world system studies. It identifies diversity itself as a source of cultural vitality; it demands of us that we see complexity and fluidity as an intellectual challenge rather than as something to escape from. It should point us to ways of looking at systems of meaning which do not hide their connections with the facts of power and material life. (556)

Does this mean that anywhere we find mixing, blending, syncretism, fusion, borrowing, or otherwise heterogeneous cultural practices we are dealing with a creole culture? And, if indeed this is the case, does this also imply that complementary or in opposition to these "creole" cultures exist "pure" cultures? Are Anglo-Indians also creoles? Canadian Métis? Hannerz emphasizes that, typically, creolization takes place in locales where a colonial past has led to ethnic diversity within a community and very much relies on world systems and dependency theory. His analysis also focuses very much on an area of the world that is perhaps second only to the Caribbean in terms of regional ethnic diversity and connectivity with the transatlantic movement of large populations: the West African coast. Here, on the periphery, in Hannerz' model, anything can and often does happen in terms of ethnic creativity, but the end result is usually some recombination of dominant European linguistic "traits" with "traditional" contributions from the native. He also notes that "in the end, it seems, we are all being creolized" (Hannerz 1987, 557).

Creolization as a social science concept has its roots in linguistics. Most creole languages are based on European ones with substrate elements from African, Oceanic, or Amerindian populations, though there continues to be significant debate in linguistics as to the extent of the linguistic contribution of the non-European substrate to the language itself (Chaudenson, Mufwene, and Pargman 2001; Mufwene 1998). Among both anthropologists and linguists, creolization was not a commonly used concept until the late 1960s and early 1970s, most notably after contributions in Dell Hymes' volume *Pidginization and Creolization of Languages* (1971). After this, linguists and anthropologists alike started to see the process of creole language formation as first and foremost a consequence of social phenomena that could not be understood, linguistically speaking, without reference to historical factors (Jourdan 1991; Thomason and Kaufman 1988), such as those found on the plantation. Hymes' argument in his 1971 volume – a work produced after a conference on pidgins and creoles held at the University of the West Indies in 1968 – was that creolization needs to be understood in the framework of a very particular socio-historical context in which groups of peoples were brought together for the sole purpose of extracting labour from an imported population. Out of this social nexus were born new cultural and linguistic forms that the world had, up to that point, not yet seen. This model has come to be used by anthropologists to explain and explore ethnographic contexts beyond the Caribbean framework in which it was constructed. The work of Knörr (2008), which builds on the Mintz-Price model, on Hannerz' work, and on linguistic studies, attempts some of this conceptual repositioning:

> Creolization is a process in which ethnically diverse people become indigenized ... distinct from other forms and processes of cultural mixing because it involves ethnicization and indigenization ... It allows for both ethnic *and* transethnic identification within contemporary, ethnically heterogeneous societies. (14)

I certainly do believe, as Knörr does, that the concept has much to offer an analysis of social contexts such as those found in the ethnically complex and culturally multilayered societies of West Africa, but I believe some degree of clarity about what socio-historical conditions lead specifically to creolization is necessary and Knörr's analysis does not provide this. The annals of anthropology are littered with the corpses of many an overused concept and theoretical abstraction, such as the folk-urban continuum, ethnoscience, cultural materialism, syncretism, or the organic/homeostasis metaphor. Overused in that through expansion and reorientation towards ever-increasing arrays of situations and contexts, the concept comes to lose much of its analytical vigor. I very much share Knörr's call for a deeper understanding of creolization's hermeneutic potential, but we must be careful again about spreading the concept too thin. Mimi Sheller (2003) has explored exactly this kind of repurposing and redefinition of the creolization concept in some detail and remarks on the problems with reorienting this concept to other ethnographic terrain in which cultures have become mixed, intertwined, or blended:

> Creolization ... is not simply about moving and mixing elements, but is more precisely about processes of cultural 'regrounding' following experiences of violent uprooting from one's culture of origin. It is deeply embedded in situations of coerced transport, racial terror, and subaltern survival ... Creolization is a process of *contention*. (189)

In other words, the conditions found specifically in the slave plantations of the Americas and Caribbean. Sheller concludes, essentially, that the work of theorists such as Hannerz serves to rob Afro-American and Caribbean societies of the historical agency that the more socio-historically specific form of the creolization concept afforded these populations and also diminishes its analytical power. By relocating the unique cultural strategies forged in plantation societies specifically to deal with the toil and whip of American and Caribbean slavery up to the level of "global culture," Sheller cautions that theorists such as Hannerz (1987) and others (e.g., Clifford 1992, 1994, 1997), whose work sees the whole world as undergoing creolization, are weakening or making irrelevant the historically specific form of creolization found in communities of enslaved Africas.

Slave Routes

In a 2005 article in the Brazilian journal *Revista Brasileira De Ciências Sociais*, Patricia de Santana Pinho called for a decentering of studies about Blackness, away from a United States-biased perspective. In this article, de Santana Pinho asserts that Salvador in particular should be considered an important nexus, a world city or *cidade mundial*, and a "Mecca" of negritude. Ironically, though, she invokes the name of Herskovits and mentions his sliding scale of Africanisms and Salvador's high ranking in this list, and goes on to rely on the importance of other North American and European scholars like Verger (2005, 40–3). To be sure, Brazil's historic contact with Africa was limited to certain areas – the West African "Slave Coast," along with Angola and other Portuguese colonies. But, in de Santana Pinho's presentation of Salvador as a new centre for Blackness, distinct from places like Atlanta or Harlem, cast not in the trope of the plantation-based African ethnicity, but, rather, in the contemporary context of a dialogue between Black worlds, she falls back on the usual suspects: Yorubaness, Nigeria with a *soupçon* of Angola, and *capoeira* thrown in for good measure.

This pattern finds replication in the work of many scholars and writers on the Africanness of Salvador and of Brazil in general (see Ayoh'Omidire 2005; Bacelar 2001; Beata de Yemonja 1996; Dantas 1988, 2002; Dzidzienyo 1999; Ojo-Ade 1999; Wesolowski 2006) and is, from both a historical perspective and in terms of the strategies of Black resistance, completely understandable. The societies of the Lagosian lowlands, the Bight of Benin, the Guinea Coast, and further south along the Angolan coast contributed the vast majority of individuals to the transatlantic slave trade. Consequently, those cultures found, through so-called survivals or through processes of creolization and later on, dialogue and reinvention, dominant expression in Brazil and elsewhere in Latin America and the Caribbean. Furthermore, I am not questioning the importance of Yoruba religious traditions, for example, in both the origins and quotidian practices of, for example, the *Candomblé terreiro* – for this study is not explicitly about Afro-Brazilian religiosity (instead, see Capone 2010; Parés 2004). Rather, I am suggesting that when these cultural and historical elements are highlighted – both by cultural elites and scholars – in order to forge contemporary identities that seek to articulate a more global and unified idea of what it means to be a descendant of African peoples, other identity constructions are inevitably muted.

In this, the Brazilian articulation of an African-oriented Blackness is not too different from the one found in the United States. The difference, however, is that in the United States, Yoruba culture is often replaced with the symbols, language, and culture of the Asante people of Ghana as key markers of Blackness and Africanness. For example, the *kente* cloth of the Asante people of Ghana has come to serve as a powerful symbol of Africanness for African Americans and also as an important "ethnic" modifier in the repertoire of African American material culture.[4] Those who wear or display *kente* or use Asante names are very much articulating an African-oriented expression of Black identity. From Bill Cosby sporting *kente* bowties and cummerbunds on *The Cosby Show*, to Bill Clinton wearing *kente* over his wool suit in the tropical heat of Accra, from the historically African American colleges use of *kente* in graduation robes, to the proud display of *kente* during Kwanza, the Asante have become a key symbolic reference point for the popular expression of Africanity in the United States. Yet, as Bruner (1996) and others (Hasty 2002; Lake 1995) have shown in their studies of African American travel to Ghana, there appears to be a considerable gulf between the popular construction of Asante and Ghana in the American imagination and the expectation of what life in this prosperous, though still developing, West African country is really like. Bruner (1996) writes:

What most Ghanaians want from tourism is economic development, including employment, new sources of income, better sanitation and waste disposal, improved roads, and a new harbor. Expectations are high. The regional planning agency wants the tourist dollars to remain in the Central Region for the benefit of the community … For many African Americans, the castles are sacred ground not to be desecrated. They do not want the castles to be made beautiful or to be whitewashed. They want the original stench to remain in the dungeons ... Ghanaians want the castles restored, with good lighting and heating, so they will be attractive to tourists; African Americans want the castles to be as they see them – a cemetery for the slaves who died in the dungeons' inhuman conditions while waiting for the ships to transport them to the Americas. Ghanaians see the castles as festive places; African Americans as somber places. (291–3)

Visitors talk of the pride and strength they receive from these places, these Black "places of power," where their ancestors suffered so much sadness and brutality. A woman who was born and raised in New York, christened Joan, but who had taken the Akan name Ama later in life told me in Cape Coast: "This is our true homeland. This is where my heart comes from, where a Black woman can be Black and proud and not have to worry about white American society. This is an African country and we are Africans. We've always been Blacks in a white land. That's why this place is so important to us."[5]

Many Ghanaians who work at the forts are often at a loss as to how to communicate with these travellers. One Ghanaian tour guide informed me that he was told by an African American tourist, "You can't understand, you live here – but we're coming home." In response, the tour guide informed me that he felt frustrated and a little bewildered. I offered to my Ghanaian informant that, in the African American experience, especially in literature, return to Africa has taken on something of a mythic quality, almost like a Garden of Eden or a promised land. Importantly, this story illustrates a number of important aspects of Black Atlantic dialogue. It demonstrates that many of these so-called roots tourists or Black travellers actively consume scholarship that seeks to articulate new definitions of Blackness and Black identity. It also shows that the dialogue between different areas of Blackness, in this case, the United States and the Ghanaian coast, is sometimes fraught with asymmetries and disagreements – there is frequent misunderstanding or misalignment. Indeed, in Bakhtin's dialogic model for understanding discourse, there is no emphasis or prerequisite for harmony or accord between participants engaged in dialogue. Crucial to the usefulness of a Gramscian perspective on the diverse voices of Blackness present not just in Brazil but throughout the diaspora is Bakhtin's (1981) assertion that dialogue is often dissonant and cacophonous as voices interact and seek to establish or contest meaning. Finally, although the two parties engaged in this dialogue sometimes disagree on how symbols such as *kente* or the plantation or the spirits that are venerated in Afro-Brazilian houses of worship, the *orixás*, should be used and interpreted – they are, after all, decidedly contested symbols – both sides use these symbols to frequently articulate a generic and homogenized image of Africa. Although my informant, the tour guide, frequently complains about the attitude of many travellers, he employs and refers to the legacy of slavery or the importance of something like *kente* in a conventional narrative that travellers demand and expect. He certainly has very different feelings and beliefs about these symbols – for him, the history of slavery is not an important part of his identity, but it is a part of his daily life as a tour guide. In his work as representative of the slave castles and of the Ghanaian government's tourism board, he uses and negotiates the key symbol of slavery in an ongoing dialogue with African Americans about what it means to be Black, and so contributes to a continually globalizing idea of Africanized Blackness.

Globalizing Blackness, then, is about an African-oriented expression of Black identity, but also one that emphasizes a very American (and I use the word here in its broadest sense) idea of what Africa is about. American, in that it conforms to the kind of perceptions and interests that have stimulated transatlantic dialogues over the past 150 years: one that generalizes and essentializes African ethnic identities; that imposes notions of purity and unity on African ethnic groups that – in the context in which they are found – hold no such beliefs about themselves; that creates idealized African types, whether they be Yoruba in Brazil or Asante in the United States; and that seeks to impose these identity constructions on all perceived constituents. This is, in other words, what Sansone (2004) calls "Blackness without ethnicity," in that it seeks to build on a formulation of identity that uses the symbols and practice of a particular African culture, but wants little or nothing to do with the in situ realities of life in that society. Africa here becomes a place without states, without polities, without rulers, without a history of colonialism, and, in the words of many travellers to the West African forts, a place where Black people have lived without the pressures of life on the plantation and all that it begat: without violence, without oppression, and without sadness. In this sense, globalizing Blackness is a considerable departure from the work of Du Bois or Césaire. For, although these authors did their share of generalizing about what Africa could mean to communities of Black people throughout the diaspora, they were equally aware of and engaged with the regional nuances of African life. Du Bois understood the different histories of countries like

Guinea, Mali, Ghana, Nigeria, and the differing impacts that French and British colonialism had wrought on these fledgling nations. Césaire too was intimately familiar with locally specific manifestations of French rule in different parts of Africa. Neither could be accused of homogenizing the diversity of the African continent.

In its attempts to re-situate the boundaries of Blackness towards the inclusion of a generalized notion of Africa that builds on key symbols of Blackness negotiated through transatlantic and transregional Black dialogue, globalizing Blackness is indeed a continuation of creolization. This process began in the Maroon communities of Jamaica and Suriname; in the *quilombos* of Brazil; in the plantation societies of Bahia, Cuba, and Louisiana; in the Gullah low country of South Carolina; and, indeed, wherever diverse communities of Africans with different languages and different cultures found themselves living cheek-by-jowl with each other. Similarly, the globalization of African-oriented Blackness builds upon the global proximity of diverse Black communities who have come to share a similar set of basic ideas about what it means to be descended from Africa and to be Black. This process is ongoing, it is alive, and it is dynamic – it is carried out in the music of American hip-hop artists and Brazilian *sambistas*; in Parisian tenements filled with migrants from French West Africa; on Canal Street and Broadway in New York City where Senegalese, Malians, and Guineans work as touts engaging American – including African American – customers looking to buy all manner of consumer goods and in turn serve to "Africanize" New York (Stoller 2002, 2003), and, finally, in Salvador, where Africans – frequently Nigerians – are involved, certainly not in developing or reinventing Afro-Brazilian religion identity, but in contributing a new vocabulary and set of ideas about what it means to be in a dialogue with the idea of Africa and with Africans.

Methodology

This study is based on ethnographic fieldwork carried out in the state of Bahia in Northeast Brazil and in the West African coastal cities of Lagos in Nigeria, Ouidah and Cotonou in Benin, and Accra and Cape Coast in Ghana from January 2003 through March 2006, and then again in the summer of 2011. Ethnographic work in West Africa attempted to follow the path of leaders from diaspora community groups and religious organizations engaged in so-called roots tourism or cultural rediscovery trips to West Africa. These "pilgrimages," if you will, primarily consist of groups of tourists from the diaspora and typically

involve visits to sites along the Guinea Coast from Cape Coast and Elmina in Ghana eastwards to the former slave port of Ouidah in what is
now the Republic of Benin, to Lagos in Nigeria. These sites are usually
home to slave forts or castles built by European powers that were involved in the transatlantic slave trade such as the Portuguese, Dutch,
Danish, English, French, and others. Most of these locations have now
been made UNESCO World Heritage Sites as part of that organization's
Slave Routes project.[6]

What started as an informal movement of Black literati from the
United States in the period after the first African nations achieved independence has been transformed into a structured tourist market that
includes travel and tour companies in the Americas, Africa, and Europe
dedicated to providing an authentic "roots" experience. The Ghanaian
government emphasizes the slave castles as master symbols of the
country's connection to the slave trade and to the descendants of slaves
in the diaspora. To this are added Ghana's history of pan-Africanism,
the legacy of Kwame Nkrumah and his long-standing interaction with
African American intellectuals, and Ghana's place as the first independent nation in Africa. In Benin, the main attraction is the so-called *route
des esclaves* or slave walk, which retraces the route taken by slaves from
the central slave market in the town of Ouidah, where slave traders se-
lected and purchased slaves destined for resale in the New World, to the
embarkation point some four kilometres away on the coast. Slaves were
branded according to the mark of the purchaser at what is now billed to
tourists as the "Tree of Forgetting". Tourist literature available in Ouidah
and interpretive material presented by guides describes the tree as a
place where slaves were forced to "forget" their African homes. The
slave walk continues along the coast until it arrives at the shallow water
harbour where slaves were loaded onto longboats and taken out to the
slave ships – here, there is now a large monument to the slave trade
erected by UNESCO known as the "Point of No Return." Among Benin's
attractions are also "authentic" displays of the religious activity of Fon
– the largest ethnic group in the region –and that tradition's connections
with Haitian *Vodoun* and tours of the *Casa do Brasil*, the residence of a
Brazilian slave trader. In Nigeria, slave tourism is little developed, ow-
ing primarily to security concerns in the country, but more adventurous
"roots" tourists are increasingly making their way to Lagos. Attractions
include the Brazilian quarter where Afro-Latin slave returnees took residence and the "shrine" of Afrobeat musical pioneer, Fela Kuti.

Although these tourist routes are aimed primarily at African Americans, increasing numbers of travellers and tourists from other parts of

the Americas are now visiting these Black cultural heritage sites in West Africa. A small, though growing, group of travellers from Brazil can now be found frequenting the slave route along the West African coast. In contrast to African American tourists, these Afro-Brazilian groups are interested primarily in engaging the traditional religious practices of the Yoruba ethnic group and Fon/Ewe complex of the coastal region, which stretches from the border between Ghana and Togo through to the Lagosian lowlands of Nigeria. Although much of their journey, like that of African Americans, is oriented around the major slave heritage sites, these travellers are primarily interested in contacting leaders and devotees of the different deity cults of the Yoruba, Fon, and Ewe. To this end, Afro-Brazilian travellers can typically be found interacting with religious leaders in Lagos and Ouidah.[7]

Following research in West Africa, extended ethnographic research in the Brazilian state of Bahia was focused on the city of Salvador and the rural town of Bom Jesus da Lapa.[8] Interviews in Salvador were conducted in neighbourhoods throughout the city, including Curuzu-Liberdade, Engenho Velho da Federação, and Brotas, which are primarily Black working-class neighbourhoods, and the old town of Salvador called Pelourinho. I also attended and interviewed people at Black consciousness rallies held at carnaval associations, churches, the Universidade Federal da Bahia (UFBa), and Afro-Brazilian religious centres or *terreiros*; lectures and events held at UFBa's Centro Estudos Afro-Orientais (CEAO); and marches and public manifestations held throughout Salvador for the month of Black consciousness and to celebrate the memory of famed maroon slave leader Zumbi dos Palmares.

Additional extremely valuable sources of information during field-work were the interactions with West Africans living and working in Salvador. Included among these individuals were instructors of the Yoruba language at UFBa and Nigerian students studying in Bahia. This community also features a number of individuals from West Africa that have, through an array of extremely colourful experiences, found themselves living in Bahia working as tour guides, interpreters, importers of West African artisan goods, and, occasionally, as impromptu priests and ad hoc experts-for-hire on African – especially Yoruba – society. Interviews conducted in the town of Bom Jesus da Lapa focused on rural perceptions of Salvador as the arbiter of all things Black and African in Brazil. Here, I also explored the extent to which a discourse about Africa and Black consciousness penetrates the interior of Bahia.

Figure 1.2 Map of Brazil, highlighting the state of Bahia.

Chapter Two

West African Cultural Brokers in Northeast Brazil

Just as Cape Coast was once a major point of embarkation for thousands upon thousands of Africans, captured and shackled, leaving for the plantations of the Americas, it was also the starting point for the life of another man from the West African coast who today labours under a Brazilian sun. In the introduction to the present work we met Georgia from Cape Coast. He is part of a small – approximately 120 individuals, primarily from Nigeria, Angola, Mozambique, and Ghana – but growing and influential community of West Africans living in Bahia that are actively involved in aspects of "roots" tourism; in the importation of West African handicrafts; in serving as experts on Africa, African religion, and West African cultural traditions; and, most importantly, in engaging in a dialogue with the African-descended peoples of Brazil on what it means to be Black.

These individuals are contemporary representatives of a transnational community that extends back through time and that travels back and forth across the Atlantic between cities like Salvador and Lagos, New York and Accra, and Havana and Cape Coast. They are a community rooted in the transregional space of the Atlantic world; a community that includes writers such as W.E.B. Du Bois, Richard Wright, and Maya Angelou; politicians like Nkrumah and Touré; and musicians like Paul Robeson, Fela Kuti, and Gilberto Gil. However, the community also includes less illustrious, though in the local cultural sense no less influential, members such as the following: our street-hustler friend Georgia, teachers of the Yoruba language at the Universidade Federal da Bahia, and representatives and visiting leaders of other Yoruba-inspired African traditions from Cuba, the United States, Canada and, of course, Nigeria. These Black men and women actively engage in negotiating ideas of Black identity articulated through some connection – real or asserted – with the African continent. I assert that these individuals, like Benedict Anderson's "pioneers" (2006, 47–65), are involved in continuing a transatlantic dialogue, furthering the ongoing process of imagining and creating communities of Blackness, and in interjecting the idea of Africa into formulations of Black racial consciousness in Bahia. However, in the dialogue between the Americas and Africa, it often seems to be the American – used here in the pan-continental sense – voice and the American meaning that carries the most weight and comes to be dominant in the exchange. To make this point, I'd like to reintroduce Georgia and some of his West African comrades who live, work, and study in Salvador.

Georgia's Story

"Wo hö te sɛn?" – a common Akan greeting of the language spoken by the Asante and Fante people of Ghana – were the first words I said to Georgia when I met him in the old neighbourhood of Bomfim in Salvador in 2005. "Oh!" he remarked. "How did you learn to speak Twi?" I had heard about Georgia from a group of Brazilian friends that I had met at a concert celebrating the work of Nigerian Afrobeat pioneer Fela Kuti and his contribution to Black struggles around the world. I had related to these individuals that I had spent extended periods of time in Ghana, to which they responded that I should meet Georgia. I was quite surprised to learn that there were Ghanaians in Salvador. I had expected, from previous experiences in Ouidah and Lagos, to find Yoruba speakers from Nigeria in Brazil, but I had not counted on finding a man from the Ghanaian coastal city of Cape Coast. For although this city once held a small community of "Afro-Latin" (Amos and Ayesu 2002) slave returnees from Brazil, it is not really a prominent part of the Afro-Brazilian imaginary landscape with reference to Africa.

Cape Coast, founded in the fifteenth century by the Portuguese, is now perhaps one of the most important, if not *the* most important, stops on West African "roots" tourist packages that transport groups of travellers, primarily African Americans, on pilgrimages through the major West African ports where slave ships, laden with human cargo, departed for the Americas. The other important sites for these slave routes include Gorée in Senegal and Ouidah in Benin. However, Ghanaian locales find little coverage in Brazilian depictions of Africa and so to find a Cape Coaster transplanted to this new and increasingly important

American nexus for "slave" and "roots"-oriented travel – Salvador – was a welcome surprise. I kept hearing about Georgia and kept being referred to this charismatic jack-of-all-trades: at public lectures organized by the Centro de Estudos Afro-Orientais (CEAO); at community groups; in the tourist-oriented old city of Salvador-Pelourinho; in a particular "roots-reggae" bar that he frequented; and in a *terreiro* that regularly received groups of African American tourists. However, it was not until about two months after first hearing his name that I finally got the chance to meet Georgia. I soon discovered that he had left his home in Cape Coast in his teens and has only very recently in 2013 and 2014, after decades away, returned to his natal homeland – though this time with groups of Brazilian travellers looking to engage with and discover Africa through Georgia's expertise. In his mid-thirties, Georgia has lived in Nigeria, Malaysia, the Philippines, and Brazil. He still has fond memories of Cape Coast and we spent much of our first day reminiscing about that most hospitable of Ghanaian cities – its geography, the colourful *asafo* sodality shrines, the twin forts of Cape Coast castle and Elmina, and famous landmarks like the Savoy Hotel that, though not as distinguished as its London namesake, still serves as a nightspot for highlife music and fresh palm wine. Since Georgia left home, "to make money," he tells me, he has spent most of his time with and around Nigerians. "I love Ghana. Ghana is my home and my brother is still there, along with many of my sisters and my mother is still alive," Georgia says, "but you know, people in Ghana have a bad idea of Nigerians. They think Nigerians are too wicked and too fast. But you know, Nigerians are the best at making business. Nobody can beat Nigerians in business. Ghana can learn so much from Nigeria."

These comments are ones that I am familiar with. Throughout much of West Africa and indeed much of sub-Saharan Africa, Nigeria is seen as an economic powerhouse. Nigerians are often inappropriately essentialized as sharp entrepreneurs wherever they ply their trade; from Senegal to Kenya, from Sudan to South Africa, Nigerians have developed a local reputation throughout the continent as businesspeople. Georgia continues:

> Nigerians, especially Yoruba and Igbo, are an important group in Brazil, like in Africa. Most of the Africans here in Brazil are Nigerians. There are maybe a hundred Nigerians living here in Salvador and they all are involved with either the tourist business or with selling handicrafts or with petroleum and many of them are even sanctioned by the Nigerian

government. Ha! You think Ghana would pay for me to be here! But Nigerians they come and some of them, the government support them.[1]

The University of Ile-Ife, now known as Obafemi Awolowo University, has for some time maintained an exchange and collaboration program with the Universidade Federal da Bahia (UFBa). This program includes a boarding house in the Salvador neighbourhood of Nazaré, brightly painted in the green and white of the Nigerian flag, where Nigerian students are housed. It also features the semi-regular secondment of a Nigerian scholar to UFBa and the CEAO group to teach Yoruba courses, both as part of the university's regular curriculum and as part of CEAO's outreach program to the broader community. Though most of these students receive a small stipend from the Nigerian government and their room and board is covered in the boarding house, these provisions do not cover much beyond the bare necessities. Consequently, many of these students also sell their services as Yoruba tutors to enthusiastic devotees from different *terreiros* who are eager to learn an African language. On the subject of moonlighting as a Yoruba instructor, Georgia informs me:

> I speak Yoruba, too. I lived in Lagos for a long time. But my trouble is I can't really write it … plus, I speak like a Lagos man and so it is *mostly* Yoruba, but in Lagos, we have people from everywhere … from Dakar, from Freetown, from Abidjan, from Cape Coast, from Conakry, too, from Accra, from Lomé, from Cotonou, from Harcourt. I suppose maybe some will say it isn't pure Yoruba. So I can't really teach people Yoruba, like the Nigerians, so that is one thing they have. But you know that's it. Me, as a Ghanaian here in Brazil, I'm an African businessman. Many Brazilians, especially the ones that go to the *Candomblé* – they want to know Yoruba. Someone else came here, some person, she was French, I have her card here (he rummages through his wallet for a torn and folded business card). Look, it says "Ethnologue," is that like you? (I nod and say yes) She came here and could only speak English and French and no Portuguese and wanted to know from me anything about the *terreiro*. Some of the Nigerians who teach Yoruba pretend to be fetish priests. Some people will believe because they want to know about Africa.[2]

Georgia appears to be of two minds about his place as an African in Salvador. He seems to be upset about the fact that few of the Brazilians whom he knows are aware of Ghana, of his own ethnic group, the

Fante, or of other places in Africa. This is slowly changing, and Georgia's involvement with the Salvador music scene has been helpful in popularizing African and, specifically, West African musical styles such as highlife and Afrobeat. However, at the same time, he is always perfectly willing to tell stories that speak to an appetite for tales of Black Africa. Georgia's hometown of Cape Coast is about 140 kilometres from the small coastal town of Winneba. The Winneba economy is based on fishing and on tourism surrounding the annual deer hunting festival, or *Aboakyer*, of the local Akan-speaking ethnic group, the Effutu. The festival is a celebration to mark the arrival of the Effutu people in Winneba, or Simpa as it is locally called. The story surrounding the event is that upon arrival in Simpa, the Effutu's chief deity, Otu, demanded that the family of the chief sacrifice one of its sons each year as thanks for bringing them to this sacred land. In response, the people cried that they could never kill one of their princes and so they demanded that a wild cat be substituted for the human being. However, after the first hunt, the cat killed so many people in their attempts to capture it that a second appeal was made to Otu – that a deer be killed in place of the cat. Otu accepted, and to this day the Effutu people ritually capture and slaughter a mature antelope in honour of their god and as thanks for continued prosperity. This event has become a major tourist attraction in Ghana in early May, drawing people from all over the country and from the "roots" tourist groups who may be visiting Ghana at the time. Indeed, many "roots" or "cultural heritage" tours include the Winneba Aboakyer festival as an example of "wild" and "untamed" (careful not to use the word "savage") Africa. I have attended the festival a number of times and have conducted interviews with "roots" tourists visiting the event, and I know it well.

Georgia, however, has his own take on the story that he tells to groups of tourists at *terreiros* and to his small entourage of young people eager to know something about Africa. He often tells the story in a Portuguese-Fante-English patois for the benefit of the individuals – often tourists from the United States – who cannot speak Portuguese and who may have come to visit a local *terreiro*. It's usually an eclectic group – some of them are from more affluent backgrounds with college educations, travellers, tourists, and members of Georgia's band and crew, Sistema Kalakuta Afrobeat Ensemble, the house band and DJ crew at Sankofa Africa Bar in Pelourinho. Georgia begins:

One of the reasons I came to Brazil is because in Africa there is too much blood. All the time when I was a boy, I had to see sacrifice. You hear about chickens and goats and even here, in some *Candomblés* they will take a fowl and kill it for the gods, for these *orixás*. But this is nothing. In Africa, we do it much more. Like, where I used to live in Ghana, there is a place Winneba where they make a sacrifice every year – just like you make a sacrifice to Ogun or Xangô, these people in Winneba, they make a sacrifice. The Winneba people are Fante like me – they are like the Asante and also there are many Ewe people there in Winneba, they come for the fish. You know, the Ewe have some small connection with your Jeje *terreiros*.[3] But you know, really they are all the same peoples in Ghana, we get along, we don't make war like other countries ... we're peace loving. So you have all these groups living there in Winneba, but every year they have to make a sacrifice of a deer ... But you know, in Winneba they used to kill humans as the sacrifice. They had to kill the prince of the royal family to make the god happy and for a long time they killed young boys like me, because they were going to be chiefs. As for me, you know my father was a chief, and so you can call me some kind of prince. That means in the old days I could be killed. Even when I was a small boy, I remember my cousin that they wanted to kill. But then it changed. When Nkrumah came in, they stopped the human sacrifice and changed it to a tiger hunt. The area around Cape Coast was once full of tigers, but now they have all been killed. So they changed it to a deer. That is better, but I know that there are still people who wish it was a human. They say that their *orixá* Otu is never pleased with a deer and that is why the fishing is getting worse, and so some people, in back rooms and in the villages around Winneba, away from the tourists, they still sacrifice human beings. That's why I left – I thought I would be next. Too much blood, too much blood!

The Ghana tourism board markets the story in a different way, certainly with less blood, but they emphasize many of the same motifs and symbols to appeal to the large number of "roots" tourists who must pass through Winneba on their way from Accra to Cape Coast. The Effutu claim that the Aboakyer is a seasonal ceremony that is intended to increase the productivity of their fields or the bounty of their nets. However, the event has become a highlight of the tourist calendar in Ghana and many in Winneba orient their entire life around preparing for the inevitable glut of tourists that invade the town each May. In the way it is presented to Black travellers, elemental manifestations of African Blackness are accentuated. Wild animals are prominent in the imagery and although the prey is a harmless antelope species, all of the men featured in tourist literature and in descriptions of the event are typically clothed in leopard or other wildcat skins. As well, drumming,

African spirituality, and sacrifice are placed front and centre in the tourist materials and Ghana is presented to the eager and enthusiastic travellers as a place where African rituals still survive. The event is largely marketed towards those travellers looking for an authentically African experience – one that articulates notes and elements of a broadly configured notion of African Blackness. The images used in publicizing the Aboakyer are invariably the same. Representations of overtly sensualized and virile Black, African masculinity abound in printed and Web descriptions of this event. Indeed, it is hard to find any description of the Aboakyer without also encountering images of glistening, male African bodies shouldering the slain or soon-to-be-slain bushbuck – a more profound mingling of ideas about wild Africa and the illusion of "tribal" Africa is hard to imagine (see Wyllie 1994 for more on the Aboakyer). In 2013, Georgia led his first tour of Ghana for a company based in Salvador called AfroTours. The marketing for the tour features Georgia prominently wearing Ghanaian cloth, painted face, and dreadlocks, but no images of Ghana or of any of the destinations offered in this travel package. This new aspect of Georgia's work includes visits to all of the slave forts of the Ghanaian coast, a tropical forest refuge and canopy tour, along with eight nights in Ghana for just under R$5,000. This is a significant investment for most Baianos and one that seems entirely oriented towards a certain view of Africa – one with Georgia front and centre as negotiator and translator of Africanity.

When Georgia tells his version of the Aboakyer story he is able to cast quite a spell. Questions that are fired at him afterwards include "Oh, so the Fante have *orixás* also, like the Yoruba?" or "Is this still done today?" or "Do the Yoruba have human sacrifice?" Now, it is not that these individuals are uncritical, uninformed, or gullible "pigeons to be plucked" (a phrase that Georgia often uses), so to speak. Many of them have been educated about aspects of African societies through information they may have received in the *terreiro* or through events organized by Afro-Brazilian community groups, but their thirst for any information about Africa is powerful. Moreover, two aspects of Brazilian popular awareness about Africa colour their perspective: one is the Yoruba-oriented Afrocentrism of the *terreiro*, the other is is the type of media and popular constructions of Africa that broadly permeate the Brazilian consciousness.

Most Brazilian media outlets are based either in São Paulo or in Rio de Janeiro. In these two giant cities, the tropical and African elements of

Brazil's Northeast are regularly played up and emphasized as important parts of Brazil's history. This finds expression in television programs like *Nigéria, Terra Mãe da África* (Nigeria, the motherland of Africa), a documentary series aired repeatedly on the country's largest and richest network, TV Globo, from 2005 through 2011. Hosted by one of Globo's few Black women hosts, Glória Maria, the series – aired between segments about new musical acts and political corruption on a 180-minute Sunday night variety show called *Fantástico* – follows Maria throughout Nigeria. The first episode takes us to the old slave market of Badagry, which was, according to the host, "the principal port of departure for slaves to the United States and Brazil," and is also a place where "many Brazilians can find their origins." Subsequent episodes examined scenes of Nigeria including the terrible lives of Nigerian women who have children outside of marriage; recently discovered Nigerian "mountain tribes" who live in isolation and celebrate death as a *festival de alegria* (festival of happiness); and, finally, a retrospective episode on Nigeria as a country that few people in the world know or are familiar with – Nigeria as an unknown and mysterious land with hidden tribes and strange rituals. Throughout the series, Yoruba religious practices such as the worship of the familiar *orixás*, the history of slavery, and connectedness with Brazil and especially with Salvador are presented in a kind of hodgepodge grab bag of ideas and images, all of which are reduced to "Nigerian culture" or, more frequently, "African culture." In addition, video footage of the numerous festivals and religious "rituals" is usually brimming with images of young, scantily clad – sometimes naked – Black African women, emphasizing the exotic and overtly sexual aspect of Nigeria/Africa.

In a more recent incident, on an episode of the very popular *Programa do Jô*, a nightly chat and variety show aired on TV Globo, television host Jô Soares interviewed a Portuguese adventurer visiting Brazil to promote his new book, a supposed "ethnographic" account of Angolan women. However, instead of an academically charged interaction, the ensuing on-air discussion about the book was filled with ribald and comedic commentary about Africa, savage behaviours, African women's genitalia, African "rituals," and racist and sexist comments about Africans and Black people in general. Surprisingly, the titillating travelogue was treated in the interview as if it were an important contribution to ethnographic knowledge and a way for Brazilians to understand their connection with Africa. Angolans, again one of the few African nations that Brazilians are familiar with, become a generalized model for all Africans and their "rituals" become a pattern for how all-African religions are practised. The media moguls behind TV Globo have long seen themselves as public guardians of Brazilian culture and regularly produce documentary specials and public service programs that allege to explore Brazil's unique history and culture. Crucial in this programming line-up are *telenovelas* – soap operas. These serialized dramas are extremely popular throughout Brazil and it is not uncommon to find a slowdown in activity on the streets, in bars and restaurants, and in other evening places of work during the hours that these programs are aired. Typically, *telenovelas* interweave multiple storylines of love, romance, and betrayal, but also speak to "working class aspirations" of "making it" in the big city while maintaining "Brazilian values." The *telenovelas* also reflect ideas about Brazil's racial composition in a way that perpetuates the sentiments of "racial democracy," and the central importance of the Catholic Church in this ideal of Brazilian life. The centrality of the Catholic Church in Brazilian life was emphasized during the non-stop media coverage on TV Globo of the election of Pope Benedict XVI in 2005 and, more recently, in 2013 during the election of the first Latin American pontiff, Pope Francis. It was also very much on display in Globo's media war during the 1990s against the growing evangelical church, Igreja Universal do Reino de Deus (the Universal Church of the Kingdom of God), their leader Edir Macedo, and the church's media arm at the time, TV Record. Essentially, this battle was not so much about ideology or commercial success, but about issues of "cultural hegemony" and who got to speak for what counts as Brazilian (see Birman and Lehmann 1999).

Throughout Globo's history as a major national broadcaster they have sought to steer definitions of Brazilian identity. From productions like the 1976 telenovela *A Escrava Isaura*,[4] based on an 1875 novel by Bernardo Guimarães about a slave-girl named Isaura and the life of Africans – all of whom speak a smattering of Yoruba – on plantations, to more contemporary productions like *Decadência*, a popular *telenovela* that "unmasked" the corruption found in a fictional evangelical megachurch, Brazil's TV Globo repeatedly casts itself as an arbiter of Brazilian culture and "Brazilianness." However, although Globo and their programs like *Fantástico* and *Programa do Jô* are broadcast nationwide, from Amazonas to Bahia, from the poor middle states like Espírito Santo to the agricultural South, they are very much oriented to the fishbowl of the industrialized Southeast – Rio and São Paulo. In this part of the country, comments like those aired on Soares' show are commonplace and tolerated. Consequently, there was no public outrage or anger expressed at these remarks in newspapers or online. In Bahia, members of local *Afrodescendente* and *Movimento Negro Unificado* (MNU) groups whom I corresponded with after the event said that, although they knew about the episode, they commented that "it wasn't such a big deal," and one even told me that the book discussed on Soares' show wasn't "that bad."[5] Considering the 2007 public castigation of U.S. radio and television host Don Imus in the United States after he made several comments on-air about the Black members of the Rutgers University women's college basketball team, this non-action in Brazil seems notable. Imus' comments, though offensive and objectionable, were mild compared with those bandied around on *Programa do Jô*, yet no formal reaction occurred in the wake of this event from any quarter of Brazilian society.

This event did not take place in a media forum reserved for the rich, elite, or well connected. Most Brazilian families own a small television set. The evening meal, as in many other societies, is often enjoyed around the TV and one cannot follow the fortunes of the Brazilian national football team without one. Further, Soares' comments were aired just after "prime-time," while Imus' remarks were confined to early morning cable TV and radio networks. Why the difference? First, although there is a considerable amount of "formal" and public obeisance paid to Brazil's "racial democracy," racism is commonplace in the workplace, in the media, and in society at large. Second, because of, rather than in spite of, the work of groups like MNU, the *terreiros*, popular music, art, and tourism, many Brazilians are familiar with and have become accustomed to generalized and highly homogenized images of Africa – much in the same way that early twentieth century Britain or France was familiarized with overtly racialized and caricatured representations of peoples from throughout their respective empires. For Brazil, the construction of Africa that they know and that is presented on a regular basis is one of mystical places, secret rituals, spirits, gods, *orixás*, blood sacrifices, and strange sexual habits.

Stories of Zimbabwean political corruption, vote rigging in Kenya, civil war in Sudan or the Central African Republic, peaceful elections in Ghana or Botswana, resurgence in the cocoa and coffee markets in West Africa, or a thousand other stories have little appeal. And to be sure, this is no different from most news coverage of Africa in North

America or Europe. Stories from Africa are rarely deemed newsworthy in the notebooks of most reporters, be they Brazilian, North American, British, French, or otherwise. But what is interesting is that throughout Brazil – in Bahia, Rio, São Paulo, Minas Gerais, and elsewhere – Black community groups and religious organizations are actively involved in trying to articulate an African-oriented identity, one that embraces the African, while also engaged in buying into and helping to manufacture – sometimes hand in hand with the media – a generalized and homogenized image of Africa. Most community groups and movements that seek to articulate Blackness through Africanity seem intent on sticking to a generalized and romanticized image of Africa that reduces the incredible richness and diversity of that continent into a few key concepts and ideas.

Consequently, many Brazilians approach an interaction, a dialogue, with someone like Georgia holding an idea of Africa built not on regional, political, and cultural nuance – something that despite his tall tales, Georgia is quite familiar with – but of ideas and symbols born of a homogenized and generalized construction of African-oriented Blackness. There is no need for members of Georgia's audience to travel to the cities of Cape Coast or Winneba or Ouidah or Badagry to hear stories of leopard hunts or slave castles. They are available, in an eminently personal, interactive, and dialogic format right in their own backyard. Moreover, they are not filtered and processed through the lens of the popular media, but recounted, person-to-person, by an African who, from the point of view of the audience, has first-hand knowledge of these experiences. This, then, is the context within which we must understand Georgia's Münchausen-like tales of African bush, gods, chiefs, princes, and "tigers." Georgia weaves his tales in the way he does not because he truly believes that his audience is naïve or that he himself believes these stories. Rather, he, like any good storyteller, knows what his audience wants to hear. His narrative of the Aboakyer is configured precisely to mediate ideas about Africa that Georgia knows will be devoured by those listening. The story itself is a note in the ongoing dialogue between Africa and Afro-America, and contained within are symbols that are seen by those taken by Georgia's charisma as thoroughly African.

Moreover, these stories are part and parcel of his main source of income. Working as, in his words, a "Rasta-Africaman Guide to Africa in Brazil," his clients include African Americans visiting "Brazil – Outpost of Africa," tourists from São Paulo, Rio, and other parts of Brazil and

South America, and European visitors who need a tour guide who can speak English. Through these jobs Georgia makes his contacts and connections with *terreiros* and community group members seeking to learn about Africa or who want to have an African as a friend. He also meets with carnaval associations or bar owners in this capacity who patronize *terreiros* and might be able to give an African "master drummer" like Georgia a job playing at a function or in their establishment.

I accompanied Georgia on a number of evenings as he guided and regaled his small groups of tourists to *terreiros*, usually groups of African Americans, who typically resided in the *pousadas* and guest houses of the neighbourhoods surrounding Salvador's old city – Pelourinho. Georgia makes sure that many of the hotels, restaurants, and other hospitality establishments around his home neighbourhood of Saúde have his number and business card. Georgia conducts his business entirely by mobile phone and on more than a few occasions, I would be out with him enjoying some cold beers when he would get a call from some small hotel or restaurant operator that they had a group of people who wanted a real *terreiro* tour or an "authentically" African tour of the old city, not like, in his words, the ones offered by the big travel agencies in Pelourinho. When the restaurateur or hotelier informed their guests that he could provide them with a "real African" to guide them, the opportunity was usually snapped up – this is what Georgia relied upon. Georgia has no steady salary or income – one week he may be playing Afrobeat and reggae music at a Pelourinho bar, the next week, providing *terreiro* tours, and the next, working to try and import West African handicrafts from either Accra or Lagos for sale in Pelourinho shops.

In 2006, Georgia informed me that his dream is to save up enough money to open his own bar that he intends to call "Sankofa." Sankofa is an Akan word that means "return" or "go back and take," and is represented by an Asante Adinkra symbol that depicts the necks of two swans turning their heads backwards to form a heart image. Adinkra symbols are used by the Asante to express proverbs and philosophical ideas and Sankofa has since been adopted by African American "roots" and "back to Africa" groups as a symbol of return to an African cultural source. Georgia hoped that his bar would attract the increasing numbers of African American tourists visiting Salvador and also Afro-Brazilians looking to, as he puts it, socialize "in an African environment." He tells me he has dreams of painting the bar in bright green, red, and yellow colours, with portraits of great African and Black leaders on the walls like Kwame Nkrumah, Nelson Mandela, Muhammad Ali,

Malcolm X, Martin Luther King Jr., Sekou Touré, Haile Selassie, Bob Marley, Gilberto Gil, Zumbí, and others. He tells me:

> We have to try and get African beer like Guinness Malta, Star, or you know, when I worked the ship out of Lagos, we always got this beer from Kenya called Tusker with an elephant on the front. Plus, we can try and have bands come from Lagos, Accra, Dakar, and Guinea-style dancing and *orixá* music or *Afoxé*.[6]

During one evening tour to a *terreiro* that Georgia had been hired to conduct in January 2006, he asked me if I might help him out as two of the individuals in the group he was to lead only spoke French. Many tourist companies and travel agencies offer *terreiro* tours for they are considered one of the essential experiences of any visit to Salvador. Georgia's angle is that he can offer a viewpoint that no Brazilian can: an African perspective on what is presented as an eminently African tradition. We all gathered at a bar just off Pelourinho's *Praça da Sé*, and set off walking towards Georgia's home neighbourhood of Saúde. We descended out of the old city on the cobblestone streets, across the famous *Baixa dos Sapateiros* or "cobbler's low area," up towards the Igreja da Saúde, and then down into some twisting alleys and back roads until we arrived, about forty-five minutes later, at a small cinder-block building tucked in behind an auto mechanic's garage and shaded by a number of large and overgrown mango trees. We entered the small *terreiro* and took seats on white plastic chairs with "reserved" notes placed on them and began waiting.

As noted earlier, the present work is not about religion or religiosity, and so I do not recount here the many elements of ritual and practice that make up a typical *Candomblé* ceremony. Further, I will not dwell on the anthropology or psychology of trance and possession. This has been covered far more capably in other work and is of no direct relevance to this study (see Boddy 1988, 1989; Bourguignon 2004; Boyer-Araújo 1993; Corin 1979; Edge 1996; Halperin 1995; Hess 1989; Lambek 1980; Lehmann 2001; Lewis 1971, 2003; Van De Port 2005; Wafer 1991). Rather, this study is about how Black peoples in Bahia use the *terreiro* as one mode of reconstructing collective self-identity towards Africa and towards the engagement of other Black communities in the Americas in a discourse about African-oriented Blackness. To that end, I include here only a very rudimentary description of the richness and variety of ritual action that occurs during the course of an evening session of worship and celebration. Most *Candomblé* rituals are divided into two main parts: the preparation and dressing of the *terreiro*, which is considered worship in and of itself, and the actual possession ritual. The preparatory phase for a *Candomblé* ceremony can start anywhere from one day to one week in advance of the actual event and during this period initiates and devotees will wash all of the white clothes to be worn by participants, decorate the house with paper flags and candles in colours appropriate to the *orixás* that are to be venerated, and prepare food for the banquet. Domestic animals such as fowl and goats may be slaughtered and offered in honour of particular deities or lesser spirits and, finally, on the morning of the ceremony, the *jogo de búzios*, or cowrie shell divination, is performed for petitioners. During the possession phase of the public ceremony, *filhos dos santos*, or followers-in-saint, will enter a central area of the house and begin dancing and chanting to a repetitive drum rhythm. Under the leadership or a *pai de santo* or *mãe de santo* (father or mother in saint), the *filhos* or initiates will, one by one or sometimes, several at once, become "mounted" or possessed by different *orixás* and *exus* or messenger spirits. The ceremony comports with the pattern of therapeutic cults worldwide, the purpose of which is to spiritually cleanse and heal those participating and those who have come to petition the *orixás* for their divine intercession. The ceremony is not over until the last *orixá* has fled his or her host. After this, a banquet is held in honour of the deities "work" here on earth.

Instead of the details of religious practice, I wish to focus on the ways in which Brazilians and African American tourists present spoke of the ceremony and the *imprimatur* of authenticity that Georgia's presence seemed to provide for certain members of the congregation and, most certainly, for the group of travellers we brought to the *terreiro*. I focus on Georgia and his friends, as they appear to be touchstones for identity discourses about Africanness and Blackness. Through Georgia, groups of travellers who wish to engage in an African-oriented expression of their Black identity find someone who can vouch for their legitimacy, someone who, at the very least, can be used as a signifier or marker of ethnic membership or be used as a proxy for an African experience that most residents of Salvador will never experience. This is what draws people to Georgia, what makes him a popular tour guide and musician and why his name is known in *terreiros*, Black community centres, carnaval associations, bars, restaurants, and hotels throughout the city. Ethnographically, Georgia and his Nigerian friends are important nexus points of information and data pertaining to Black identity discourse in Bahia. As emphasized earlier, I take Scott's (1991) exhortation that we focus on how concepts like Africa pattern and configure the processes of identity construction most seriously. In Georgia, I could have found no better conduit for this kind of talk.

During the banquet after the evening's celebration, I sat down with Georgia and the *mãe* of the *terreiro*. The *mãe*, a woman in her sixties, knew Georgia well and she told me that he is the only person she will allow to bring foreigners or outsiders into the *terreiro*. Hers is not a large *terreiro* nor particularly famous, as she explained:

> We don't have famous luminaries like other *terreiros*. Here, we have only the poor, the people of the street and those that work for a living. We are a poor community and 99.99 per cent of our devotees are Black. But, many of the participants of the rich *terreiros* are politicians, professors, or other rich people. I allow Georgia to bring foreigners here because we need the money, and we want to show our traditions, our heritage for other populations descended from Africa, like you from Cuba, or you from the United States. Georgia understands this, because he's from Africa. He understands our rituals and he can be a good example for our children – an African man.[7]

I questioned the *mãe* about Georgia's role. How could Georgia, who is Fante from Ghana, be a good example for your group if *Candomblé* was based on Yoruba practice and on the Yoruba *orixás*? She responded that she believed that all Africans have a shared understanding of spirits and mystical beings and that people descended from Africa have the same insight. Simply through being around Georgia, engaging and conversing with Georgia, the members of her congregation, the *mãe* told me, could learn something about Africa. Georgia chimes in: "In Africa we have more than gods and spirits, but we also worship the ancestors with shrines. That is why a 'Ghanaman' can talk to 'Yorubaman' about the spirits because we all believe in the ancestors, like what you would call your great, great, grandparents." One member of the tour group, a young Afro-Brazilian student, Salvador resident, and friend of Georgia added, "You just can't understand. We are all linked through being African in our heart. Georgia and all Africans have so much to teach the world about respect and pride and the beauty of being Black. Black people have to accept that they are Africans, and not Americans or Brazilians or Cubans." There is no air of scepticism about

Georgia's right to speak to tour groups, to young members of the *terreiro* or to the leaders of these houses of worship on just about anything pertaining to Africa. He appears to have carte blanche to say just about whatever he wants when it comes to the subject of Africa.

Candomblé houses have been an important part of the Bahian and broader Brazilian religious scene for quite some time. They are not young or fledgling peripheral cults looking to rediscover ritual practice and long-lost mystical formulae. The *terreiros* of Salvador are a religious and political force to be reckoned with and most are rightly self-confident in their position within Bahian society. Few *terreiros* have need of an imported African expert to tell them how to do things "properly," and indeed some emphasize that Africans need to come to Brazil to learn how real African culture, unsullied by the evils of colonialism, have been kept alive. Brazil is home to more than just *Candomblé* – other religious forms, such as *Umbanda* and *Xangô*, also embrace the pantheon of Yoruba deities and give them divine standing alongside the spirits of Amerindian warriors, departed slave spirits, and Catholic saints. These religious forms are fully developed and mature forms of religious activity that have become, for the most part, fixtures on the Brazilian religious landscape and accepted as an alternative – especially for Afro-Brazilians – to Christian denominations. To be sure, they still receive occasional backlashes from militant evangelical groups, such as a recent event in Rio de Janeiro state in which four members of the small but vociferous Igreja Evangélica Nova Geração de Jesus Cristo (New Generation Evangelical Church of Jesus Christ) broke into an *Umbanda terreiro* and smashed all of the status and icons of the *orixás* (Menchen 2008). Many *terreiros* have come into the open and no longer hide from religious persecution in the same way that they did during the years of military rule in Brazil, or they seek to confront such racial and religious intolerance. Indeed, without the *terreiros* and the symbols of Africanity that it provides as a major attraction, the income earned by Bahia in tourism would likely be significantly reduced.

The fascination and special status attached to Georgia and other Africans in Salvador lies not in their ability to judge the veracity or authenticity of African-oriented ritual, but rather in their capacity to serve as markers of real Africanness in the identity discourse that has built up in and around the space of the *terreiro*. The *terreiros* have come of age and consequently Black communities and Black neighbourhoods attached or associated with these places of worship are actively engaged in transposing the African orientation of this religious space into the arena of identity politics. The *mãe* continues:

> Georgia can't tell me anything about the *orixás*. I'm a daughter of Ogun. He's my guide in this life, and he tells me about the secrets of this world and the next ... he tells me the secrets of mother Africa. But the eyes of Ogun are different. His perspective on Africa is not the perspective of humans. For this, we need to learn a little about African life from people like Georgia.

There is an unexpected Ghanaian nationalism that bubbles up in Georgia when he starts talking about the dominance of Nigeria in the ethnic imagination of Afro-Brazilians interested in him or what he has to say. This fervor becomes apparent on the evening of our visit to the Saúde *terreiro* when a small group of young men and women ask Georgia about Yoruba classes and the Yoruba teacher at UFBa – Universidade Federal da Bahia – named Félix. The group informs Georgia that they could not afford to take the classes taught by Félix, who they have heard is a professor from Nigeria, and they want to know if there is some alternative way for them to learn how to speak Yoruba. Georgia tells them that they should go find one of the Nigerian students that live in the Nigerian house in the neighbourhood of Nazaré. This, Georgia tells me, is where he always loses out. He informs me that he doesn't have the ability to teach the Yoruba language to Brazilians in Salvador:

> They want to learn Yoruba. Many think African equates to Yoruba. There are also some Afro-Brazilian Muslims in Salvador and they want to learn Arabic, but 99 per cent of all Black Brazilians in Salvador who want to learn an African language think of Yoruba. I do what I can. Try to make money. But I can't get in on this market. This is where those Lagos boys succeed.[8]

During one evening celebration, held in late November 2005 at the Saúde *terreiro*, during the *Mês da Consciência Negra* (Month of Black Consciousness), the *mãe* held an informal, though quite well attended Black consciousness rally in the small plaza adjacent to the centre. Georgia and I took part in this event, enjoying the cold drinks and freshly cooked "African" food – the popular street food, *acarajé* – being served. Speakers included the *mãe* of the *terreiro*, some businessmen in the neighbourhood who were members of the congregation, and a graduate student in history from CEAO who was also an infrequent attendee at the *terreiro*. The speakers discussed the need for all people of African descent in the neighbourhood to be proud of their African traditions, to be proud of their African heritage, and *sangue de África* (African blood). They noted that they were pleased to have with them tonight an anthropologist who had worked in West Africa (referring to me), and a famous *"personalidade,"* known to all, direct from Africa. They were referring, of course, to Georgia. They went on to describe him as someone who was intimately familiar with the gods of Africa and who had lived in Lagos, an important city for the Yoruba people and for the *orixás*.

The loudspeakers blared *afoxé* music along with Brazilian reggae and James Brown's funk anthem, "Say It Loud – I'm Black and I'm Proud," which seemed to be looped into the mix approximately every twenty minutes. The presenters were all extremely charismatic and all spoke to a need for Brazilian society to "finally" come to terms with the horrors of slavery and for *"Afrodescendentes"* to stop apologizing for their mixed heritage and to proudly assert that are *"negros."* They need to be, the *mãe* added, like Georgia – *"negro e orgulho"* (Black and proud). Many individuals came up to Georgia during the evening to ask him how to say "hello" in Yoruba, how to say "thank you" in Yoruba, about Yoruba clothes, about Yoruba food, indeed, about almost anything to do with his time in Lagos. Words like *preto, pardo,* or others are being replaced in the identity language surrounding a site like this *terreiro*, in bold and decisive ways, with a single phenotypic descriptor to describe all people with even the slightest possibility of African heritage – *negro*, or Black. For this group of Afro-Brazilians, Black meant a public expression of Africanity. Of course, this small community of Salvador residents did not want to start speaking Yoruba as the principal language of communication, wearing printed West African cloth, giving up eating staples such as *feijoada* and *churrasco* (beans and barbeque) or stop cheering for the Brazilian football team. Politically significant and public assertions of identity are rarely about the mundane quotidian aspects of life, but rather about the cultural practices and idealized notions of heritage that a community strategically and deliberately chooses to overemphasize as markers of membership. For this community, those key markers or points of contention are Africa-oriented articulations of Blackness that dwell primarily on *elements* of Yoruba religious practice.

I emphasize *elements,* as it is important here to guard against conflating the reinterpretation of elements of cultural practice sourced from another society with some kind of extrapolation or remapping of the geographical territory occupied by that original society. Emphasizing aspects of public identity, learning Yoruba, or engaging in religious activity that incorporates or – as in the case of some *terreiros* that claim "purity" – replicates aspects of another culture, does not make the population *members* of that other society. Matory (2005), in *Black Atlantic Religion*, comes very close to asserting that because Yoruba culture was born out of transatlantic dialogues – and he presents convincing evidence to suggest that this is the case – Yoruba culture is, therefore, perhaps the first truly Atlantic culture and the Yoruba people can be found on both sides of the Atlantic. However, are Afro-Brazilian communities that practise *Candomblé* and that assert an African-oriented Black identity truly members of Yoruba *society*? Brazilians engaged in these redefinitions of ethnic identity do not reckon kinship like the Yoruba, get married like the Yoruba, recognize the political authority of regional and village *obas* or chiefs, or participate in any meaningful way in Yoruba social life – they are and remain, Brazilians. Yet through the processes of conversing and engaging with individuals like Georgia and, as we shall see, other, more clearly defined agents of Yorubaness, they are being increasingly drawn into a global community of individuals who reckon Blackness through similar key symbols – of which Yoruba religious practice and basic linguistic ability are just two. But mediation of these *elements* of Yoruba culture does not imply membership in Yoruba society. Rather, through the process of transatlantic dialogue between agents of Afro-Brazilian and West African society, both sides are increasingly involved in redefining and globalizing what Blackness can, and for those invested in this process, *should* mean for all Black people.

Certainly, we live in a globalized world in which the boundaries of identity, collectivity, nationality, and other such social formations have become transregional. Yoruba, as an ethnic group, is no different, as it has large contingents living in London, New York, Toronto, Frankfurt, and elsewhere that maintain important economic and political connections with the homeland. But although African ethnic identities are tricky and slippery things at times, *orixá* worship does not a Yoruba make. Ask any Ghanaian what Asante means, a Nigerian what Yoruba means, or a South African what Zulu means and you will likely get an array of answers. "Someone born in Kumasi," or "Someone born in Lagos," "a person whose father is Yoruba" or "whose father is Zulu" or

Figure 2.1 Georgia in his element at Sankofa African Bar. Photo courtesy of Kweku Aidoo.

"whose mother is Asante" might be among the range of responses that one might receive. Ethnic identities in Africa, like those elsewhere in the world, shift and move according to context and historical circumstance. However, there are certain elements of ethnic identification across the African ethnographic record that seem to hold fast as key signifiers of group membership. Among these, although it no longer holds the pride of place it once did in the discipline of anthropology, is kinship. It is still very hard to understand how African communities – especially at the village level – work without an understanding of that society's patterns of kinship. Afro-Brazilians who speak of Yorubaness, of the Yoruba language and religion as important components of their Blackness, are in no way implicated in Yoruba patterns of kinship or in any other aspect of daily life in a Yoruba village – unlike expatriate communities of Yoruba emigrants living abroad. They must then be understood, first and foremost, as Brazilians.

Now in 2014, Georgia's dream has become a reality. Georgia is now one of the founders of the Pelourinho-located Sankofa African Bar and is also the de facto house DJ. Sankofa African Bar is very much as Georgia described it would be in 2006 – festooned in flags from around the African continent; painted in green, red, and yellow; and decorated with maps of Africa and generic African masks. Sankofa plays – thanks largely to Georgia's influence – a mixture of contemporary African music, Afrobeat, reggae, and other music oriented specifically towards creating, in Georgia's words, an "African cultural space." Regular events include Festa Afrobeat, a celebration of Afrobeat and African music; Black Poetry slams; and Black consciousness rallies and events – in short, Sankofa has become the centrepiece of Georgia's efforts to be a representative of a particular construction of the Africa-idea. In many ways, Sankofa has come to occupy a new, specifically African-oriented, cultural space within the highly commercialized and contested space of Pelourinho. As former long-time residents, new businesses, restaurants, bars, cultural institutions, UNESCO World Heritage Sites, and myriad representatives of the tourist trade all compete for every tourist dollar in Pelourinho (see Collins 2008), Sankofa African Bar seeks to make its mark by catering specifically to the desire for spaces that speak to what Brazilians understand of Africa. Here, Georgia is of particular importance. For every performance as DJ or as a member of Kalakuta, Georgia will typically dress in some form of robe made of colourful West African printex cloth. He will also adorn his face with daubs of white face paint in geometric patterns – none of which is attributable to a specific West African, or African in general for that matter, society, but all of which contributes to his role as a mediator of Africanity to an audience that is eager for such overt and ritualized performance of a particular identity.

Yoruba Language Instruction in Salvador

If Georgia is involved in the formation and development of *general* ideas of Africanness and Yoruba culture in communities like Saúde and other locales, then Félix Ayoh'Omidire, a now former Yoruba teacher at UFBa, is actively engaged in promoting a specific form of dialogue between Black communities in Salvador and the Yoruba homeland of Ile-Ife. Félix is a scholar of European languages and in addition to speaking the English, Yoruba, and Hausa of his native Nigeria, he also speaks Spanish, French, and Portuguese. For almost six years he was seconded to the languages department of UFBa and in this position he was also a

fellow at CEAO – the Centro de Estudos Afro-Orientais, a research institute within UFBa's Faculty of Philosophy and Human Sciences. Félix
took up his position in Salvador with a long tradition of Yoruba instruction already in place at UFBa.

The exchange program between Obafemi Awolowo University in Ile-
Ife and UFBa was started in the late 1970s with the help of the distinguished historian of Brazil in Africa and Africa in Brazil, Olabiyi
Babalola Yaï (1997). Yoruba instruction at UFBa began in 1959 (Parés
2004) when the first language classes were offered at CEAO, but it
wasn't until Yaï's arrival in the 1970s and formalization of exchanges
between Brazilian and Nigerian universities occurred that an emphasis
on Yoruba culture and sociolinguistics began to be incorporated into
the curriculum. These courses were frequented by religious officiants
from various Afro-Brazilian congregations – especially *Candomblé terreiros* – who "besides learning the religious songs, also wanted access to
esoteric knowledge, attributing to their African teachers a religious status which they sometimes did not have" (Parés 2004, 200). Yaï has since
become enshrined in CEAO's pantheon of intellectuals who were actively involved with *terreiros* and with the place of CEAO as an important champion of African-oriented religious expression. Yaï's (see 1997)
position in the history of UFBa and the Black communities of Salvador
anticipated Félix's involvement and was very much a contemporary
recapitulation or reworking of the subject of his own research – Atlantic
dialogue between Africa and the Americas. During the ceremony held
for CEAO's forty-fifth anniversary in 2004, much of the evening was
taken up by former students of the centre, many of them now members
of larger and more dominant *terreiros*, others now professors at UFBa,
and some, members of Salvador's Black movement. They spoke of Yaï's
dedication to teaching Yoruba and to educating the people of Salvador
about their African heritage. The Yoruba instruction program was presented, during this event, as one of CEAO's most important contributions to battling racism and religious intolerance in Salvador.

During his time in Brazil, Félix actively continued Yaï's legacy at
CEAO by becoming an enthusiastic and important authority on the
Yoruba people, unofficial Yoruba ambassador, and all-around expert on
every aspect of African life relevant to the activities of Afro-Brazilian
communities in Salvador. Félix, however, did not worship at *terreiros*
in Salvador and did not, like some other Nigerian men in the city, market himself as a *babalaô* or fetish priest to *Candomblé* centres looking for
African authenticity. Indeed, Félix actively speaks out against the small
group of Nigerians from Lagos who tried to sell their services as official

representatives of the *orixá* traditions in Nigeria. These individuals, most of them young men who now reside in Brazil with little means or desire to return to Nigeria, will charge for official naming ceremonies for start-up *terreiros* or will bless and sanctify smaller centres. One such individual named Nwafor, who was only in Salvador for a few short months before making his way to São Paulo, informed me:

> I'm no *babalaô*. I'm not even Yoruba. I'm an Igbo, but it doesn't matter. I can speak perfect Yoruba, you know. Everyone in Nigeria can really speak Yoruba. This is the biggest problem with Brazilians and Europeans. They can only speak one or two languages. In Africa, when we are small boys, we can speak four or five languages. So now I'm here, I can go to this one *Candomblé* in Ondina [a Salvador neighborhood] and make some money. People don't understand how many *Candomblés* there are in Salvador. There are the big ones that everybody knows, but there are thousands of small ones. That's what people don't know. You don't realize how many *terreiros* there are. That's where I can make some money. You can't go in to Casa Branca and pull this stuff. More than anything they want me to come and just sit there as an African presence.[9]

These "impostor" (Parés 2004) African priests can be found throughout the country, and both Gonçalves da Silva (1995) and Capone (2010) note their predominance in southern cities like São Paulo. However, because of the growing tourist trade and the increased emphasis on Bahia as a major nexus point in transatlantic Afro-American tourism, it would now seem that Salvador is increasingly a focal point for such operators. Another such "impostor" priest with whom I spoke in 2011 is Adebola, who does indeed spend time between Rio de Janeiro and Salvador working, as he puts it, "in whatever style" people want:

> I can do Jeje, I can do Yoruba, whatever you need. I have the clothes and I know what to say. They don't want anything or me to take over. It is just that they believe my presence makes some people believe that the African gods are really with us. I get a few *reais* and move along to the next place. I got to Brazil via Cuba. I went to school in Cuba for a little while and I discovered these religions over there. Now I'm doing this to save money to go college here in Brazil.[10]

Georgia confirmed for me that some "Lagos boys," as he calls them, are engaged in this kind of activity in Salvador and he is disapproving of this behaviour. However, he also realizes that many of the West

Africans in Salvador are there in an undocumented capacity and are looking to make money through whatever means possible. Apparently, one such individual who did not speak Portuguese very well even tried to induct Georgia into his operation, telling him that they could split the profits if he acted as his translator and assistant. Georgia asserts: "This guy was no *babalaô*. He told me that if I translated his Yoruba into Portuguese, that we could make some money. But this was too much for me. This guy was a real "419er."[11]

In my first meeting with Félix, I had mentioned that I became aware of him through my interviews with Georgia. Félix spoke kindly of Georgia, noting, "Georgia – he works very hard and has he told you his dream of the 'African' bar? He's always working some angle. He never tries to pretend he's a *babalaô* like some of my countrymen here in Salvador." Félix continued:

> I've been here for six years now. I've seen many anthropologists and soci-
> ologists come and go. They come here constantly and all they want to do
> is dive headlong into the *terreiro*. Many of the ones that come here, they
> already believe! Half the researchers that come here looking to do a study
> already practise one of these religions or practise *capoeira* in their home
> country, and so come here deeply invested in *Candomblé*. Every time that a
> *terreiro* has a celebration or anniversary or a Black consciousness rally, or
> the university holds a seminar about "African" presence in Brazil, or there
> is a *palestra* [colloquium] about the *orixás* or religious intolerance, I'm at
> the top of the invitation list … My schedule is constantly booked and I
> have to always keep my *gbariye* [the handwoven smock worn by Yoruba
> men] clean. Once a week, I'm at some event talking about Yoruba customs
> and the *orixás*. I know about them because I am a Yorubaman, but so many
> people find it hard to believe that I am a practicing Christian. They think
> that because I am learned and an African, that I must practise traditional
> African religion. I am here as a linguist, not as a fetish priest, so I will go to
> the *terreiro* openings and anniversaries, I will attend the lectures, but not
> as a believer, just as an observer, a supporter of Yoruba identity and social
> scientist.[12]

"Why then do you wear the *gbariye* to these events if you don't want to come off as an authority on the Yoruba and their culture?" I asked. Félix continues:

> When I first came here, I treated my job as just another teaching appoint-
> ment. But after seeing the way that so many people want to use the *terreiro*

and Yoruba culture as a way to be proud, I had to participate and contribute as much as I could … These people see my culture, Yoruba culture, as a way to talk about being Black. That, as a Yorubaman, makes me feel pride in my own culture. The Yoruba kings are the most renowned in all of Africa. You can be like the historians at UFBa who go to the *terreiro* and believe that what they do has been preserved by slaves and Blacks in Brazil through the centuries, or you can be like Fry [he means Peter Fry] and say that the whole Yoruba emphasis in the *terreiros* was invented by Ramos and Nina Rodrigues and so on, or you can believe, like Matory, that Bomfim and his so-called English professors not only created the Yoruba emphasis here in Brazil, but also created the Yoruba culture in Nigeria. But it doesn't matter what perspective you take. These people here are crying out for a new way to think about race and about identity. They are crying out to be something other than *mulato* or *preto* or *"café-com-leite,"* and if they can find it through Yoruba culture then that is fine by me.

I asked Félix a number of times about his own place in this ongoing dialogue between West Africa and Bahia. He is reluctant to admit that he is involved and implicated in the process of Africanizing the discourse on identity in Salvador. However, he is quick to point out that he thinks such a process has certainly guided the development of Afro-Brazilian culture. Félix is every bit the cultural broker and mediator of identity that Georgia is – Georgia operates at the street level, working in bars and restaurants, at musical events, in local *terreiros* and at Black consciousness rallies; whereas Félix is a scholar, and due to his former academic position as a teacher of language at UFBA, he is very much an elite negotiator of African and Yoruba-oriented Blackness. Félix is emphatic about the details of his own African culture and, more than anything, he is directly involved in the dissemination of the Yoruba language among young Afro-Brazilians. His classes at UFBa and CEAO were always overflowing with students and invariably there was a waiting list for registration. While at UFBa, he typically taught one class at the main UFBa campus and another at the CEAO offices that were up until recently located in the old city of Pelourinho.

I joined Félix just after one of his classes ended and the experience seemed something like escorting a celebrity or rock star away from one of their performances. Félix was mobbed with students asking him about this verb and that noun in Yoruba, about a particular Yoruba phrase they had found on the Internet or saw written on a fetish doll that they had purchased at Abitoks, an "African" boutique in Pelourinho run by another Nigerian resident in Salvador.[13] He tells me that this is a normal occurrence and that it usually takes him at least an hour after each class to deal with all of the questions and concerns of the students. "They are very enthusiastic," Félix tells me, but he does sometimes lament on the fact that all they ever want to know about Yoruba society are the *orixás*. "They become interested in Yoruba society because all of the prominent Black leaders in Salvador who speak of Africa or incorporate Africa into their political agendas emphasize the same cultural elements," Félix explains. "Not only that," he adds, "there are some leaders here who think that they have a *purer* form of Yoruba culture here in Brazil [emphasis his]." Félix makes an important observation here – he replicates the phrase "purer Yoruba *culture*" as used by many local Black leaders to describe *terreiro* activity and the concomitant identity discourse, not stronger or more devout expressions of religious belief, but rather stronger *culture*. The metonymical substitution of the entire Yoruba culture for elements of religious praxis is, I think, analogous to suggesting that because members of a particular society are devout and fervent adherents of Catholicism, that those individuals are somehow representative or embody Roman culture, or that ardent practitioners of Sunni Islam are in some way "carriers" of "bearers" of Arab Bedouin society. It is a mistake of conflation that, as mentioned earlier, is committed with considerable regularity in Salvador.

During 2005's *Mês da Consciência Negra,* I accompanied Félix to Salvador's famed carnaval association Ilê Aiyê in the neighbourhood of Curuzu-Liberdade where he was to speak at a special seminar and public rally entitled "Reconnecting with Africa." I met Félix at his home and waited for him to dress in his best golden *gbariye* with matching black with gold trim soft cap before we made our way to the carnaval hall. When we arrived, Félix was taken aside and greeted by all of the leaders of the association or *bloco*. He was received with a great deal of formality and was introduced to the other speakers in something that seemed like a royal receiving line. "Professor Félix," as he was called, had come "all the way from Africa" and was presented as a noted authority on the Yoruba people, their language, and their customs. When the evening finally got underway, Félix took his place at the panelists' table along with two professors from UFBa, a Black community organizer from the nearby Northeast state of Sergipe, an *iálorixá* from a major *terreiro* in the neighbourhood of Engenho Velho da Federação, and a Catholic seminary student from Angola who happened to be visiting Salvador.

The event began with a vigorous discussion of the recently enacted Lei 10.639 (Law 10.639). This piece of legislation is widely seen as a crucial victory for Afro-Brazilian community groups as it enshrines in law the need for the teaching of Afro-Brazilian and African history in the national education system and recognizes the place of Black society in the formation of the Brazilian state. In the words of one of the speakers, the *terreiro* leader: "The law is our instrument of pressure, and it gives us the ability to be proud of our Black identity. With this law, we can teach our children about their motherland – Africa." Those present concurred with this assertion, suggesting the models for instruction of African-oriented material should come directly from the kind of community development and after-school programs run by *blocos* like Ilê-Aiyê and many of *terreiros* in neighbourhoods like Curuzu-Liberdade or Engenho Velho da Federação.

Using *cadernos* or workbooks that focus on art, poetry, stories, and parables, primarily composed by community leaders or translated from African writings into Portuguese, Ilê-Aiyê has run a very successful children's program that emphasizes the importance of African culture and pride in an Afro-Brazilian heritage. In one of Ilê-Aiyê's recent *cadernos* entitled *África: Ventre Fértil do Mundo* (Africa: Fertile womb of the world), that is still used in the program, one finds discussions of the predominance of nature in African religions, the possibility of a Black origin for Egyptian civilization, West Africa's *griot* tradition, Islam in Africa, different African celebrations, Africa's oral traditions, war and disease in Africa, and other subjects. Here again, key symbols of Africa's connection with spirituality, nature, and orality are emphasized as the fundamental building blocks of an African-oriented Black identity.

There is much to admire in this thin children's workbook and certainly it could serve as a good starting point for a major shift in the Brazilian education system in terms of diversification and broadening horizons. Moreover, I cannot imagine that an increased awareness of other societies and other parts of the world through the use of course materials such as this book can have anything but a positive effect on the intellectual development of young people. In terms of the processes of identity construction that are taking place in Bahia's Black communities, the *caderno* very much reinforces a generalized and totalizing view of Africa as connected with nature, as a *"continente primordial"* (Ilê Aiyê 2001, 10) and a place that produces *"jorrando vida, conhecimento, espiritualidade, ritmo, música, de seu Ventre Fértil para o mundo inteiro"* (a gushing out of life, knowledge, spirituality, rhythm, and music for the whole world in its open womb) (13). Through these kinds of programs, the speakers continue, Brazilian schools can learn how to incorporate African material into the curriculum.

After this interaction, Félix starts to speak. Immediately he begins by addressing the need to recognize more than just the general African contribution to the Brazilian society but specifically the Yoruba contribution to the religious traditions and culture of Black Bahia. If anything is to be taught, he asserts, let that be taught – let teachers speak to their students of the kings and queens of Africa, but let us not forget, he reminds us, where the most important kings and queens reside: "You must not forget that the African originators of your traditions were the priests and leaders of the Yoruba." Félix suggests that the actions of many of the larger *terreiros*, who are increasingly asserting an anti-syncretistic and pro-Yoruba approach to their religious practice, are on the right track, that they are reclaiming their heritage from a past of "mixture and blending." Similarly, Félix believes, if Black community groups want to assert an African element to their identity let it be a Yoruba element and not some watered down notion of Africanity. Throughout the Americas, Félix suggests, all Black societies have found their connection with the Yoruba people, whether it be in the practices of US-based groups like American Yoruba-Revisionism Movement, Oyotunji (see Palmié 1995), in the *regla ocha* or *Santería* of Cuba, or *"os grupos negros do Brasil"* [the Black groups of Brazil]. Although Félix sometimes resists his celebrity status as the most recent agent of Yorubaness in Salvador, he is very much aware of his role and his position, which he seems to use to support and encourage the privileging of Yoruba culture as the centerpiece of Black identity discourse. Whether through his courses of language instruction, his participation in events like the one described here or through his frequent appearances at *terreiros*, Félix has taken on a central role as an agent, indeed as a promoter, of Yorubaness in the Black milieu of Salvador. To be sure, It would be hard to underestimate just how well known this one language professor has become. During my time in the city, I could not find one *terreiro*, one community centre or carnival association that had not heard or met Félix.

Félix, Georgia, and other West African – primarily Nigerian – residents in Salvador have been responsible in helping to build a continued emphasis on Africanity in the public representation of Black identity in

Bahia and thus contribute to a continually globalizing notion of African Blackness. They have become important points of coalescence, charismatic individuals who are seen as embodying, quite literally, Africa and true African Blackness. Further, for groups like the *terreiros*, community organizations like Ilê Aiyê, and Black leaders, these individuals provide a contemporary source of knowledge about African culture and African knowledge – one that is accessible and convenient. For although some groups have been able to fund the travels of their leaders to West Africa, to cities like Lagos and Ouidah "in search" of African tradition, for most their only connection with this "motherland" is through reports on television and through their religious traditions. Félix, Georgia, and others have become embodied proxies for an entire continent; physical representatives of everything that those involved in making Black identity in Bahia want or require of Africa. They have become, through their talk and action, powerful allies in the movement to emphasize and mobilize the African orientation of many Black communities. Georgia uses storytelling, tours, and performances at "reggae-roots" bars; Félix, in his role as a venerated elder of the Yoruba people, living and working in Brazil, employs other means, most notably his regular classes in Yoruba language instruction. However, both individuals are implicated as preeminent participants in a continuing dialogue between Africa and Afro-America, specifically Afro-Brazil, about what Africa means, and what an idea of Africa means to the notion of Blackness. Blackness not just in Brazil and confined to Afro-Brazilians, but to African interlocutors, to Cuban travellers, African American tourists and exchange students, and others from throughout the Black Atlantic world.

Chapter Three

Manifestations of Afro-Brazilian Blackness

Blocos and *Terreiros*

"Africans have to come to our city, Salvador!
To drink at the font of True Africa
Here, in Brazil, exists the pure African culture!"

Valdina Pinto (Salvador, Bahia, Brazil, 2007)

These words were uttered by a noted religious leader and professor in Salvador at the "Reconnecting with Africa" forum held at the famed *carnaval bloco*, Ilê Aiyê, in Salvador in November 2005.[1] Ilê Aiyê is the oldest *bloco carnavalesco* or carnaval association in Salvador devoted exclusively to the city's Black population and is widely regarded as the most "African" of these organizations.

From a narrative perspective, this chapter picks up precisely where the previous one left off. Not just in terms of the continuing story of how African-oriented expressions of Black identity are manufactured and negotiated in Salvador. The opening scene of this chapter is from the same event where we just left Félix emphasizing the importance of Yoruba culture in the Black community's incorporation of Africa into their identity discourse. Here, I seek to explore how intellectual and cultural elites – conforming very much to a Gramscian model of non-organic intellectuals – within the Black community have been able to assert a powerful influence on the direction that they believe Black identity in Salvador should take. In returning to the "Reconnecting with Africa" event at Ilê Aiyê, I begin a discussion of the impact that organizations such as this powerful *carnaval bloco* have on manifestations of Blackness that incorporate globalized ideas of Africanized Blackness.

In the community of Black associations and movements in Salvador, there are many divisions and tensions – some of them quite extreme. In the Afro-Brazilian religious sphere, minor cleavages exist between the different *terreiros* that claim origin from specific *nações* or fictively constructed African cultural origins. However, Yoruba or Nagô traditions are dominant and individuals like Félix are helping to increase the prominence of this form. All *terreiros* in Salvador, whether they claim Nagô, Jeje, or Angolan heritage, worship *orixás* – the name for the spirits or deities that comes directly from the Yoruba *órísá*. Indeed, there are few concepts in the Bahian Afro-Brazilian religious vocabulary that are not of Yoruba origin. The real divisions in the Black movements pertain to the influence that African-oriented groups – such as the *terreiros* – exert and the extent to which articulations of Afro-Brazilian identity should include African concepts and culture. There are many – perhaps even a majority of Black Bahians – who do not agree with the inordinate amount of attention afforded the Africa-centric movement and the dominant position that their assertions of Blackness assume within Brazilian society.

During the 1920s, as Freyre and others were writing about what it meant to be Brazilian, particularly in the context of the country's growing urban environment, community leaders in Rio de Janeiro attempted to reinvent the annual February carnaval as an expression of national culture and something uniquely Brazilian. Part of this reinvention was to try and organize the mass confusion of the pre-Lenten festival into some kind of order. The cultural elite of Rio organized carnaval participants into a hierarchy of organizations with the exclusive and invariably white-only *sociedades carnavalescas* or *grandes sociedades* at the top and more populist *blocos*, *ranchos*, and *cordões* at the lower end. Brazilian anthropologist Roberto DaMatta (1984) has written, "It was not Brazil that invented *carnaval*; on the contrary, it was *carnaval* that invented Brazil" (245). There's considerable insight in this assertion, for although *carnaval* has become a stereotyped, clichéd, and all-too commercialized display of everything that is good, bad, and exotic about Brazil, there are few better manifestations of Leach's (1954, 15) observation that ritual makes the social structure explicit. *Carnaval* is Brazilian society writ large and in it, all of the nuances of Brazil's eternal albatross – race relations – are played out again and again each February.

For much of the twentieth century, the racial hierarchy of Brazilian society was replicated in the organization and presentation of carnaval. Only in the late 1970s, as Brazil started to move away from the extremes of military rule, did movements aimed at mobilizing and radicalizing the Black population start to emerge. It was an uphill battle as the ideology of racial democracy asserted that such a struggle was, of course, unnecessary (Skidmore 1993). Eventually, however, a diverse array of politically motivated organizations aimed at derailing the myth of racial democracy and fighting for Black people in Brazil started to coalesce in locales like Rio, São Paulo, and Salvador. These groups, like the *Movimento Negro Unificado* (MNU), emphasized Black consciousness, valorization of Afro-Brazilian religious forms, and activist viewpoints that stood in sharp opposition to the dominant racist social institutions of Brazil – including *carnaval*.

In 1974, Antônio Carlos dos Santos Vovô – also known simply as "Vovô" – founded Bloco-Afro Ilê Aiyê in Salvador. Ilê Aiyê was the first carnaval *bloco* composed of, and dedicated to serving the Afro-Brazilian community in Salvador – especially Curuzu-Liberdade, an urban neighbourhood of Salvador that boasts the largest Black population in Brazil. Vovô had been inspired by the Black Power movements in the United States and by the inchoate Black cultural groups in Rio and elsewhere to create a new kind of space in Brazil – one only for Black people and Black culture. Further, this would be a space that would be Afrocentric and one that would seek to emphasize the global contribution of Black peoples to world history, much like the vindicationist work of the Harlem Renaissance. Vovô was also much inspired by the events of the 1977 Second World Black and African Festival of Arts and Culture in Lagos, Nigeria or, as it is commonly known, FESTAC '77. FESTAC was a cultural high-water mark in the ongoing dialogue between Africa and the Black world at large. Leaders, community organizers, musicians, and cultural elites from Brazil were all present at the event. The main attraction of the festival were the daily musical performances, but these were complemented by daily debates and colloquia attended by Black scholars from around the world, including Brazil, who discussed the need for dramatic and immediate change in global Black society – to "reawaken" Black society, as it were (Foundation for Research in the Afro-American Creative Arts 1977). In the wake of this event, Black community groups and the Black movements in Brazil were re-energized and revitalized by FESTAC with the belief that Africa must be an important part of their future. FESTAC set a defiant and strident tone – one that would be echoed in work of community organizers like Vovô in the early years of Ilê Aiyê.

Racial classification in Brazil has evolved significantly since the 1970s, but is still very much based on subtle and specific gradations in phenotypic indices. Three decades ago, though, during the founding of

Ilê Aiyê, the test for admission was simple, emphatic, and perhaps represented the surfacing of a more dichotomous approach to race. An individual petitioning for admittance into the *bloco* would have their skin scratched: if it turned grey-white or "ashen grey," then they were permitted to be a member; if their skin did not change colour after being scratched, they were considered white and not allowed for membership[2] – the idea here being that only people of African ancestry had the kind of skin that turned grey when scratched. Though this test is no longer used, Ilê Aiyê still only accepts members of Black heritage. At a public forum held for a visiting Nigerian journalist at Ilê Aiyê in March 2005, an Ilê Aiyê member noted:

> Ilê Aiyê has always been a group that only accepts people of African descent. Critics say we are being racist, that we are fighting racism with racism. But we are the only *bloco* that has succeeded in resisting the pressure to admit non-Blacks. This is because Ilê Aiyê exists to serve the Black community of Curuzu-Liberdade. Here in this neighborhood, where there exists so many *terreiros*, we have the strength and support to stick to our principles.[3]

Ilê Aiyê's involvement with the Salvador carnaval since 1974 has very much served to "Africanize" the event. Now a number of other so-called *blocos afros* exist in Salvador. Groups with names such as Ara Kétu, Gunga, Malê Debalê, Malcolm X, Mundo Negro, Olodum, Oriobá, Quilombo, Tempero De Negro, and others have become regular fixtures on the streets of Salvador during *carnaval*.[4] All of the *blocos afros'* groups take their name from some aspect of African or Afro-American culture. Some reference the history of Black resistance in the Americas through the evocation of the famed African American civil rights leaders like Malcom X. Others use names that hearken back to the era of the *quilombo* or the maroon slave communities – the most famous being Palmares. Other groups such as Ilê Aiyê and Ara Kétu take their names from concepts or phrases in Yoruba, and assert a direct link with the *Candomblé terreiros* and with Yoruba culture.

Ara Kétu, certainly one of the more upscale *blocos* with a modern boutique that sells music and paraphernalia in the rich and tourist neighbourhood of Barra, takes its name from a cognate of the Yoruba ethnonym Quêto, or Kétou. Kétou is a specific Yoruba town close to the border with Nigeria in the People's Republic of Benin and a chiefdom within the broader Yoruba kingdom. Slaves shipped to Brazil from

Porto Novo in Benin were often labelled with this *nação* or "nation." Olodum, another popular *bloco afro* and cultural group, takes its name from an *orixá* and has become particularly famous abroad for their performance with the musician Paul Simon. Due to this, Olodum has become a major attraction in Pelourinho, putting on major concerts every Tuesday in the central plaza of the old city. During carnaval, Olodum's drumming ensemble is a major participant, but members also see their involvement in carnaval as a political statement. Olodum maintains a children's educational program, like Ilê Aiyê, for young people living in the poorer, primarily Black neighbourhoods, and members openly describe their mission as one of defeating racism and, according to their website, "*o desenvolvimento da cidadania e preservação da cultura negra, oferecendo um saber afro brasileiro e novas formas de conhecimentos adicionais àqueles adquiridos no sistema formal de ensino*" (Olodum 2008) (development of citizenship and the preservation of Black culture, through the delivery of Afro-Brazilian knowledge and new ways of knowing that supplement those found in the formal education system). Olodum's principal mode of communication with the public is through its drumming performances in Pelourinho, during carnaval and at other events, in service of movements like *Mês da Consciência Negra* (Month of Black consciousness), or for the tourist industry. Olodum is explicit that drumming, especially their particular brand of powerfully rhythmic and syncopated drumming that has become synonymous with Salvador and its carnaval, is essentially African in nature – that this kind of drumming speaks to the African "spirit"[5] of Bahian society. Here again, we see an example of Africanity in Salvador being reduced to certain key metaphors, such as "drum" and "spirit," as markers or signifiers of Blackness. A teenaged girl named Francesca, a member of Olodum whom I interviewed after one of their performances in Pelourinho, put it best when she told me: "*Olodum é como os tribos da África. Como o Ioruba ou Jeje, Olodum é meu tribo!*"[6] ("Olodum is like the tribes of Africa. Like the Yoruba or Jeje, Olodum is my tribe!")

Of all the *blocos*, Ilê Aiyê remains perhaps the most famous in Salvador. The group takes its name from a Yoruba phrase that translates to "life," "the world," or – according to many of the young children who can frequently be found running through the halls of the cavernous building that houses the organization – "big house." Ilê Aiyê overtly emphasizes the importance that Bahians of African descent should, though are not required to, be participants in one of the Afro-Brazilian religions of Brazil, or at the very least be sympathetic to the *terreiros*.

Though not involved with outward proselytizing, the *bloco* is actively involved with *terreiros* throughout Salvador and maintains a special relationship with the Ilê Axé Jitolu *terreiro* in the neighbourhood of Curuzu-Liberdade.

Ilê Axé Jitolu claims to be a house of the Jeje-Nagô "nation" or *nação*. By this, it is meant that the religious practice of this *terreiro* largely follows the patterns of the Nagô or Yoruba and the Jeje – the combined ethnic complex of the Ewe and Fon speakers that borders Yorubaland to the west. There are very few houses in Bahia that claim to be exclusively Jeje in practice and most of them now incorporate aspects from the more popular, famous, and influential Nagô houses. Indeed, Jeje practice is, on the whole, in decline in Salvador, with very few houses claiming to be "purely" Jeje in practice (Parés 2001). Today, such little difference actually exists in the practice of Nagô and Jeje houses, that to assert clearly defined ethnic origins to their traditions is to essentially reify categories that no longer truly exist, if they ever did. Mãe Hilda, as the *mãe de santo* or *iálorixá* of the Jitolu *terreiro*, up until her death at eighty-six in 2009, was a prominent figure in the religious and political life of Salvador and also enjoyed a degree of prominence at the national level for her work in championing the construction of a memorial for the maroon slave leader, Zumbí dos Palmares. In 1988, Mãe Hilda, along with Vovô, started a one-room remedial school for children from impoverished Black families in Curuzu-Liberdade who had failed in Brazil's public education system. Called Escola Mãe Hilda,[7] it is located within the grounds of the *terreiro* and is aimed at improving literacy skills among neighbourhood youth. Now, however, the school has become one of the primary community outreach projects of the *bloco*, outside of the yearlong preparation for and participation in the carnaval. The *escola*, in addition to teaching basic academics, also involves students in religious education and emphasizes the importance of the *terreiro* and "African" religious life for all *Afrodescendentes* or "peoples of African descent." In conversations and interviews conducted with a former teacher at the school, I was informed:

> Students at the school learn to live with the natural world, which is the space from which African spirits come from and start to have new attitudes and "postures" towards the value of their Black culture, their *African* culture. Even though we have students here that come from different religious backgrounds, it is important that they learn the principles of the *terreiro*: respect for elders, respect for each other, and respect for the

natural world and environment. These are values from Africa … especially respect for elders. These new attitudes are reflected in the families … we hear reports from families and they say that the students' behaviour improves. These are not things that the students can learn in Brazilian schools. Only in our school, because it is more African.[8]

From Ilê Aiyê's website:

Ilê Aiyê, through music, recounts the history of pre-colonial Africa, describing its kingdoms and empires; singing the story of Black people in the construction of Brazil and North America; singing of Black revolutions fought for equality and to end prejudice; of leaders and heroes; composing songs that elevate and raise the esteem of the Black population; contributing to the reduction of racial inequality and promoting education through history and culture.[9]

Ilê Aiyê is now much more than merely a carnaval association – it is a cultural juggernaut in Bahia, eulogized in popular songs and television programs, and known throughout the country not only as the most African *bloco*, but also as the *bloco* that has the most contemporary connections with Africa. It is also known nationwide for another reason – it is the only *bloco afro* in Salvador that has received "official" sponsorship from Brazil's largest beer company.[10] Ilê Aiyê is a force actively involved in shaping and, to some extent, prescribing a construction of Blackness in Bahia and in Brazil that emphasizes the slave past and Africa as key signifiers of Afro-Brazilian ethnic identity. Ilê Aiyê receives funding from a number of government agencies in Brazil for its projects, including the Ministry of Culture. The former "Ministro de Estado da Cultura" – minister of culture – in Brazil was the world-famous *Baiano* musician and entertainer Gilberto Gil, who has been involved with musical collaborations in the United States, Europe, and Africa and was present in Lagos at FESTAC '77. His personal commitment to the *bloco* has ensured the group's prominence on the Brazilian stage and invariably, when the national media wants commentary on Black issues, the leaders and members of Ilê Aiyê are often first on the list. Ilê Aiyê also receives funding and support from a special agency within the Ministry of Culture – the Fundação Cultural Palmares. This foundation is named for the *quilombo* of Palmares and, as stated on its website, its mission is to promote the preservation of what they term Black "cultural, social and economic values" and the "*influência*" of Black society in the formation of Brazil (Funação Cultural Palmares 2007). Ilê Aiyê, in all aspects of its work, attempts to conform very much to this mission statement. Much of the external funding that Ilê Aiyê receives goes towards the educational project, but it also helps support projects such as *Mês da Consciência Negra* (Month of Black consciousness), *Beleza Negra* (a Black beauty pageant), lectures, forums, and a calendar full of other events, all aimed squarely at advancing the idea that Blackness in Brazil should be about reconnection with Africa as a source of identity and culture.

However, Ilê Aiyê is not alone in terms of the influence it wields in the area of Black identity discourse. It forms, along with other carnaval associations and *blocos afros*, an important part of the complex of leaders, religious elites, government agencies, entrepreneurs, literati, and intelligentsia in Bahia who are active participants and stakeholders in directing and determining public discourse about Blackness in Brazil. Members of these groups include religious leaders from the powerful Nagô *Candomblé* houses such as Ilê Axe Opô Afonjá and Casa Branca; a new generation of anthropologists, historians and other social scientists from the Universidade Federal da Bahia; the *blocos afros*; government agencies such as Palmares; and more recently, cultural brokers and entrepreneurs from West Africa such as Georgia. These groups seek to define not only what it means to be Black in Brazil, but also attempt to limit and curtail what aspects of Black Brazilian society are relevant to the general discourse on national identity and unify the often differing ideas about Blackness into a singular, totalizing message.

The *blocos afros*, like Ilê Aiyê and Olodum, along with their patrons in government and the academy, represent the popular or secular aspect of the African-oriented approach to redefining Black identity in Bahia. However, they cannot and should not be understood as independent operators. Most *blocos afros* in Salvador, although engaged primarily in cultural and political mobilization, stress the importance of the Afro-Brazilian religious traditions in the reconfiguration of the ethnic paradigm in Brazil – in Salvador this means, first and foremost, *Candomblé*.

The most famous and some of the oldest centres of Afro-Brazilian religious practice are to be found in Salvador. Many of these *terreiros*, such as Ilê Axé Opô Afonjá, are well funded, have schools on the premises, and *orixá* shrines that are large and ornate. Also, a number of these richer centres count among their members famous Brazilian and foreign celebrities, politicians, and even a number of academics – many of whom are anthropologists. Though they once started as loci for a subversive or hidden religion – what Lewis (1971) might call a "peripheral" cult – centres such as Opô Afonjá have now become cathedrals of Afro-Brazilian religion, the priests and leaders of which have become celebrities on the Salvador social scene. Importantly, *terreiros* such as Ilê Axé Opô Afonjá openly denounce syncretism and claim, like Valdina Pinto at Ilê Aiyê's "Reconnecting with Africa" event, to be more African than Africa. Towards this end, they do their best to eliminate or diminish Catholic or Christian elements of religious practice and to reintroduce instead elements that they believe represent more authentically African (Yoruba) traditions (Capone 2010; Skidmore 1993).

Chief among the exponents of the re-Africanization movement is the *mãe* or *iálorixá* of Opô Afonjá. Maria Stella de Azevedo Santos, known as Mãe Stella de Oxóssi, is well-known throughout Salvador as a vocal critic of Catholic syncretism in the *terreiro* and, despite the success and frequency with which she attracts rich patrons, the commercialization of Afro-Brazilian religion in Salvador. She decries the regularized tours of *terreiros* in and around Pelourinho and the use of Yoruba images and slogans in public places. However, she has been very much responsible for the degree to which the Yoruba cultural vocabulary has permeated the popular consciousness of Salvador.

During the era of military rule in Brazil, *terreiros* were secretive about their religious practices and about their membership. Today, association with a *terreiro* provides eminent public figures such as sports heroes, politicians, actors, and musicians with a certain cache of authenticity and "street credibility." Images of the *orixás* are displayed prominently throughout the city and well-known words and phrases from the liturgical canon of the *terreiro* such as "Axé," which means "positive energy" or "power," are taken as brand names for everything from health tonics, to major municipal bus lines, to pop music produced in Salvador. In this way, *Candomblé* and Afro-Brazilian religion in general has been made mundane, part of the ordinary, and has lost much of the mystique and the aura of *feitiçaria* or witchcraft that surrounded it for much of the twentieth century. This folklorization, as Selka (2007) calls it, of *Candomblé* is of great concern to leaders like Stella and her adherents: "Those who are selling our traditions, they are destroying the heritage of Africa in Salvador and in Brazil."[11]

The irony here is that many of those who object to the trivialization and folklorization of *Candomblé* are often the ones who have

Figure 3.1 Two public expressions of "Yorubaness" in Salvador. A bus company, whose vehicles bear the company's name "Axé," and one of the many large statues of the *orixás* that decorate the Dique de Tororo in a park near the city's old football stadium.

participated in making *Candomblé* more palatable to a wider Brazilian audience over the past twenty to thirty years. They have done this through a concerted campaign to place Yoruba cultural tropes at the centre of all aspects of Black culture *and* popular culture in Bahia and, in doing so, have gained widespread support from influential sectors of society in the process. By embracing the aid and patronage from diverse sources – including the Palmares Cultural Foundation, the culture and tourist ministries at both the state and federal levels, prominent figures like Gilberto Gil and fellow *Baiano* singer Caetano Veloso, and the Brazilian social science academy at large – *terreiros* like Opô Afonjá, along with *blocos afros* like Ilê Aiyê, have sought to assert if not formal then certainly symbolic control over who gets to speak only for the Afro-Brazilian religious community in Bahia. In repeated conversations with members of Olodum, Ilê Aiyê, Casa Branca (another influential *terreiro*), and former members of Opô Afonjá, I invariably heard similar sentiments: that the Black movements in Bahia *needed* the *terreiros*; that without the strength and guidance of these religious spaces, the Black movements in Brazil would be dead. This type of discourse is, for Gramsci, symptomatic of social movements that are undergirded by an emphasis on progress and advancement against oppression through the embracement of an ever purer, ever more distilled and refined understanding and application, indeed, a consciousness, of opposition to all that stands in the way of overthrowing hegemony – or, as Hanchard (1993) suggests, "Afro-Diasporic intellectuals" are not "immune" to the influences of the enlightenment (96). In the Yorubacentrism and "Nagôization" (Parés 2004) of Bahian Black movements, in the Afrocentrism of Asante (1988), even in the Pan-Africanism of Nkrumah, Touré, and Selassi, we see a tendency for the leaders of these movements of resistance and counter-hegemony to discount the diversity of voices within their own constituencies as they develop sophisticated critiques of the dominant power structures – state-based and cultural – while at the same time replicating the enlightenment-rooted emphasis on progress through the obliteration of previous *or* alternative forms of existence and consciousness.

In addition to Mãe Stella, one of the strongest voices for antisyncretism is Deoscoredes M. Dos Santos or, as he is more commonly known, Mestre Didi, also of Opô Afonjá. Didi (published as Dos Santos 2003) urges, in his work as a priest of the ancestor cult or *Egungun*, as an author, and as a public speaker on Afro-Brazilian issues in Bahia for members of *Candomblé* centres to abandon syncretic practices in favour of a particular Yoruba *orixá* or patron. Syncretic associations, he asserts, were made by the older generation and now that the *terreiro* has gained acceptance, practitioners should abandon such distortions. Didi and Stella also enjoy the support of Nigerian scholars such as Félix, the Yoruba teacher at UFBa, who often referred to them in our discussions as "representatives" of the Yoruba culture in Brazil. Both Didi and Stella also regularly participate in world conferences of *orixá* worshippers that bring together devotees of *Candomblé*, *Santería*, and Yoruba from Nigeria for discussions of how Yoruba "culture" is being increasingly globalized.

For individuals like Stella, Didi, and their devotees, anti-syncretism and re-Africanization is about asserting the authority of Black people in their own religious space – an African space that does not need to be sanctified or authorized by a Catholic priest. In discussions with members of one *terreiro* that boasted members who had visited the cities of Lagos in Nigeria and of Ouidah in Benin, I was told:

Our *terreiro* and others, like Casa Branca ... our leaders, they know Africa well. Our *mãe*, she used to visit Africa for many years. She knows Nigerian politicians, chiefs of Yoruba villages, even famous Yorubas like Wándé Abímbólá – he's a professor of Yoruba in Nigeria and now he is the chief of the global congress of Yorubas ... What she discovered in Africa is that our traditions are more pure, more authentic, because the slaves in Brazil preserved everything! The traditions in Africa were ruined by the British ... You ask me about "re-Africanization," or whatever you call it, Africans need to come to Salvador to be "re-Africanized"![12]

For this informant, the idea of re-Africanization was not even relevant to her *terreiro* as she felt that her practices were more authentically African than those found in the Yoruba homeland. However, this has not stopped the leaders of many influential *terreiros* and *blocos afros* from becoming a small, but growing part of a network of Black travellers engaged in what can be conceived of as "pilgrimages" to the source of Africanity.

Dialogue on the West African Coast

Bruner (1996), Hasty (2002), and others have explored the place of African American tourists that visit Ghana and other West African sites as part of a personal journey to reorient themselves towards an African articulation of identity. During research conducted along the West African coast, I encountered a small number of Brazilians in the port city of Ouidah, in Benin. These groups of Brazilians were composed of people from throughout the country, from Rio de Janeiro, São Paulo, and one group composed entirely of individuals from Salvador. The group from Bahia was composed primarily of middle-class, affluent individuals who were Lebanese-Brazilians, along with younger members who referred to themselves as *Afro-Brasileiros*, and all self-identified as practitioners of *Candomblé*. They told me that they had come to West Africa for two reasons: for the Lebanese-Brazilians, they wanted to visit family who managed a hotel in Lomé, Togo,[13] and, more importantly, they wanted to visit the place that their *iálorixá* had visited the year before. They explained to me that they had helped to pay for their *terreiro* leader to visit Lagos to take some courses in the Yoruba language and to learn a little about how the Yoruba themselves worshipped *orixás*:

"Opô Afonjá and Casa Branca are attracting so many members in Salvador," one of the group members told me near the "Point of No Return" monument in Ouidah, they've got so many rich patrons that our

small *terreiro* is being left out ... Plus, we are losing members to these larger *terreiros*. That's why we are here. To understand more about Africa and
take it back home to our religion.[14]

All members claimed to be *candomblecistas* and the leaders of the
group all spoke very passionately about the need to rediscover the ancient African secrets of the Yoruba and Fon people of Benin who, according to one of the women present, "were closely related to the
Yoruba,"[15] and about the need for Black communities in Brazil to recon-
nect with Africa. Upon further questioning, I discovered that the two
young men were children of a leader at the group's *terreiro* and that the
community had paid for their round trip fares from Salvador to São
Paulo to Johannesburg to Lagos so that they could return with a message about "true Africa" for the young people of the community. The
group leaders were senior devotees and former residents of São Paulo
where they practised *Umbanda*. When they relocated to Salvador, they
quickly became attracted to what they told me was the "Africanness" of
Candomblé and found it to be more "in-tune" with Brazil's past than
Umbanda – so they converted. *Umbanda* is another of Brazil's African-
derived religious traditions. It is practised throughout the country, but
enjoys prevalence in the industrialized Southeast states of São Paulo
and Rio de Janeiro. *Umbanda*, like *Candomblé*, incorporates the religious
pantheon of the Yoruba, but also gives equal weight, unlike *Candomblé*,
to the spirits of Amerindian warriors, *caboclos*, and the kindly, departed
spirits of elders from the slave plantation, the old Blacks or *pretos velhos*.
In addition, *Umbanda* has integrated the ideas of European spiritism
developed in the mid-nineteenth century by French religious innova-
tor, Allan Kardec. *Umbanda* is often decried by religious purists in the
Candomblé terreiros of Salvador because, they assert, its syncretic incli-
nations diminish and pollute the "proud traditions of the Yoruba in
Brazil."[16]

Purists may be dismayed by the kind of à la carte approach to religion exhibited by these travellers – especially towards a religion that
they sincerely believe provides them with a conduit to their ancestors
and a venue for proudly asserting their Blackness separate from Christian symbols and European ideas such as syncretism. But in their attempts to exert power over what *Candomblé* is about or, rather, what
they believe it *should* be about, such individuals have been responsible
for helping to diversify the religious marketplace so that opposing categories like "purity" versus "syncretic" have both become legitimate

options for Paulista migrants to Salvador. Furthermore, they must surely accept that the positioning of a "purely African" form of religious practice as a desirable avenue for Afro-Brazilian people to express their Blackness will – when connected with noble ideals, ministries of culture, carnaval associations, and noted celebrities – become attractive to other elites within a society. This must be true especially when that society has gone out of its way to emphasize and folklorize Blackness and Afro-Brazilian culture as some of the most important aspects of its heritage. For those who emphasize anti-syncretism and deny that they even need to be re-Africanized, here's the rub: they have, at the same time, succeeded in making these concepts an important part of the contemporary discourse on Black identity in Bahia to the extent that many *Candomblé terreiros* vie for members within their home communities based on whether or not they are more syncretic or more pure. Those that assert "purity" – other than the large and well-funded *terreiros* – are forced to pull together whatever means they have at their disposal, including admitting rich patrons from São Paulo who have the funds to finance "pilgrimages" to West Africa. They have, if you will, created a trajectory for progress within the Black movement that culminates in a perfect point of Foucauldian tactical reversal (Thompson 2003) where all resistance is brought under a unified and singular message of opposition.

There is a clear parallel, I would suggest, between the syncretism versus African purity debate and the one that continues between academic partisans of the African survivals in American societies' perspective and those who advocate the Mintz-Price model of rapid creolization. Further, scholars in Bahia who support the changes in *Candomblé* practice being urged by Mestre Didi, Mãe Stella, and others very often align themselves with the neo-Herskovitsian approach. The best example of this is Bahian historian Ubiratan Castro de Araújo (1992, 1999, 2000, 2001, 2006), a former director of CEAO and Fundação Cultural Palmares, who has written extensively on the need for the recognition and acceptance of Bahia's and Brazil's "essential" Africanness and on the need for slave reparations. He is something of an intellectual godfather to many of Salvador's Black movements and is venerated throughout the city in *terreiros*, *blocos afros*, and community groups as a tireless advocate for these communities.

At a public discussion and Black community event held at Vila Velha community theatre on the relevance of Africa to Black societies in Brazil and entitled, quite simply, *África*, Castro de Araújo spoke about his historical investigation into slave records, missionary accounts, and colonial records on, specifically, patterns of scarification among rural slave communities. His research, apparently, suggests that African cultures were able to hold on to more than just scraps of religious activity and what Mintz and Price (1976) would term "grammatical principles." Rather, he asserts the slave communities were able to hold on to African cultures *in toto*, including aspects of kinship, political authority, cosmologies, and aesthetics. This is what he feels must be understood about the religious space of the *terreiro*: that they are contemporary concatenations of whole, "pure" cultures of Africa, not some "schizophrenic"[17] amalgamation of Europe and Africa.

In discussions with some of Castro de Araújo's students after the seminar, we talked about the strong connections that are maintained between academics in Salvador – particularly social scientists such as anthropologists and historians – and the *terreiros* and *blocos afros*. I asked them whether the profound commitment that CEAO scholars and UFBa social science in general has towards the *terreiros* and the Black communities clouds their objectivity. Without exception, members of the group informed me that social science in Brazil has a history of being involved with the community. Even though most of them despise and reject the work of Freyre (1933) and the idea of racial democracy, one of them told me, "You can't deny the power of his ideas – they have extended into every part of Brazilian life."[18] This is the legacy that many of these students want to inherit: an approach to social science that has a direct impact on the communities under study. The idea of social science research for curiosity's sake or purely for the notion of expanding human knowledge was, one of them offered, "antisocial and antiquated."[19] Furthermore, all of the students have adopted Castro de Araújo's dedication to demonstrating how much African practice still exists in Brazil, not just in the *terreiro*, but also throughout Brazilian society. The eldest student in the group, Nelson, who was born in the nearby town of Feira de Santana and who had come to study at UFBa with the assistance of a scholarship told me: "Our mission is not to reconstruct little pieces of African cultures, but to help to reconstruct an entire culture that the Europeans couldn't destroy."[20]

To be sure, Brazil is still a country with a deeply systemic and institutionalized racism problem. Individuals who are visibly Black, those who are of Amerindian descent, or anyone who falls somewhere in between in the vast spectrum of colour that defines Brazilian racial categorization will likely face far more challenges, economically and socially, than those Brazilians with fairer skin colour. Moreover, the discourse of Africanized identity and Black vindication articulated by the elites of Salvador explicitly takes on these challenges and seeks to free Black communities, like Curuzu-Liberdade, from the oppression and hatred imposed by this racism. Black society in Brazil is one that has been and continues to be "historically on the defensive" (Gramsci 1971, 273). Consequently, much of the rhetoric of anti-racism and Black consciousness movements is not just about realizing the rights and promises of the Brazilian republic, but also about emphasizing and ul-timately bringing about the negation of the inherent privileges con-tained within the cultural forms – political, economic, and religious – that oppose them. However, because the African-derived culture of Bahia and the Yoruba-centric identities that these elites espouse have become a part of the mainstream cultural vocabulary of Brazil and no longer just symbols employed by the oppressed and dispossessed, I contend that many leaders like Stella have been transported out – meta-phorically and ideologically – of the marginalized communities they once occupied to the level of celebrity. Stella, Vovô, Didi, and Castro de Araújo articulate philosophies that have helped create a powerful com-plex of African-oriented symbols. These individuals deploy a set of ideas about race and identity that now serves as a pervasive cultural trope in Bahia – one that now uses the same techniques, methods, and categories of the dominant power structures within Bahia and beyond in broader Brazilian society.

The majority of individuals in the communities represented by these leaders still live an impoverished life and must, on a daily basis, deal with the adversities of racism. Yet the elite status enjoyed by these lumi-naries is one that is founded on the folklorization of exactly these chal-lenges and some of the solutions they have developed to deal with them – folklorization of what, in Brazil, amounts to forms of social pov-erty and exclusion: Africanity, Blackness, and actual economic poverty or disenfranchisement. The gulf that exists in these communities be-tween the elite leaders and the people they claim to represent can per-haps best be represented, both figuratively and literally, by an event I documented during a musical concert held at a well-known landmark in Salvador, the Barra Lighthouse or Farol da Barra in 2006.

Salvador sits at the tip of a triangular peninsula that juts southward into the Atlantic. At the apex of this tip, guarding the mouth of the bay, sits the Barra Lighthouse. Surrounding the lighthouse is a large green space overlooked by tall apartment buildings and casinos that line the city's famed Avenida Oceânica. In 2005, then minister of culture

Gilberto Gil organized what was supposed to be a musical extravaganza of African and Brazilian talent entitled Festival África-Brasil. The line-up included Olodum, Ilê Aiyê's band, Cesária Évora from Cape Verde, Brazilian jazz great Carlinhos Brown, popular Brazilian acts like Margareth Menezes and Daniella Mercury and, highlighting the festival, Miriam Makeba from South Africa – who ultimately never attended. The event was very well funded, with many corporate sponsors, including a large Brazilian bank, a national mobile phone carrier, the federal and state governments, and a major Brazilian construction company. Although the park surrounding the Farol is large, the ground is sloped and can accommodate only a few thousand people at best. However, despite these limitations, in the middle of the audience space, a raised VIP platform was erected for dignitaries and celebrities to view the event. Consequently, individuals from throughout the city had arrived only to find that unless they were within about fifty metres of the stage, their view would be obstructed by the VIP platform. I was unable to gain access to the guarded platform, but included in the list of invitees were prominent leaders and members of Opô Afonjá, Ilê Aiyê, and other *blocos afros* and *terreiros*, professors from UFBa involved in the Black movement, Félix the Yoruba teacher from CEAO, the honorary consul generals of Nigeria and Angola resident in Salvador, and a cavalcade of local celebrities. Now, there is nothing new or particularly noteworthy in the observation that those who achieve power and influence often find themselves removed from the people for which they fight. What is of importance here is that these individuals have risen to prominence through the ironic folklorization of the lifeways of a marginalized and – in most parts of Brazil – second-class social group. In this sense, the Africanized and folklorized culture of Black people has become a culturally dominant symbol that enjoys primacy in Bahia, but the bearers of that culture remain a subaltern and in many cases, unrepresented, class.

A brief treatment of how Gramsci viewed folklore is, by extension, appropriate here before we consider the ways in which intellectuals have sought to promote particular Afrocentric permutations of Black identity in Bahia. Gramsci (1985) understood "folklore" as a conception of the world – "implicit to a large extent in determinate (in time and space) strata of society and in opposition (also for the most part implicit, mechanical and objective) to official conceptions of the world" (188). Further, such conceptions of the world (*concezione del mondò*) were necessarily "many-sided" and filled with "different and juxtaposed elements" while also being internally stratified (Wainwright 2010, 189) and rooted in everyday activities essential to political and economic life. These "conceptions of the world," then, can be seen as crucial to formation of identities and ideas about identity and racial consciousness in terms of how human societies "make themselves" for, as Gramsci (1971) asks and asserts, "what we are and what we can become; whether we really are, and if so to what extent, 'makers of our own selves,' of our life and of our destiny. And we want to know this 'today,' in the given conditions of today, the conditions of our daily life" (351). Subaltern conceptions of the world – multi-sided and at times contradictory – are created then through the actions of those seeking to define their own lives and view of their position in life vis-à-vis the dominant class; one that is in opposition to "official" conceptions of the world.

Gramsci continues that for educators and intellectuals who must contend with the alternative conceptions of the world, such folklore should neither be eliminated – as the state is wont to do – nor preserved as some romantic, picturesque, element of the past. He writes: "Folklore must not be considered an eccentricity ... but as something which is very serious and is to be taken seriously ... so that the separation between modern culture and popular culture of folklore will disappear" (Gramsci 1971, 191). Crehan (2002, 109) suggests that this erasure between modern culture and the popular folklore of a subaltern class flows from Gramsci's assertion that a new culture may be forged by integrating the positive aspect of folklore into society at large. Moreover, in Gramsci's estimation, intellectuals are crucial to any process where such a new culture – a culture where a new class comes into being or formally a dispossessed and enslaved class is liberated – comes into being. Intellectuals are those who have the ability to organize and mobilize conceptions of the world, to transform society through a bridging of the production of knowledge [cultures] through a "genuine understanding of the conditions of life experienced by 'the popular element'" (131).

Academic Inventions of Yoruba Religious Purity

The overarching narrative in the history of Africans in the Americas that has been transmitted both to scholars and Black communities is one that was first articulated by Herskovits and the network of Black researchers in Latin America and the Caribbean with whom he collaborated. In this tale, slaves separated by time and space from their African homelands were able – in spite of the brutality and cruelty of slavery – to "remember" and hold on to their culture. Members of Ilê Aiyê, other *blocos afros* like Ara Kétu and Olodum, and *terreiros* in Salvador such as Casa Branca and Ilê Axé Opô Afonjá assert that the culture they have maintained and thrived upon is the ancient, pure, Yoruba culture. Further, they maintain that this culture should take pride-of-place in any definition of what it means to be Black in Bahia. Although the use of the Yoruba ethnonym itself is relatively recent (Parés 2004, 187), since the early work of Nina Rodrigues (1932), Ramos (1934), and Freyre (1933), the culture and specifically the religion of this West African chiefdom – both in and out of the *terreiro* – has taken centre stage in discussions of the African cultural repertoire of Bahia. Scholars have attempted to provide a number of reasons for why Yoruba cultural practices have been ascendant in the former slave societies of Brazil and elsewhere, such as Cuba (Matory 1999, 76). Pierre Verger (2002) and Roger Bastide (1971) have suggested that the reason why Yoruba culture is so prominent in Brazilian manifestations of Africanity is because of the more recent arrival of members of this society, and because large numbers of this captive community were high-ranking religious elites who were preoccupied with maintaining cultural distinctiveness from the existing slave population. This perspective flows, it would seem, directly from Herskovits' (1930, 1941) assertion that the predominance of any particular African culture in any former slave region of the Americas was a direct result of the numerical superiority of the bearers of that particular culture.

However, we cannot assume that this is necessarily what took place in Bahia and elsewhere. Most evidence seems to indicate that those who were enslaved and who arrived on American or Caribbean shores first generally had a greater impact on the generation of new identities and communities within the context of the plantation (Mintz and Price 1976). For example, Phillip Morgan's 1998 *Slave Counterpoint*, a massive work which explores the development of slave-culture in North America, demonstrates that ethnic identities among the slave population, as per the Mintz-Price model, faded quite quickly. These distinct groupings were quickly replaced with a new creolized, plantation-specific sense of solidarity and, crucially, new slave arrivals were quickly assimilated into this collectivity, learning the ropes from the old creole hands (Morgan 1998, 460–1). Ira Berlin's *Many Thousands Gone: The First Two Centuries of Slavery in North America*, also published in 1998, similarly emphasizes the importance of the original slave groups in the plantations for the formation of Black communities. Berlin describes differential patterns of slave arrival, creolization, newcomer arrival, brief periods of re-Africanization, and subsequent re-creolization, but concludes that all of this inexorably led to the formation of new communities in which there was a general absence of an idea of "Africa" and which prevented the intact "transfer of any single African nation or culture to the Americas" (Berlin 1998, 410).

Gwendolyn Midlo Hall (2005), although explicitly not in favour of the Mintz-Price model, has also shown that original slave communities, not newly arrived groups, ultimately exerted the most influence on the configuration of African American societies in the southern United States. Further, Roquinaldo Ferreira (2007), focusing on microhistories of slaving interactions between particular regions of Brazil and Angola, suggests that Angolan ties with Brazil were as important as those forged with the Bight of Benin, and asserts that the majority of Africans imported into Brazil came, in fact, from Angola towards the end of the nineteenth century. Given these findings, the date of arrival of any so-called Yoruba slaves in Brazil may not have had any relevance on the ethnic or cultural focus of the plantation society.

A recent development in the study of Afro-Brazilian culture and Black identity has looked at the impact that European, North American, and Brazilian intellectual elites had on the invention of "Black" tradition in Brazil. Central to this body of inquiry is the assertion that so-called Africanisms in Brazil owe more to the influence of cultural elites and their efforts to replicate a pure form of Yoruba practice in the *terreiros* with which they had become associated, than to the agency of Black Brazilians and their enslaved ancestors. These so-called white "negotiators" of Brazilian Blackness include Brazilian individuals such as Arthur Ramos and Edison Carneiro and American anthropologists such as Ruth Landes.

Advocates of this position reject that the demographics of the slave plantation or that the regional microhistories of slavery had anything to do with the ascendance of one particular African culture over another and argue, instead, that the pre-eminence of Yoruba practice in the *terreiros* of Bahia and elsewhere in Brazil and the Atlantic world is a direct consequence of white fascination with Africanness. In this model, white and foreign elites attempted to make their chosen religious alternative – *Candomblé* – as authentic as possible and for them, authenticity implied Yorubaness. Proponents of this model – drawing on their experience with a state that now openly endorses the Africanness of Brazil in public manifestations of *patrimônio negro* in performing arts, musical festivals like África-Brasil held in Salvador, *carnaval*, and tourism – assert that the emphasis placed on Yorubaness in the *terreiro* was brought about by European, North American, and elite Brazilian scholars' attempts to associate themselves with alternative religious forms that they could modify and reorient towards ideas of a sophisticated African religiosity and force the houses to shed any association with black magic (Brown 1999; Fry 1982; Hayes 2007).

Matory (1999) calls this position "wrongly posited" in that it depends "on the powerlessness of all Blacks over every part of their lives" and argues that "a more carefully drawn history will ... reveal the role of Afro-Brazilians in creating a trans-Atlantic culture, with consequences no less revolutionary in Africa than in Brazil" (79). He argues, along with Palmié (2007) and Clarke (2002), that Black societies throughout the Americas have not only been responsible for reinventing and incorporating "Africanisms" into their religious practice and identity discourse, but have also influenced, in some respects, the formation of some forms of ethnic identity in West Africa. In Matory's model of Yoruba ethnogenesis, an active dialogue between the northeastern littoral of Brazil and the West African coast resulted not only in an emphasis on Yoruba purity in the Afro-Brazilian religious congregations of Bahia, but also in the consolidation of the unified Yoruba ethnic group itself. He asserts that "Afro-Brazilian talk and action helped to generate a so-called Yoruba culture in West Africa that is in fact younger than its Brazilian diaspora" (Matory 1999, 81). Matory's intent here is to counter claims of Euro-Brazilian agency in the creation of Yoruba purity in Bahia with a model in which a class of literate and well-travelled Black Brazilians employed in transatlantic travel and trade helped to bring ideas about a pure Yoruba culture and Yoruba traditional religion *from* Brazil *to* West Africa, and thus brought the same into existence in and around Lagos.

The first appearance of this model was in the article *The English Professors of Brazil* (Matory 1999). Here, the author presents a reconstructed version of the origin of the Yoruba people, one that focuses on the period called the Lagosian Cultural Renaissance of the 1890s. Matory asserts that during this transformative epoch, the Yoruba came to be unified as a bounded ethnic group, celebrated both in West Africa and in the Atlantic world as a powerful and politically complex kingdom. The thesis is premised on the assumptions that, before the nineteenth century, the unified Yoruba kingdom as we know it today did not exist and that, second, there was nothing like a pure or unified culture or religion that spanned all of Yorubaland. Matory's assertion is that a transnational movement of the Bahian emphasis on the "purity" of the Nagô form of *Candomblé* found in many of the oldest *terreiros* of Salvador like Opô Afonjá to the Lagosian coast during the nineteenth century was instrumental in solidifying and unifying the widespread speakers of the different Yoruba dialects in the southwest and central parts of what is now Nigeria into an organized kingdom. This florescence of new ideas about group identity, the growth of a Yoruba literary canon that included not only the bible, but also a transliteration of the Yoruba founding myths, and the success of returnees made Lagos the new capital of a consolidated Yoruba ethnic group that many British colonialists, Matory (2005) argues, saw as superior to other African societies. Here, Matory (2005) cites the former governor of Lagos, Alfred Moloney, who commended groups of returnee Afro-Latin "Yorubas" for having kept their dignified and ancient "Yoruba" language alive in Cuba and Brazil (55). Upon their return to Lagos these "returnees" helped to stimulate what Matory calls the Lagosian Cultural Renaissance within which ideas of Yoruba superiority and cultural unity were initially generated. Freed Brazilian slaves who had been hired by traders and merchants then communicated these ideas, along with an emphasis on the importance of learning the English language, back across the Atlantic into the *Candomblé* houses and Black communities like Curuzu-Liberdade. Chief among such agents or vectors (as Matory styles them) of such Yorubaness is Martiniano Eliseu do Bonfim, whom Matory describes as one of Bahia's "towering leaders and perennial informants quoted in the literature on Afro-Bahians from the 1890s to the 1940s" – he was one of Matory's so-called English professors of Brazil (2005, 46; see also Palmié 2007).

According to Matory (2005), such "professors of English" deliberately explored and exploited their connections within the Lagosian Renaissance and other cosmopolitan affiliations and returned to Brazil with ideas about the ascendance of a growing Yoruba culture. Subsequently, ideas about the purity and superiority of the Nagô tradition flourished and were distilled in Brazilian communities and then reimported back to Africa to help refine and solidify a unified Yoruba kingdom. Now, there appears to be no doubt that individuals like Bonfim and others, such as Nina Rodrigues' friend Lourenço Cardoso, another Afro-Brazilian traveller who translated works from English to

Yoruba, were instrumental in negotiating and solidifying a sense of Yoruba purity on both sides of the Atlantic. I place the Yoruba literary critic Wándé Abímbólá, whom more than a few informants that I spoke to in connection with anti-syncretism were familiar with, in the same group, along with Olabiyi Babalola Yaï. Indeed, Abimbola, a former professor and vice-chancellor of the University of Ile-Ife, a *babaláwo* diviner, and an important member of the global *orixá* movement, has been called a "new Martiniano" by Matory (2001, 187). To this company one must add Félix Ayoh'Omidire, the Yoruba teacher at UFBa, Georgia, and the hundred or so of other Nigerians – even "imposters" such as Nwafor and Adebola – and West Africans living and working in Salvador, engaged in reprocessing and – to use a metaphor suggested by Palmié – "cooking"[21] ideas of Africa and Yorubaness for the appetites of Black communities in Bahia.

However, to suggest that it was the labours of these Black identity entrepreneurs alone who brought about the emphasis on "Yorubaness" in the *terreiros* of Bahia and ultimately in the neighbourhoods, community groups, and *carnaval* associations is to neglect the fact that many of these individuals actively *used* anthropologists and other social scientists – both Brazilian and American – in bringing about this focus on purity. Bonfim actively engaged anthropologists such as Ruth Landes (1947) and Edison Carneiro (1948) essentially as press agents for his quest to elevate his *terreiro* – Opô Afonjá – and its leader at the time, Mae Aninha, to the status of being the *only* Afro-Brazilian religious congregation that could speak with authority about Africa. To be sure, there is agency here and Black agency at that, but slowly the anthropologist also becomes implicated in the process of remaking Africa for Brazil. In this sense, both Matory and those who suggest that white intellectuals created the emphasis on Yorubaness in the *terreiro* are right, for one could not exist – in the context of a Brazil committed to the use of social science as a source of legitimization for nation building – without the other.

"Respected" scholars like Ramos and Nina Rodrigues along with anthropologist-activists like Landes and Carneiro provided the "pure" *terreiros* with an opportunity for their practice and devotion to championing Black communities in Bahia to be tolerated by mainstream Bahian and the broad Brazilian society. Negotiaters of Africanity like Bomfin were very much responsible for helping bring about the emphasis on Yoruba purity in many of Salvador's Blackest neighbourhoods, but individuals like Landes, Carneiro, Ramos, and later, Pierre Verger and Roger Bastide, helped legitimize this emphasis during the course of twentieth-century Brazil. In his 2005 synthesis of this argument, *Black Atlantic Religion*, Matory emphasizes that both West African travellers and their academic interlocutors both played a part in creating Yoruba centricity while also emphasizing the importance of local Black agency. In a chapter of this volume entitled "Para Inglês Ver: Sex, Secrecy and Scholarship in the Yoruba-Atlantic World," Matory (2005, 188–223) argues that Landes, guided by a feminist perspective, was single-handedly responsible for transforming Bahian *Candomblé* into a religion governed primarily by a matriarchy of powerful women priests. Further, Matory (2005, 189–95) suggests it was Landes herself who recapitulated, backwards in time, the "cult matriarchy" of *Candomblé* so that practitioners began to see the matriarchal form as the truly "African form" – here he also asserts that Landes also brought about the construction of male *adé* priests as homosexuals within the space of the *terreiro*. Nevertheless, "Black Atlantic Religion" is a praise song for "pure" Yoruba-form *Candomblé*. It places this form over all others and regards syncretism as a step backwards – again, as part of a revolutionary struggle – for Black identity. Matory dismisses the extremely popular Afro-Brazilian practice, *Umbanda*, which is found in Brazil's Southeast and Amazonian delta regions and brings together Yoruba deities with Amerindian entities, Catholic saints, and European spiritism in an eclectic – and largely urban – religious fusion, as a "watered-down" version of *Candomblé* (Matory 2005, 165).[22] While writing eloquently about how foreign intellectual elites played no role in elevating Yoruba practice to the exalted level it now enjoys in Black Bahian society, he is himself engaged in this very activity.

The point here is that academics, especially anthropologists, have been and continue to be vitally important in manufacturing and disseminating much of the mystique of the *terreiro*. Not just in the rarefied atmosphere of the academy, but also within the societies they study. Palmié (1995), in his study of Fernando Ortiz' nation-building project in Cuba, has shown how informants and research participants are quick to start incorporating and manipulating anthropological ideas and concepts into their own political, economic, and social agendas. Black communities in Bahia have been equally successful in using the anthropological fixation with the Afro-American *problématique* – in particular, Afro-Brazilian religious survivals and how to "explain" them – into their own projects of social mobilization and cultural legitimization. Scholars on both sides of the debate concerning the historical origins of Africanity and Yorubaness in the diaspora – Africa-centric historians versus creole theorists – seek to emphasize the place of local Black agency in the maintenance and preservation or the invention of African traditions in Brazil as a corrective to interpretations that place the "creation" of Africa in Brazil and elsewhere at the feet of Herskovits and his followers. However, whilst down among the ethnographic "weeds," so to speak, it is extremely difficult to deny the looming presence that many of these early social scientists still possess – many leaders in the Black community of Bahia still invoke the legacy of these white negotiators of the Black Atlantic. Individuals such as Ruth Landes and Pierre Verger and their affluent Brazilian interlocutors are often mentioned or talked about with considerable frequency in Salvador. I speak here not just of elites in the *terreiros* like Opô Afonjá or in *blocos* like Ilê Aiyê, but of young men playing football on a small plaza in Curuzu-Liberdade; of women working in restaurants close to the large *terreiro* of Casa Branca in the neighbourhood of Engenho Velho da Federação; or of schoolchildren visiting the old quarter of Salvador, Pelourinho – everyday people whose familiarity with ethnographers and ethnography is often surprising, to say the least.

I recount here an interaction with just such a group of schoolchildren that had emerged from an art gallery in Pelourinho, on their way to see a performance of Olodum. The gallery they were visiting is part of the Fundação Pierre Verger. An organization whose purpose, according to its website, is to "improve the exposure of the ethno-photographer's work" that is based on, in Verger's (2014) own words, his "love for two places: Bahia and the region of Africa located within the Gulf of Benin. The Foundation's purpose is to enhance this shared heritage by revealing to Bahia the knowledge of Benin and Nigeria." The presence of the Verger Foundation can be seen everywhere in Salvador. From museum openings, to Black consciousness events, to *terreiro* celebrations, it is a powerful and ubiquitous cultural force. In addition, the foundation also makes money by selling artwork, photo books, and T-shirts emblazoned with the photographer's images. All of the images used on the shirts are of Black Brazilian men and women engaged in work or in after-work relaxation, or are of African men, women, or children, shot in stark settings and always rendered in black-and-white. There is no interpretive or ethnographic material attached to the images printed on the T-shirts and they definitely appear to be the most popular item for sale in the gallery/boutique. The shirts have become quite a common sight throughout Salvador.

Upon emerging from the gallery, a number of the students were grasping recently purchased T-shirts or had already put them on, so I asked them about what had just transpired and why they bought the shirts at the boutique.

AD: Why did you buy these shirts?[23]

INFORMANT: Pierre Verger is very important. He helped teach many people in Salvador about Africa, about why people in the *terreiro* do their rituals. The spinning, and the singing and everything.

AD: So, he taught *Baianos* about Africa?

INFORMANT: Exactly! He showed the *Candomblés* what part of Africa their rituals come from. They are from Nigeria. You have two kinds. The Jeje and the Yoruba. He showed them the difference. Well, I think my teacher goes to a *terreiro*. But I'm not sure. I don't think he would tell us. But it is important to help support the Pierre Verger Foundation because he did so much for *Baianos*. Especially for us "*Afrodescendentes*."

AD: Okay, so you bought the T-shirts because of Verger.

INFORMANT: Yes, but also because of the Africans on them. We're all Black – Africans and Brazilians and we have many things in common. So I wear this because it is chic, but also because I like to show Black beauty. You see the scars on this girl's face? Well, I would never do that, but this is what it means to be beautiful in Africa!

AD: Do you think that scars like these (I point to the shirt) are common in Africa?

INFORMANT: That is what they do throughout Africa, especially in Nigeria. I saw it on *Fantástico*.

This exchange left me thinking about the extent to which figures like Verger still penetrated the everyday discourse about race and identity in Salvador.

Verger is perhaps the most oft-cited member of the cadre of foreign intellectuals responsible for popularizing and romanticizing the space of the *terreiro* in Bahia. In every bookstore in Salvador, Pierre Verger's books, especially *Fluxo e refluxo do Trafico de Escravos entre o Golfo do Benin e a Bahia de Todos os Santos dos Séculos XVII a XIX* (2002), are

Figure 3.2 T-shirts and photo books displaying images of Blackness for sale at the Pierre Verger gallery-boutique in Pelourinho.

available for sale. Bookstore employees informed me that they always have to restock Verger's titles on a monthly basis and that they are regularly reprinted in Brazil by the large Salvador-based publisher Corrupio. At every event I attended that promoted Black consciousness, awareness of African heritage, religious tolerance, and antiracism, Pierre Verger's name was always, without fail, invoked by important speakers or organizers. At an event promoted by UFBa and organized by a religious tolerance community group, one prominent Black leader who is a member of a small, but "proudly Yoruba" *terreiro*, proclaimed: "Pierre 'Fatumbi' Verger was my *babalaô* and he taught me everything about the *Orixás*."[24] This individual spoke expressively and passionately about the importance of Black society finding its own way in Brazil and of Black people in Brazil being proud of their African heritage. However, he sanctioned and authenticated his place in the Afro-

Brazilian religious hierarchy of Bahia not through a visit he had recently made to West Africa, nor through knowledge of the Yoruba language, but rather through a connection with a French amateur anthropologist and photographer whose principal legacy in Bahia is a foundation and gallery that earns money through the sale of photographic representations of Blackness and T-shirts.

In the suburb of Lauro de Freitas, a former student and member of Verger's entourage who is also a *babalaô*, Balbino Daniel de Paula, founded the *terreiro* Ilê Axé Opô Aganjú in 1972. Balbino is an important community leader in Salvador and often speaks at major events in the city that are connected with the Black movements and with religious tolerance. His is an extremely well-known and popular *terreiro* that counts among its devotees a number of important politicians and businessmen. Balbino regularly speaks about the need for greater religious tolerance in Bahia and in all of Brazil, especially given the increasing strength and power wielded by the large evangelicalchurches, many of which are openly hostile to the *terreiros*. He is, along with Mãe Stella and Mestre Didi, one of the most famous and influential protagonists of Africanity in Bahia. At a 2006 event commemorating the institution of a new law aimed at protecting all religious spaces from any form of discrimination, Balbino declared, in the presence of a number of visiting state dignitaries, local governmental officials, and visitors from Nigeria, including Félix, that none of this would have been possible were it not for the initial support and encouragement that he received from Verger.[25] Dead now for over a decade, Verger's name is still everywhere in Salvador: in daily newspapers, on schools that bear his name, on television, and in connection with many aspects of the Black movement. With this kind of daily bombardment, it is unsurprising to find that even among lay people and schoolchildren, the name "Verger" has become synonymous with "Africa," "Blackness," "Yoruba," and *"orixá."*

Verger is not alone. Almost as popular is the name of Ruth Landes. Though professionally blackballed in the United States by Herskovits with the assistance of Arthur Ramos (Yelvington 2006b), Landes' legacy is still quite potent in Bahia. Landes has come to be something of an unofficial icon of feminine power in the *terreiros* that claim to practise a pure Yoruba form, and she is exalted as the one who finally "showed the world"[26] a society where women were in control and where the "feminine communed directly with the divine."[27] In a film entitled *Cidade das Mulheres* (2005), that takes its name from Landes' (1947) similarly titled *City of Women*, the American anthropologist is lauded and celebrated as a woman who truly understood the feminine soul of Black Brazil and also of African society. Indeed, the film proudly proclaims itself as a homage to Landes and to the other proud women of Salvador. Funded by the Brazilian national oil company, Petrobras, the Government of Bahia, and the Federal Government's Culture Ministry (again, Gilberto Gil's portfolio), the film was written and produced by Cléo Martins, a well-known minor celebrity in Salvador, a close associate of Mãe Stella, and a devotee of Opô Afonjá – the *terreiro* that Matory (2001) singles out as the most pure Yoruba house of worship in all of Brazil. Consequently, the message of Yoruba purity comes through loud and clear. I mention the sources of funding to demonstrate how the message of Africanity and African purity are increasingly being seen as mainstream in Bahia. Petrobras, essentially an organ of the Brazilian government, is one of the largest philanthropic organizations in Brazil. They regularly fund films, television, concerts, and other "cultural" projects throughout the country and are often connected with overt public manifestations of Brazilian nationalism. For them to be openly associated with a film that presents a racial and historical narrative that runs contrary to the dominant ideals of racial democracy marks a shift, albeit a small one, in the public image of the company. In 1984, an application was made by a unified coalition of Brazil's Black movements to the oil giant for funding to support the Zumbí movement. Petrobras declined the application, as Zumbí was seen as too divisive and did not represent "racial democracy" (Burdick 1998a, 71). Twenty years later, and Petrobras appears to be more than willing to fund a project that speaks to a racial agenda very different from the harmonious ideal they previously espoused.

Cidade das Mulheres opens with a series of animated sequences that place images of Ruth Landes among shots of Black Brazilian women carrying water, cooking, and engaging in religious activity. Intercut with these images are scenes of Asante women in Ghana wearing *kente*, Edison Carneiro walking the streets of Salvador, and an image of the Statue of Liberty – indicating Landes' home in New York. This opening sequence then fades into a shot of an actress portraying Landes "writing up" her fieldnotes on an old typewriter with a narrator, speaking in Landes' voice, quoting from *City of Women*. The film, rather than echoing Matory's suggestion that Landes created the emphasis on femininity and homosexuality, suggests rather that Landes uncovered this basic "truth" of African societies. Either way, it becomes clear that Landes, and now Ayoh'Omidire and Matory, are all implicated in the ways in which groups like the Yoruba-centric *terreiros* and other similarly influential community groups understand and represent themselves to society at large.

Ethnography and Identity

From Herskovits to Landes, Freyre to Ramos, Verger to Bastide, these so-called white inventors of Brazilian "Africanness," although not entirely responsible, as Fry (1982) suggests, for inventing ideas of Yoruba purity or Africanity in Black Bahian society, cannot be ignored or omitted from an analysis of the construction of Africa-centric and Yoruba-centric identities in Bahia. These individuals remain as powerful touchstones for local Black leaders and are used to legitimize totalizing and unified ideas about Africanity. Even when speaking to members of activist groups and Black organizers, it appears that prominent leaders cannot help but invoke the names of these researchers in order to lend some degree of anthropological credibility to their claims of African descent. The continuing reliance on individuals whose ideas and theories, in the annals of academic social science, may have been all but forgotten or rejected reminds the anthropologist that, as much as we are involved in the describing and ethnographically inscribing societies, we often get implicated in new ethnographic realities, born of ideas such as identity, purity, syncretism, and creolization. Surely, this is as much a dialogue, one that is transacted between the authors and those communities who read and consume ethnography, as the one that Clifford (1986) insists is embedded on the page.

Yelvington (2006a) traces the use of the dialogue metaphor in anthropology to Tedlock and Mannheim's (1995) introduction of Russian literary critic Mikhail Bakhtin's theories in the mid-1990s. Bakhtin was principally concerned with consciousness and tropes of language in literary works. He asserted that language had both a creative and interpretative aspect, but also held that language had the capacity to elicit contestation and struggle over meaning. Any context in which consciousness or world view is altered or in which a discourse is contested and negotiated is inherently dialogic in that it is interactive and continually producing new meanings. However, the use of Bakhtin's dialogic metaphor, especially in relation to how it informs our understanding of discourse, can be traced even further back to the work of the Writing Culture group (Clifford and Marcus 1986). It should be noted that their introduction of the dialogic approach is primarily concerned with the production of ethnographic text and the inscription of culture, but Clifford's (1986) note that dialogical processes "proliferate in any complexly representative discursive space" is well taken (15). He is referring here primarily to the polyphonic and multivocal collaboration that this group of scholars believes ethnography *must* be: a construct in which different voices demand attention – attention that was denied and restrained in so-called traditional ethnography. Nonetheless, the dialogic processes that Clifford and Marcus (1986) suggest exist in textual collaborations or textual *products* seem to miss the dialogue that takes place in the actual ethnographic encounter. It is in this way that anthropology finds its place within the polyphonic discussion about which so much ink was split during the 1980s. Clifford and Marcus (1986) called for a reassessment of ethnography as text and the place of the ethnographer as author of culture. Fox (1991) and others responded that such interpretative exhortations missed the point – that the call for polyphony, reflexivity, and dialogue were, to some extent, overwrought attempts to deal with the essential reflexivity that Watson (1987) sees as the sine qua non of the ethnographic endeavour.

More importantly, though, what the Writing Culture project appears to neglect is that the dialogue of importance is not one that is inscribed within the pages of an ethnography. The dialogue that ultimately has a far greater impact in *making culture* is the one that occurs when subject communities read and embed the ethnography, as a final product, and the personality of the ethnographer within their own identarian quests. *Writing Culture* (Clifford and Marcus 1986) rightfully draws our attention to the politics within text, but does not recognize, as the writers in *Recapturing Anthropology* (Fox 1991) seminar suggest, the politics surrounding the reading and reproduction of text. This reproduction takes place in a cultural milieu in which anthropology has been part of the process of understanding and creating culture and history – and this has certainly been the case among Afro-diasporic intellectuals and leaders. Indeed, it is *history* that the Writing Culture group seems to understand least. This key insight, one that Weber was also keenly aware of, seems to elude Clifford and Marcus in *Writing Culture* (1986). Weber (1915), like Gramsci (1971) after him, understood the creation of knowledge as a social phenomenon that led to the formation of human hierarchies. Science, anthropology included, must be understood within a historical framework, a context that involves understanding

ethnography "as a historical phenomenon ... associated with social, political, and material circumstances" (Vincent 1991, 47). Surely this is the
dialogic at its unfiltered best – or worst. A dialogue in which inscribed
culture – the ethnography – becomes a note or phrase, sentence or
speech, song or, at its very best, concerto, in a continuing, though sometimes lopsided, interaction that makes identities, cultures, and histories. Crucial to this dialogue is that ethnography is read not only by
scholars and intellectuals, but is also increasingly read by the people
about whom it is written.

In the context of a dialogue between Africa and the Americas, and
between locales within the Americas where Blackness finds different
expressions, ethnography and ethnographers – sometimes amateur
ethnographers – are part of a broad network of ideas and communities,
all of which are engaged in defining and manipulating ideas of what it
means to be Black and "of Africa" in the modern world. Anthropologists have become part of the call-and-response of identity politics in
Black America, not in the least because anthropology – especially
American anthropology – has been so intertwined with the aspirational
and emancipatory agendas of oppressed and minority populations.
Handler (1993) finds this connection unsurprising: "nationalism and
anthropology have common origins in Euro-American romanticism
[much of which provided grist for Boas' notion of culture]" and that
"social scientific analyses of ethnicity and nationalism were almost always cast in the same terms that ethnic and nationalist movements
used to describe themselves. In other words, social scientists and na-
tionalists spoke that same language" (68). Furthermore, informants and
the communities from which they arise do more than simply read what
is written about them. They are also able to, with great skill and dexter-
ity, manipulate agendas, ideas, and data to their own ends.

Ethnography is consumed by both those *for* whom it is written and
by those *about* whom it is written. As Sidney Mintz (1974) notes, Afro-
American cultures were born in the midst of incredible brutality and
oppression, born of "disturbed pasts," and delivered to a future of racism and intolerance. In using the work, ideas, and names of these researchers, we see an attempt, on the part of those who invoke them, to
infuse these pasts with meaning.

Many leaders of the Afro-Brazilian society in Bahia are so intimately
familiar with the process of ethnography, with the debates present in
the history of Afro-American societies, and with the work of major
anthropologists working their terrain, that one is almost reticent to

self-identify as a member of this most peculiar tribe. "Another one?" is a phrase I received more than a few times – Salvador is, quite literally, teeming with anthropologists and ethnologists, many of them working and reworking the same well-trodden ground. There is, of course, nothing wrong with this. If anthropology is indeed a social *science*, then repetition and confirmation of past research with fresh eyes and fresh ideas is a pre-requisite for the discipline's validity. But should it then come as any surprise when anthropologists and their work start to be incorporated into local histories and agendas?

Clifford (1986, 118) argues that what frequently passes for the local or native's perspective in ethnography is, more often than not, only the beliefs, ideas, and assertions of the anthropologist who, in the act of inscribing culture, serves to suppress the native's world view. Writing ethnography becomes, therefore, an expression of power and control and provides, ultimately, authority to speak for the native. On the other hand, what happens when both the work and the personality of the anthropologist become a primary resource for mobilizing, legitimizing, and manipulating communities? What happens when the labour of ethnography is subsumed by activism? Clifford called for ethnography to be dialogic and polyphonic, but what happens when, as part of this dialogue, local communities – the object of our study – take one "version" of their story as authoritative and run with it at the expense of other voices within the community?

In the process of reflexively inserting the self into the ethnographic "fiction" – motivated by particular political agendas, beliefs, or by the desire to avoid the kind of omniscience they believed flawed so much modernist ethnography – anthropologists like Clifford and those that have followed have created an *ultimate* kind of authority. With biases revealed and agendas made visible, ethnographers, their involvement and commitment to the community now made visibly explicit in the text, become the community's official narrators and possessors of the truth. Why? Because subject communities and societies know, as one of my informants sardonically points out, how to read. In both their texts and in their lives in Brazil, Landes and Verger made their personality and authority as anthropologists potent and palpable, and successfully presented themselves to their fieldwork community, through local elites like Bonfim and Balbino, as "artisans" of ethnography (cf. Fox 1991, 9). For Landes, Verger, and now also for a whole generation of Brazilian and foreign academics involved as champions of the *terreiro*, of Blackness, and the Africanity of Black Brazil, so much of themselves and what they believe in is invested in their ethnography and in their personal involvement with their community.

Beyond the evocation of heroes such as Landes and Verger, it now seems virtually impossible for any public activity, whether an art opening, a community reinvigoration project, the commemoration of a slave hero such as Zumbí, African reconnection projects, or any of a host of other events to take place in Salvador without some connection with the scholars at UFBa's Centro de Estudos Afro-Orientais (CEAO). CEAO has become a clearing house for all things connected with Africa and Afro-Brazilian scholarship in Salvador and they have, through their courses in Yoruba and Arabic that draw students, both young and old, from throughout the city, extended their influence deeply into community organizations and *terreiros* in many neighbourhoods.

Moreover, many of the scholars and students associated with CEAO are devotees of a variety of different Afro-Brazilian religious congregations: some of them members of "pure" Yoruba-centric *Candomblé terreiros*, others practitioners of *Umbanda*, and some openly "eclectic" about their religious beliefs. A relationship – one might say dialogic – has developed between those who seek to be representatives of an African-oriented identity for Black Brazilians living in Salvador the scholars and scholarship that advocate understanding of the truly "African" quality of Black society in Brazil.

Intellectuals for Gramsci (1971), insofar as they are important in shaping culture and contributing to social movements, are present in every class within society: "Every social group ... creates together with itself, organically, one or more strata of intellectuals" (5) and that "the intellectuals of the historically (and concretely) progressive class, in the given conditions, exercise such a power of attraction that, in the last analysis they end up subjugating the intellectuals of the other social groups" (60). Scott (1985) has likewise argued such intellectuals – within the frame of societal "progress" – serve to define standards of rightness, beauty, and morality, building a "symbolic climate that prevents the subordinate classes from thinking their way free" (39). Now to be sure, the cultural elites of Bahia engaged in making Blackness part and parcel of the image of this "most African of states" are not oriented towards the material exploitation of a particular underclass. Indeed, many of these writers and activists have worked tirelessly to rid Brazil of the blight of racism and to enhance tolerance and acceptance of Brazil's African heritage. However, as Selka (2005) notes, "forms of resistance that are based exclusively on the direct contradiction of dominant representations and classifications are often unsuccessful in eroding structures of domination" (90).

Popular Christianity and Brazilian Blackness

Despite the pre-eminence and celebrity-like status accorded individuals like Mãe Stella, Mestre Didi, Balbino, and others, the *terreiros*, the *blocos afros* and their counterparts in the academy do not exert a monolithic influence on Salvador's and Bahia's Black communities. There are other voices and other perspectives on how Black communities should be mobilized to fight racism and alternate identities available for Black individuals to engage and articulate. That a tension between syncretism and purity in *Candomblé* can even exist attests to the underlying fact that large numbers of Afro-Brazilians, even those who assert an African-oriented manifestation of Blackness, often still cling to some form of baseline Catholicism. A large, white wooden cross even stood on the grounds of Opô Afonjá, the stalwart of the Africa-centric movement, for a long period of time. Catholicism has more of the character of an ethnic identity for many Brazilians than a religion, and it is not one that is easily washed away.

The Africa-centric movement has certainly become culturally dominant in Salvador. However, despite this ascendancy, most Black residents of Salvador still adhere to an underlying reverence for Catholicism. One need only spend an hour walking though any neighbourhood in Salvador to quickly discover the importance of Christianity. It truly is hard to walk more than a hundred metres down any street in the city without passing at least a couple of churches. As we have seen, throughout Salvador, African-oriented aspects of Bahia's culture are placed front and centre by tourist agencies, intellectual elites, and Afro-Brazilian religious communities. They prevail in all popular depictions of Salvador and form an important part of the daily lives of many Black people in Salvador. However, although the anti-syncretic movement emphasizes that these African forms must take precedence over Christian beliefs or European ideals, this point of view, though highlighted and accentuated by scholars and media, does not always represent the realities of life for many individuals in Salvador. For many Black men and women in the city, even those who are members of proudly Yoruba-centric *terreiros*, there remains a powerful respect and reverence for the Catholic Church. Part of this is because of Catholicism's historical place as the quasi-official religion of Brazil. The other reason for this

Figure 3.3 Usage of *negro* as an identity category among Afro-Brazilians continues in different communities throughout the city.

seemingly indelible reverence to the Church is that manifestations of
Catholicism in Salvador often include their own, alternative forms of
African-oriented practice and Black identity discourse – other voices
of Blackness within the broad array of Afro-Brazilian identity options.

Vast numbers of people in the Black neighbourhoods also turn to the
growing number of evangelical churches in Brazil for religious succour.
Members of these churches are explicitly forbidden from participating
in any aspect of Afro-Brazilian worship as evangelical churches disparage these practices as devil worship and witchcraft. The Black movements very much see this intolerance and hatred of *Candomblé* and
other Afro-Brazilian religions as nothing less than racism. In the discourse of the *blocos afros* and the *terreiros*, despite the exhortations of
terreiro leaders, there is an awareness, I believe, that Catholicism is
something that can never be entirely expunged from the hearts and
minds of their devotees or from the Black community – it is too deeply
ingrained. However, the *terreiros* are openly hostile towards the evangelicalchurches, especially the megachurches, which continue to make
inroads into poorer Black communities.

The twinning of a globalizing African Blackness with the identity
rhetoric of the *blocos afros* and the *terreiros* is something that is often
rejected, both by the leaders of the evangelical churches and by indi-

viduals from Black communities and neighbourhoods who eschew African-oriented religion. Large numbers of evangelicals in Salvador are Black and they often find themselves in disagreement with friends and neighbours who rebuke them for "betraying" their people or their communities. *Candomblé*, the Black space of the *terreiro*, and the *bloco afro* have become touchstones for African-oriented Blackness, and the forms of Black identity that have emerged from these locales of resistance and opposition to power have become the dominant narrative of counter-hegemony within the Black community. Not perhaps to the expense of all other narratives, but certainly to the extent that alternative stories of resistance and opposition are often not able to fully participate in the formation of a broader sense of Black consciousness in Bahia and elsewhere – that is, these alternatives are very much part of Afro-Brazilian identity discourse, but they are often left out in constructions of popular Blackness by responsible stakeholders. Slowly but surely, the peripheral cult that was *Candomblé* and the identity discourse built up around it has become the central and institutionalized cult of Blackness in Bahia. Does this mean they have won the battle? That racism has been excised? Certainly not, rather, the dominance that these practices and beliefs enjoy is a cultural one – it exists at the level of perception and public awareness. However, it is an extremely powerful perception, one that belies the fact that membership in *terreiros* and other aspects of the Black movements are restricted to a segment of the Black community. In the recent 2010 national census, the number of self-identified Roman Catholics across Brazil was 123,280,172 individuals out of 190,755,799 – fully 65 per cent.

From this same population, 42,275,440 (22 per cent) individuals identified as members of an evangelical congregation, while 588,797 (0.3 per cent) individuals identified as practitioners of an Afro-Brazilian tradition (*Candomblé, Umbanda*, and others) (IBGE 2010, 148). Now, Bahia was and is still the state with the largest percentage of people who self-identified as Black (Preta) or Brown (Parda), 17.1 per cent and 59.2 per cent, respectively, but again, only a small portion of this community are actually practitioners of an Afro-Brazilian religious tradition. Moreover, there is disagreement within the broader Black community throughout Bahia as to what extent political and social objectives should be tied with those of a religious organization. In short, there is considerable contestation within Black communities about the place of *Candomblé* (Sansone 2004). A number of scholars, notably Butler (1998) and Burdick (1998b), have argued that the overwhelming emphasis on

Table 3.1 2010 Brazilian Census Data on Religious Affiliation by Racial Ascription (IBGE 2010, 148)

	Branca (White)	Preta (Black)	Amarela (Yellow)	Parda (Brown)	Indigena (Amerindian)	Undeclared	Totals
Roman Catholic	60,189,864	8,348,310	1,261,350	53,064,179	416,201	269	123,280,172
Evangelical churches	18,867,446	3,461,646	413,261	19,323,780	209,259	48	42,275,440
Afro-Brazilian religions	277,150	124,514	3,408	181,214	2,511	0	588,797
Totals	79,334,460	11,934,470	1,678,019	72,569,173	627,971	317	166,144,410

the religious symbols and identarian assertions of the *terreiro* is an extremely precarious and ultimately, untenable, trajectory for Brazil's Black movements. In 1998, when John Burdick wrote *The Lost Constituency of Brazil's Black Movements*, he noted: "Most of our informants, across all color categories, had little concrete notion of what we meant when we referred to the black movements ... it is inaccurate to say that 'all' participants in the black movement in Brazil are followers of ...'traditional' African religiosity" (146–7). At the end of the 1990s, in Rio de Janeiro, this very well may have been the case. In 2013, in Salvador, there is a much more acute awareness of what concepts such as *Movimento Negro, Afrodescendente, bloco afro*, African purity, anti-syncretism, and Yoruba mean – not just at a general level, but rather an awareness that entails knowledge of the political implications of these ideas, organizations, and identities. Even among Black Catholics and evangelicals who do not participate in associations as the MNU, who have little to do with *blocos afros* such as Ilê-Aiyê, and who possess little or no connection with *terreiros* other than through the activities of family members, luminaries of the Afro-Brazilian religions and broader African-oriented identity still loom large.

Maria

As the 2010 Brazilian census illustrates, Black Catholics and other Christian groups by far make up the majority of the Black community in Salvador and Bahia at large and yet, in numerous interviews, these individuals claimed that their beliefs and their Black *Brazilian* culture were not as well-known or understood broadly as representative of Blackness in Bahia. I had numerous conversations about this very issue with Maria, a fifty-two-year-old woman, and her son, fourteen-year-old Raimundo. Together, this mother and son duo sell the famed African "food of the gods," known as *acarajé*,[28] for which Salvador has become famous. Maria, like all *acarajé* sellers or *Baianas*, as they are called, wears a long white dress, elaborated with lace and cowries along with a length of white cloth tied as a turban around her head. She represents precisely the kind of folkorized image of feminine, African-oriented Blackness to which Selka (2007) refers – a woman steeped in the heritage and history of an African past. Decorating her *acarajé* stall are small statues of beloved *orixás*, notably Iemanjá, *orixá* of the sea and a deity that is usually associated with images of the Virgin Mary. Other images include stickers and flags with the pan-African colours of red, yellow, and green, along with images of Bob Marley and political decals for the PT, the governing Partido dos Trabalhadores of President Dilma Rousseff. Maria tells me:

> All my family are Catholics and that is not going to change. I wear the *Baianas'* white clothes because I am a *Baiana*. People come to Salvador for an Afro experience. That means *Candomblé* and *acarajé*. I have my son Raimundo helping me. But he cannot be the one to package up the food and give it to the customers – they expect women to be selling this food. Not men.[29]

In a survey conducted over fifteen months of ethnographic fieldwork in Salvador, I found only three out of 200 *acarajé* stalls that were run by men. During this study, I ate hundreds of *acarajé*, but the fashion in which it was prepared, packaged, and sold was consistent across the city. At each stall or *tabuleiro*, the woman was typically dressed in a long white dress with some kind of elaboration made of lace, shells, or ribbon along with a white headcloth. Furthermore, out of the 200 stalls that I sampled, only twenty-six of the sellers could be considered to occupy an ethnic category other than visibly Black. Raimundo informed me when his mother is sick and he has to run the stall he sells practically no *acarajé* except to tourists and a few other foreigners. Maria continues: "I don't believe in *Candomblé*, but I have to dress and staff the stall appropriately – that includes having a woman present. I'm a Catholic and my church is here in Pelourinho – the Igreja Rosário dos Pretos. That is where, every year, we have our Day of the *Baiana*." The Igreja de Nossa Senhora do Rosário dos Pretos (Church of Our Lady of the Rosary of the Blacks) is a Catholic church in Pelourinho that is oriented towards primarily serving the Black community of the old city. It was constructed in 1704 by freedmen and slaves who laboured in what little free time they had and was sponsored by the Irmandade de Nossa Senhora do Rosário dos Homens Pretos do Pelourinho (Sisterhood of Our Lady of the Rosario of Black Men of Pelourinho). Although the church is designed as a traditional Catholic place of worship in the rococo style, a number of motifs in the blue façade allude to the presence of African practices that existed in Salvador at the time of construction. Additionally, many of the parishioners are involved in some of the explicitly African-oriented manifestations of Afro-Brazilian religiosity. Maria adds: "Many *Baianas* attend the *terreiro* and we all respect the *terreiro*. But I'm not African, I'm Brazilian!" When I ask her whether she thought that the majority of women who sell *acarajé* in the city are Christians, she responds: "I won't say that there aren't *Baianas* who aren't part of a *terreiro*. When people ask me the story of *acarajé*, I tell them that yes, it comes from Africa, it is African in origin, but we do it differently. So you can say this is African, but I call it Brazilian. I call it Bahian food."

Maria is devout about her Catholicism and is committed to her church, Igreja de Nossa Senhora do Rosário dos Pretos. Members of the church and the Pastoral Afro[30] ministry that work within this parish are concerned with many of the same issues that have mobilized groups like Ilê Aiyê and Opô Afonjá: fighting racism; poverty in Black communities; dignity for the Black people in Brazil; and respect for Black history – but their approach is less oriented towards an explicit recreation or celebration of Africa and the African in Bahia. There are two vitally important statues or religious icons that Maria directed me to go and observe in the church that would provide me with an alternative perspective on Black religions in Bahia. One of these images was, of course, the large statue of Nossa Senhora da Aparecida. In Brazil, Nossa Senhora da Aparecida is considered the national patron saint and, like other iterations of the Virgin in predominantly Catholic countries or regions – Guadalupe in Mexico, Fátima in Portugal, and Lourdes in France – has come to symbolize contested notions of national identity.

The story of Nossa Senhora da Aparecida is one that, even in a Brazil where evangelical religions are slowly starting to gain ground on the quasi-official Catholicism of the state, many schoolchildren can recount. As the story goes, in 1717, a Portuguese nobleman named Pedro Miguel de Almeida Portugal e Vasconcellos arrived in the town that would later be called Aparecida or "appeared." In honour of his arrival, local fishermen were asked to bring in as many fish as they could from the Paraiba River. Despite treacherous weather, three fishermen, Domingos Garcia, Joilo Alves, and Felipe Pedroso, went out on the river. While on the waters, rather than catching a haul of fish, they pulled in a statue of the Virgin that had become entangled in their nets. Most notably, the effigy of the Virgin had not the pale skin of a European but rather the dark brown skin of the typical Brazilian peasant or *caboclo*. Soon after the discovery, fishing in the region became abundant, with nets overflowing with fish. The "Appeared Lady" soon became the patron of fishermen throughout Brazil and, in 1822, Pedro I raised her to the status of patroness of the empire. In 1931, when Vargas took control of Brazil from a military junta, he promoted the Catholic Church as the state's semi-official religion and the Lady as the symbol of a united

Brazil. Vargas, who was very much swayed by the notion of racial democracy, saw the colour of the Lady as one which precisely tied into the growing belief that Brazil was a country in which the different founding races – European, African, and Amerindian – would come to together to form a new and prosperous tropical society. At the same time he gave his principal Catholic adviser, Cardinal Leme, free reign in suppressing and denouncing the Afro-Brazilian religious cults.

Nossa Senhora da Aparecida has become a powerful marker of racially mixed public space, "one that was transformed through miscegenation into the folkloric shadow of the mulatto" (Johnson 1997, 128). However, over the past ten years or so, especially in Bahia, in churches like Nossa Senhora do Rosário, the complexion of most statues of the Nossa Senhora da Aparecida has shifted from one of dark brown to being decidedly Black, representing, Johnson suggests, "a new configuration of what and who, occupies the center of Brazilian public space" (140). In Bahia, it is Blackness, regardless of whether one refers to the dominant images of an Africanized religious space or the more nationally recognizable image of the "Appeared Lady" that defines the key symbols of public space, especially in an area like Pelourinho.

The other icon that Maria had exhorted me to see in the church was a shrine to Anastácia. A slave from the Angolan coast, Anastácia laboured as a house slave and became the mistress of her white master. When the slave-owner's wife discovered the affair, Anastácia was "silenced" with a ceramic disk inserted into her mouth and secured in place by a leather strap. This torturous existence eroded her mouth and led to starvation and death. Anastácia has been sanctified and venerated by thousands of Afro-Brazilian women throughout the country; devotees regard her as holy and claim miracles on her behalf, while the Catholic Church refuses to entertain her beatification. Anastácia's attempt to "voice" resistance to her oppression and her ultimate martyrdom has become an inspiration to other Black women who revere and celebrate her in the Catholic "inculturated mass." This mass is an attempt, according to Burdick (1998a), "to salvage the history and culture of Afro-Brazilians from the oblivion to which racist society seeks to consign them, by imparting knowledge about African culture" (57), but within, I would add, the context of Catholicism. The MNU and many terreiros in Salvador and many anti-syncretic terreiros are reticent about Anastácia and the inculturated mass because of its connection with the Catholic Church. Furthermore, they believe the veneration to Anastácia focuses on a narrative that provides Black people with a nihilistic solution to

Figure 3.4 A statue of Anastácia in the Igreja de Nossa Senhora
do Rosário dos Pretos in Pelourinho.

racism – one in which a Black woman had to be martyred before she
could be liberated (Burdick 1998a, 151–2). However, women like Maria
venerate Anastácia precisely because, she tells me, her story is one that
women "around the world" can relate to and because the inculturated
mass and the message of the Pastoral Afro focuses more on domestic,
everyday matters.

Black leaders point out that the inculturated mass mainly serves
women who are concerned with finding a supernatural panacea for

what ails their communities and families. This is at odds with the political agendas of anti-syncretic *terreiros* and their emphasis on Yoruba hegemony as a new identity for Black people, which is oriented towards developing a revolutionary sense of racial consciousness in the face of the historical devalorization of African culture in Brazil.

Every Tuesday, the same day that Pelourinho throws its gates open to public manifestations of Africanity such as performances by Olodum and official guided tours of local *terreiros*, an inculturated mass is held at the Nossa Senhora do Rosário. I met Maria one Tuesday and accompanied her to the service. Almost everybody who attended the mass would be considered Black or would openly self-identify as such. *Preta*, which means Black in Portuguese, was the term that was, for a very long time, used to describe the skin colour of those present at the mass I attended. Indeed, it is still the term used by the Instituto Brasileiro de Geografia e Estatística (IBGE) in the most recent 2010 census to describe people who self-ascribe as Black. However, Maria tells me that, even among Christian congregations such as hers, this word is increasingly seen as derogatory and that the more emphatic category of *negro* is preferred by her and by many of her fellows. However, the movement away from the term *preto* towards acceptance of *negro* has been a slow process in Salvador. *Preto*, although certainly a category associated with race and ethnic identity, connotes Black or dark skin colour more so than ancestry. It is analogous to the use of the word "coloured" to describe Black people in the United States prior to desegregation and during the Jim Crow era. However, *negro* has long been associated not so much with a certain skin colour but with a history of slave ancestry – to call someone *negro* in Brazil once meant to highlight their descent from slaves and their position as part of an oppressed population. However, with the growth of the Brazilian Black Power movements in the 1970s, the development of the MNU, and the increasing pro-African stance of the *terreiros*, *negro* is now associated not so much with slavery but with Africanity. To be sure, slavery is a part of the African-oriented identity articulated by the Black movements, but not in a derisive or oppressive form. Rather, descent from slaves now implies African descent. Maria and her fellow parishioners at Nossa Senhora do Rosário do not embrace Africanity, but they do embrace the word *negro* as it has come to be used by Black communities in Salvador beyond Africa-centric *terreiros* and *blocos afros*.

The inculturated mass, described in detail by Burdick (1998a) and also by Selka (2007), bears a striking ritual similarity to those performed in the *terreiro*. Maria believes most government agencies and political leaders do not understand how to talk to the Black community without talking in the vocabulary of Afro-Brazilian religiosity and the *terreiro*. She asserts many – attracted by growing tourist revenue and the spectacle of an Afrocentric carnaval – have been sidetracked by what she believes to be "purely cultural matters" and meanwhile "Black people are still poor."[31] It was Maria herself who suggested that I conduct the survey of *acarajé* sellers throughout the city and then come back and tell her what I discovered. In the survey I found that out of the 197 *acarajé* sellers who were women – I discounted the ones run by men – only twenty of them openly admitted to being members of a *terreiro*. The rest were either practising Catholics or members of an evangelical group.

Maria was not the least bit surprised by these numbers, and it is unlikely – given the recent census data – they would come as a revelation to members of other religious congregations. However, informants who were regular attendees at Ilê Aiyê informed me that, despite the work of the Pastoral Afro and churches like Nossa Senhora do Rosário, they feel that the Catholic Church is a place where non-Black or non-Afro elites are still in control and that the only places where Blacks really have a say are in the Africanized spaces such as the *terreiro* and *blocos afros*. Others have suggested that the work of anti-syncretic *terreiros* is being undone by practices such as the inculturated mass. They see any attempts to make Catholicism more "African" by adding "some drums" as ultimately "deceitful," in that it is trying to appeal to Black people and keep them in the church using "coercive" means that distort the "pure" Yoruba culture.[32] Maria believes that racism exists in Brazil and that, even with the dominance of an African-oriented expression of Blackness in Bahia, racism still pervades her home state. However, she does not equate her position in life – that she has been selling snacks on the streets of Pelourinho for over fifteen years – as a product of a racist society, nor does she view the ferment of ideologies about the place of Africa in Bahia that emerges from the *blocos afros* and the *terreiro* as a solution to her problems. There is an air of resignation to Maria and she tells me that she'll likely be selling *acarajé* for the rest of her life and no amount of politicking over religion will change that. Instead, she seems to find a certain degree of serenity in her Catholic faith, one that does present her with images of divine or sacred Blackness but that also emphasizes the Brazilian as opposed to the African.

Burdick (1998b) believes that there are two key reasons why people like Maria have become alienated from the Africanizing discourse of the *terreiro*: one is a rejection of African religiosity; the other is a lack of identification with colour categories such as *negro*. In the case of Maria and many of her *Baiana* sisters, there is a strong willingness to be openly identified as *negro* and not by one of the myriad other phenotypic categories that are replete within Brazilian Portuguese. But Burdick's assertion that the ties that bind Black political movements with African-oriented religious practice disaffect many Black Brazilians still appears to be very much the case. There is perhaps no more ubiquitous example of folklorized Africanity in the city of Salvador than women like Maria – her clothes, the food she sells, *O cheiro de dendê* (the aroma of palm oil) – all of these symbols are embodied in the *Baiana*. Yet many women like Maria openly rail against the notion that, as a Black woman in Salvador, she must necessarily look to Africa as a source of cultural authenticity for her identity. She is perfectly willing, as are the scores of other *Baianas* that sell their wares on the streets of Salvador, to manipulate and incorporate those same symbols into their dress, their manner, their speech, and onto the small wooden stalls they cart around along with the propane tanks and aluminum pots. But, she suggests, they do not define who she is as an Afro-Brazilian woman.

Through an understanding of how women such as Maria use the trope of Bahian Africanity in order to make a living while at the same time living what could only be called an eminently Brazilian existence, one that incorporates many of the aspects of a creolized Black culture, we can uncover the kind of analytical middle ground that M.G. Smith (1957) suggested that anthropologists of Afro-America needed to find: one that seeks to reconcile the positions of Frazier and Herskovits in an approach that understands how so-called Africanisms are used in daily social life. Further, this is precisely the kind of approach demanded by Scott (1991) in that it explores the symbolic and ideological labour performed by engaging ideas about African Blackness. Maria makes use of Africanity in her daily life and is proud to be associated with symbols like Anastácia, but resents the popular belief that simply because she sells "African" food and wears the white dress of the *terreiro*, that she must necessarily subscribe to those beliefs. The reason, Maria believes, for why the Black movements are unable to disassociate themselves from the *terreiro*, is a combination of the "spiritual," in her words, nature of *Candomblé* and African rituals, and the massive investment that the tourist industry in Bahia has made in making the state live up to its description as a "Black Rome." She tells me: "The tourist industry and the government are committed to this trajectory and they depend on academics like you."

In an attempt to better understand what Maria had told me, I related her story to other individuals in Salvador and their respective responses are quite instructive in understanding how different factions within the Black community view the Africanizing emphasis of the *terreiros* and *blocos afros*.

Georgia

After talking to Georgia about my experiences with Maria, his responses, predictably, were couched in the same no-nonsense and pragmatic language that I had come to expect from him. "What do you expect?" he told me, "I do what I have to do to make money, so does your friend. She knows that if she doesn't wear those clothes or put *orixás* on her stove then nobody will buy from her. She is doing the same things that I do." Georgia tells me that he knows many *Baianas* that work in Pelourinho and in Saúde and that he believes most of them are Christians of some denomination who simply see the white clothes and *orixá* statues as a necessary part of the paraphernalia needed to do their work. "No different," he tells me, "than my Haile Selassie postcards, headbands, and Fela T-shirts."[33] Georgia, more than anything, is an entrepreneur and he sees the emphasis on African culture in a very instrumental way. For him, the work of people like the *terreiro* leaders and other elites is providing him with the opportunity to bring more customers and clients into Sankofa African Bar, to get more work as an "African" tour guide, and to generally continue in his role as an expert on Africa. Georgia is certainly proud of his African heritage, of Ghana, and he loves playing reggae, Afrobeat, or highlife music to packed houses in Pelourinho, but he is not overly religious and generally doesn't think an awful lot about his role in negotiating issues of Black religiosity in Bahia – although he is certainly involved in this process. Frequently, Georgia can be quite cynical about much African-oriented identity discourse in Bahia: "We are always trying to get the white man to see and respect our culture, but often all we do is end up selling it. Like they used to buy our bodies; now they buy the culture."

Edmar

Edmar is a forty-nine-year-old woman who lives in the neighbourhood of Engenho Velho da Federação, not far from the very large and famous *terreiro* of Casa Branca. She works outside a petrol station on the busy main street of Avenida Vasco da Gama where, like Maria, she has sold *acarajé* for over ten years. Also like Maria, Edmar is a practising Catholic; however, she was for many years also a devout member of Casa Branca and, for a very short period, a member of the Foursquare Gospel Church – a second-wave Pentecostal church in Brazil. Edmar is conflicted about the ascendance of the Africa-centric movement in the Black neighbourhoods and in the Africanized public image of Bahia. She believes that they are helping to improve awareness of Brazil's African heritage, to improve the life of many Black people in Salvador, and to change the way in which the country at large thinks about Bahia. Without the *terreiros*, she says, tourists would not visit Salvador or any parts of Bahia. Tourism, Edmar believes, is key to Salvador's future and if it means selling – in Georgia's terms – a little bit of Black culture to *Paulistas*, then that is fine by her. When I relayed Maria's attitudes to Edmar, she felt that her compatriot was being a little too harsh – she believes that the *terreiros* and *blocos afros* do many good works beyond their political, anti-racism, and Black advancement work, and give many children a chance to express themselves as young Black men and women without resorting to crime and drugs. I asked Edmar if the *terreiros* have a positive message, then why did she leave? She responded:

> I still believe in the *orixás*. They are an important part of who I am as a Black woman. I tried the evangelicals, but I didn't like the way they talk about Black culture. They treat the *orixás* like they are demons and tell people to reject all of their Black traditions. I couldn't accept that. I spoke to a priest who is from Pastoral Afro at the local church here in Vasco who buys *acarajé* from me all the time. He said to come back to the Catholic Church and see what we have to offer. I went back and I don't regret it.[34]

To this I asked her to clarify what she thought about Maria's comments that some *terreiros* do not respect the Pastoral Afro or Anastácia: "I think she is right in some ways; they don't respect us. But it is not done in a hurtful way. The problem is, they want to speak for *all* Black people [emphasis hers], but they also believe that Brazil is a racist country and that they must fight fire with fire." Edmar's perspectives on anti-syncretic and more dominant *terreiros* in Salvador are echoed throughout the city among other women who sell *acarajé* on the streets. They strongly approve of the message of Black solidarity and anti-racism, and they hold respect for the African-oriented forms of Blackness that the *terreiro* and *blocos afros* represented, but did so in subtle ways. Unlike some of Burdick's (1998b) informants, there existed no reluctance on their part to discuss how many of the travails they dealt with in their daily lives were the products of a racist society, but they did not believe that the strident politico-religious message of anti-syncretism, re-Africanization, and anti-Catholicism truly resonated with them. I do not believe that any of them were still clinging to some shred of belief in racial democracy or other such ideal of harmony. Rather, Edmar and her "sisters" simply seemed more concerned with what can only be described as "bread-and-butter" issues.

Most women like Edmar are born into a society in which they are most likely destined for a job employed as a domestic worker, selling or making food, or a similar kind of service work. Indeed, most Black women born in places like Engenho Velho da Federação will rarely move out of their home community – all of this is part of a society in which racism exists in systemic and institutionalized ways. Key stakeholders in Salvador's *terreiro*-affiliated Black movements believe that only through the adoption of a Black identity that emphasizes Africanity can liberation from poverty and racism be achieved. Yet in my interviews and in speaking to *Baianas* across the city, this message does not entirely resonate with many Black men and women like Maria and other *acarajé* sellers.

One key group, however, stands firmly against this Africanizing trend and invokes a language of a different kind of religious purity, while at the same time using many of the techniques and ritual accoutrements of the Afro-Brazilian traditions. They are an increasingly powerful and large segment of Brazilian society – almost a quarter of the entire population, according to the 2010 census (IBGE 2010) – that portrays the Africanizing of Black Brazilian culture as collusion with the devil. They are also a group that is just as vociferously denounced by people like Mãe Stella and by many Catholics as foreign, as "not Brazilian," and as the agents of real racism and intolerance in Brazilian society: the fundamentalist evangelicals.

Marisol

Marisol is a member of the Igreja Universal do Reino de Deus (the Universal Church of the Kingdom of God). I met Marisol at Salvador's large bus station, or *rodoviário*, as I waited for a bus that would take me to the small interior town of Bom Jesus da Lapa in the heart of the Brazilian *sertão*. I started chatting with Marisol while we were both were waiting for the same bus, and I would later return to Salvador to interview her again. I discovered that Marisol had come to Salvador six years ago as a student from another small town in the interior. She told me that she was raised in a *terreiro*, but that *Candomblé* in rural Bahia was very different from what she found in the big city. She says that her form of *Candomblé* was one that was very private, not elaborate and showy like the big *terreiros* of Salvador that are featured in the media and in tourist websites. Still, initially, she was not turned off completely. She found a small *terreiro* in her new home community of Brotas in Salvador. After a year, however, she left the *terreiro* because, she tells me, she became weary of the continued efforts to engage in political activity and to rally against the evangelical churches in the neighbourhood. She tells me: "My mother became an evangelical and she goes to the Igreja Universal. I didn't like the way they always spoke ill of the evangelicals."[35] Marisol then joined her mother and became a member of Igreja Universal. She informed me that she now truly believes that the direction the Black community is headed in is, in her words, "evil." Furthermore, she sincerely believes that those who are leading the community down this "road to damnation" are the heads of *terreiros* and any other organization that approves of "devil worship."

I spoke to Maria and Edmar about Marisol's assertion that possession by demons can be passed on through contact with those who participate in cults like *Candomblé* or even through eating Afro-Brazilian foods, such as *acarajé*. They both responded that the link between *acarajé* and the *terreiro* is a powerful one in Salvador and, traditionally, *acarajé* vendors are seen as the *filhas da Iansã* (daughters of *Iansã*), another widely beloved *orixá*. But with the spread of Pentecostal churches, *acarajé* has become entangled in an argument that involves gender, religion, and race over who has control over this food item. Over the past few years, some *acarajé* sellers have refused to wear the white dresses and cowrie shells, refusing to put on what they call the symbols of witchcraft. Among the 200 sellers that I interviewed in 2005 and 2006, none of them, even the evangelicals, had ceased to wear the white dress, but some of them did say that what they sold had nothing to do with Africa – this is "*comida Baiana*" (Bahian food) they told me. Now, more and more *acarajé* sellers are men dressed in colourful robes or everyday clothes who explicitly seek a split from the so-called *filhas da Iansã*. Marisol then goes on to tell me, as I consumed an *acarajé* myself, that, "I only eat *acarajé* in church." She's speaking here about what has come to be known in Salvador as *Bolinhos de Jesus* or "Jesus' *acarajé*."

Terreiros and other leaders in the MNU have spoken out against this trend and take great exception to the notion that a food item so coupled

Figure 3.5 Acarajé da Alminda in front of Salvador's Templo Maior of the Igreja Universal with sign displaying "Deus é Fiel" (God is faithful).

with *Candomblé* and with ideas about an African past could be usurped by the evangelical churches when those same churches disparage everything connected with Africa as evil. Further, many Black leaders have also been angered that evangelicals who sell *acarajé*, many of them outside the large Templo Maior (Main Temple) of the Igreja Universal, are often men. The sale of this foodstuff has traditionally been reserved for women and this intrusion is another sign, for the *terreiro*, that the evangelicals have no respect for their African traditions. Further, from 2004 to 2006 there were few *acarajé* sellers outside of the large, stadium-like Templo Maior of the Igreja Universal. In 2013, a number of stalls are figured prominently in front of the main steps leading up to the "temple."Now, the normal price throughout Salvador for *acarajé* is typically around R\$3 to R\$4 with an added R\$1 for dried, salted shrimp. However, the *acarajé* sold by the largest stall outside the Igreja Universal, called *Acarajé da Alminda*, sells for an extremely low price of R\$1.50 or R\$2 with shrimp. When I asked one of the women selling *acarajé*

– dressed in red-and-white T-shirts with red caps instead of the customary white dresses – how they could afford to sell for so little she informed me: "Our *acarajé* are blessed by Jesus."

When asked why they advertised them as *acarajé* and not "*bolinhos de Jesus*," I was told, "that's the old name and it caused too much controversy in the city and in the newspapers. So, we sell it now as *acarajé* and we can get more customers because it is the cheapest, the best, and the 'most sacred.'"

Marisol suggested to me that my friend in Pelourinho, Maria, who makes a living selling *acarajé*, may not seem like a "devil worshipper", however, because she was associated with the *orixás*, she was in some way contaminated. Indeed, she even mentioned that if I were to keep eating *acarajé* sold by such women I, too, would be in danger. For Marisol, Africa truly was a land of dark magic and malevolent spirits that had to be tamed by the "sacred fire" of Christendom, just as her church was doing with the Black communities of Bahia and in Amazonia, and as it had done with herself: "Anything that is associated with Africa has the touch of evil." Nonetheless, many Pentecostal churches adopt practices and ritual concepts directly from the possession traditions. Stylistically and ritually, a Pentecostal service borrows many of the underlying beliefs and modes of religious practice found in Afro-Brazilian religions, including the idea of spiritual possession, albeit to cause harm rather than good. Marisol and a number of other self-identified evangelicals with whom I spoke seemed assured that what they did was quite different, most often because their religion did not believe in *orixás* or African spirits but only in good and evil.

To be sure, spirit possession, speaking in tongues, and emotive or ecstatic performance are part and parcel of many Christian traditions. However, the use of these techniques in the large Pentecostal megachurches of Brazil seems to owe far more to Afro-Brazilian tradition than to an awareness of Christian roots. These communities often contain many individuals, especially Black men and women who, although they may not practise *Umbanda* or *Candomblé*, have a grudging regard for the power and efficacy of its traditions. Lehmann (1998) summarizes it perfectly: "In its services the Universal Church – like other 'neo-Pentecostal' churches, adopts imprecations, gestures and symbols drawn directly from the possession cults, but without the slightest hint of a theory of identity or autochthony. It simply borrows them because the leadership or the preachers believe they will work" (613).

There is also widespread hostility towards Igreja Universal among the majority of Brazilian Catholics, especially after an incident in which a Universal Church pastor was seen kicking an image of Nossa Senhora da Aparecida during his televised ministry. The event, which was staged as a protest against Nossa Senhora as a form of Catholic idolatry, took place on 12 October 1995, "The Day of the Appeared Lady," and became a national scandal. Birman and Lehmann (1999) write: "In this incident, Pastor Sergio von Helder, head of the Universal Church in São Paulo, mocked an effigy of the Madonna and ridiculed it as a 'doll' and a 'piece of plaster,' and even nudged it with his foot, provoking outrage throughout the country" (150). Pastor von Helder went on to describe the dark-skinned image of the Virgin as ugly, horrible, and wretched and claimed this "doll" could not do anything to help the poor of Brazil and that the Catholic Church was built on a lie (Johnson 1997, 131). The verbal attacks were seen as being levelled directly at the Catholic Church, but many Black individuals with whom I spoke in Salvador about this issue – practitioners of *Candomblé*, Catholics, and even some evangelicals, even Marisol – admitted to me that they saw this as a slight against Black people and towards what the Universal Church considers the idolatrous practices of many in the Black community.

Despite this desecration of a nationally beloved religious icon, in the competitive religious marketplace of Brazil, any faith that claims it can alleviate poverty and provide solutions for working-class Brazilians will draw followers to its banner. This is precisely what the Igreja Universal claims it can accomplish. The church donates millions of *reais* to regional pastoral charities and openly points the finger at the efforts of *Candomblé terreiros*, *blocos* like Ilê Aiyê, and the Black movements in general as impotent in fighting poverty because of their misguided emphasis on anti-racism and on Africanizing Blackness.

Chapter Four

Blackness in the Bahian *Sertão*

Home to ranchers, gold and diamond prospectors looking to strike it rich, maroon slave communities, pilgrims, prophets, and messiahs of every variety, Brazil's interior, the *sertão,* has always held a powerful and central place in the imaginary of Brazil and very much forms part of the national character. In this chapter, I seek to explore how rural communities such as Bom Jesus da Lapa understand the discourse of Blackness being promulgated by groups such as the purity-driven *terreiros* and *blocos afros*. Specifically, it deals with how assertions of an African-oriented identity play in the backlands of Bahia, a place that has, historically, been home to much more integrated and creolized communities of Black Brazilians – many of whom are descendants of runaway slaves or maroons.

Sertão

The word *sertão* is difficult to translate as it does not refer to a certain kind of vegetation, lack thereof, ecotype, or landform; it does not mean, as James (1948) has pointed out, unexplored or unknown country, as he notes that the Brazilian back country has been "tramped over again and again for four hundred years, and again and again they have yielded wealth to any strong enough, brave enough, and persistent enough to discover and exploit their hidden resources" (658). Furthermore, although *sertão* is derived, etymologically, from the same root as "desert" and, in the context of Bahia and the other northeastern states, it can refer to the arid land of the interior, it is generally understood in Brazil not as a specific kind of ecological type but rather as being synonymous with "frontier" (Lombardi 1975; McCreery 2006). The place of the *sertão* in Brazilian history as both a real and imagined "frontier" is a major point of reference in the development of the Republic. Indeed, the *sertão* is very much a frontier of expansion, much like the American or Canadian West or the Argentine pampas. Territorial expansion is a major theme of Brazilian history, but the pattern of westward movement differed significantly from those found in Turner's (1928) frontier thesis of American westward movement. Despite a century of critique, leaving little of Turner's original argument intact, the frontier thesis remains an important source of inspiration for American history and has continued to prompt new explorations and investigations of how the American frontier has contributed to the building of a nation. In Turner's thesis, he asserts that the success of the United States and American identity is directly connected to the westward expansion of the country. According to Turner, America's idea of itself as a rugged and pioneering society that values individual enterprise developed in the social space between the line of western settlement and the untamed wildness of the frontier. At this juncture was forged a new kind of individual and a new society – the American was one who could tame the wildness of the West, but also someone within whom was contained that same wildness. Those who have attempted to apply Turner's frontier thesis to the Brazilian *sertão* have seen westward movement not as an advancing line of civilization, but rather what Hennessy calls a "hollow frontier" (1978, 98) – small groups of entrepreneurs striking out into the backlands in order to discover and exploit resources, then moving on after exhausting a locale, leaving behind a skeleton of a settlement.

The first real scholarly treatment of the *sertão* is to be found in the work of Brazilian author, engineer, and sociologist Euclides da Cunha. In his 1902 work, *Os Sertões: Campanha de Canudos* (Rebellion in the backlands), Da Cunha describes the Brazilian government's campaign against the millenarian "holy city" of Canudos in the interior of Bahia. His main argument in this work was that the conflict between the frontiersmen of Canudos and the Old Republic of Brazil grew out of a fundamental social difference between the society of the Brazilian coast and its interior backlands. The coast of Brazil, Da Cunha argues, was characterized by a chain of modern civilizations from the Amazonian port of Belem, down to Salvador and Ilhéus in Bahia, through to the cities of Rio de Janeiro and the state of São Paulo. The interior was primarily composed of backward and untamed societies that needed to be brought under the control of the state. Nevertheless, for Da Cunha (1902) these wild "men of the backlands" were the "bedrock" of Brazilian society in that they were born out of the ethnic mixing and pioneer hardiness of the interior (81). Here we see a clear distinction in the Brazilian and American ideas about wilderness. A difference that is articulated by none other than Theodore Roosevelt (1914): "It was not until early in the afternoon that we started into the *sertão*, as Brazilians call the wilderness ... when they reached this place they had been thirty-six hours without food ... and ... for much of the time on this trip lived on wild fruit" (209–10). For Roosevelt, John Muir, and others, wilderness meant the absence of human beings on a landscape that could be revealed to those who persevered. For Da Cunha, wilderness was a testing ground for the most rugged of individuals who represented this new society in the tropics.

Da Cunha's report of the military suppression of the Canudos settlement in *Os Sertões* is still widely read in Brazil and is often cited alongside the work of Freyre (1933) as one of the sources of root metaphors for the formation of the Brazilian sense of national identity. Yet Da Cunha's ideal of the Brazilian "race" – the image of the raw *sertanejo* – is also an ethnic stereotype that has done as much to cement, in the national ethnic imaginary, not only the idea of the primitive and rough interior but also the perceived backwardness of northeastern Brazilian society in general. *Os Sertões* painted the leader of the Canudos settlement, Antônio Conselheiro, as a demented desert mystic who was followed by a misguided band of racially mixed "primitives" who, in the end, needed to be put down in order to prevent Brazilian society in general from descending into a similar state of degeneration. Da Cunha (1902) emphasized that the ignorance and backwardness of *sertanejos* was, in part, a product of their long isolation from the coast and cities like Salvador. In the backlands, he asserted, society had been unaffected by the progress of evolution that most human societies were undergoing. Moreover, because of their removal from "civilized" society, they could not even understand their own Catholic religion – their "crude religious practices ... reveal all the stigmata of their underdeveloped mentality" (111–12).

This attitude is best articulated by historian João Pandiá Calógeras, a former federal administrator in his home state of Minas Gerais, successively minister of agriculture, finance, and war, and ultimately Brazil's delegate to the 1919 Paris Peace Conference. In his 1930 work, *A Formação Histórica do Brasil* (The historical formation of Brazil), Calógeras writes that the population of the interior is a "mixture of ignorant folk, *mestiços*, along with the stains of Indians and African slaves" and that "they follow a unique form of Christianity in which Catholic dogma is adulterated with beliefs and practices of African tribes from the 'Dark' continent, strangely altered and formed of outright pagan idolatry and superstitions of all kinds" (3). Da Cunha's work was very much driven by a kind of pseudoscientific racism about the nature of so-called tropical societies that grew out of an evolutionary framework. An important aspect of this kind of racism lay in how the environment supposedly affected the "behaviour" of different peoples, especially those of the tropics. European scientists in the early twentieth century, still energized by the growing acceptance of Darwinian models in almost every discipline of study, were quick to apply their spurious models of causation to the colonies. Greenfield (1993) writes that such approaches rationalized a "vision of the 'natives' of such places as Africa and India as children who needed firm guidance from Europeans, whose colonial endeavours essentially were fulfilling a civilizing mission ... These tenets of European tropicology merged easily with Brazilians' long-standing belief in the abundance of their nation's resource base" (38–9). Such ideas about the deficiencies of "tropical" peoples were seized by Brazilian elites such as Calógeras as an explanation for what they saw as the "backwardness" of the *sertão*. This region was seen as brimming with possibility and potentially held the future of the Brazilian republic, yet it was peopled with individuals whom they saw as "idlers, loafers, drunkards and thieves, along with freed slaves who were no better" (Do Amaral Lapa 1980, 121). Scholars of Brazilian history who have attempted to apply the Turnerian thesis to the *sertão* have, as Rausch (2008, 202) points out, either ignored or downplayed the importance of the African slave and indigenous elements in opening up this part of the country. Ironically, though, early Brazilian writers such as Da Cunha and Calógeras have made explicit that while they see the kind of racial mixing found in the interior as part of the strength of the *sertanejo*, it was also their weakness, in that it brought African practices into syncretic play with Christianity.

Recognizing the movement of escaped, freed, and former slaves into the backlands is crucial to any exploration of the ethnic texture of the *sertão* and to understanding the linkages between this region and the plantation societies of Salvador and the Recôncavo. Many Blacks along the coast saw the inland territory as a place of sanctuary, of escape from the brutalities of slavery. Consequently, throughout the *sertão*, especially in the valley of the São Francisco, congregations of ex-slaves, religious pilgrims, Amerindian groups, white settlers, and farmers gave rise to communities like Bom Jesus da Lapa, to maroon communities, to religious isolate societies like Canudos, and, importantly, to a thoroughly creolized society (Crist 1944).

Quilombos

Colonial Bahia and its sugar-based plantation economy depended absolutely on the coerced labour of African and Amerindian slaves. However, the threat of revolt and desertion was constant and much of Brazil's experience with slavery was beset with instability, resistance, and insurrection (Schwartz 1970). Indeed, throughout the Americas, wherever slavery formed the economic basis of the society, revolt was always a constant fear for white plantation owners. Most discussions of slave resistance focus on the great "Black Republic" of Palmares, a *quilombo* community of over 5,000 escaped slaves in the northeastern state of Alagoas that gave rise to the slave leader Zumbí (R.N. Anderson 1996; Chapman 1918; Diggs 1953). Palmares was a self-sustaining community and expressed its autonomy and distinctiveness from colonial rule in its social practices. Community members, for instance, spoke a unique language – a *patois* combination of Portuguese and African languages – and historian Mary Karasch (2002) contends that Palmares "challenged the colonial order ... in a way that no other *mocambo* [*quilombo*] had ever done" (106).

Zumbí was born in Palmares in 1655, but shortly after his birth, Portuguese raiding forces captured him. He was given to a Portuguese priest, Antonio Melo, who raised Zumbí as his ward until age fifteen, at which time Zumbí ran away to rejoin the *quilombo* at Palmares. He had been Christened "Francisco" and thoroughly Christianized by Father Melo, but when he rejoined the *quilombo* he changed his name to Zumbí (Karasch 2002, 113). From this point until his death in 1695, Zumbí mounted a sustained challenge to the colonial order. Palmares became famous throughout the Northeast for its military campaigns against the Portuguese, and slaves flocked to Zumbí's banner from throughout the region (Carneiro 1946). In 1693, the Portuguese decided that Palmares and Zumbí were too much of a threat and they began a two-year campaign against the *quilombo* that culminated in Zumbí's death on 20 November 1695. After his capture, the Portuguese beheaded him and took his head to Recife, where it was displayed to counter claims of Zumbí's immortality (R.N. Anderson 1996, 563–4). Karasch attributes the Portuguese offensive to a belief that *quilombos* like Palmares represented a threat to colonial society and that their "destruction ... would deter all other such attempts in the interior of Brazil" (2002, 106).

In spite of the killing of Zumbí, desertions from the slave plantations surrounding Salvador were frequent. Throughout the seventeenth, eighteenth, and nineteenth centuries, communities of runaway slaves were common throughout the captaincy of Bahia (Schwartz 1970, 209). Many of these runaways found themselves living in the small communities along the São Francisco River, while others found work on the emergent cattle *fazendas* (cattle ranches) and by cultivating cassava on the banks of the river (Crist 1944). The sheer size of Palmares and the influence it had on other maroon communities are two of the reasons why so much attention has been paid to this *quilombo*. From a contemporary perspective, however, Palmares has become of central importance because of the position that Zumbí dos Palmares occupies for members of Brazil's Black movements. The Black movements in Salvador – indeed, throughout Brazil – have elevated Zumbí to heroic status because he, unlike the figure of Anastácia, vociferously and fiercely fought against slavery. Anastácia's story is seen by Black movements as one which illustrates the brutality of slavery and the racism of Brazilian society, but she is not lionized as an icon of resistance, but rather as someone whose sad tale should be taken as symbolic of all that is wrong with Brazil and European settler society. Zumbí, however, is constructed as an African military hero. His upbringing by the Portuguese priest Antonio Melo is typically elided by those seeking to integrate *quilombismo*, what Gramsci (1985) would call a *concezione del mondò*, into African-oriented Black identity formations, or skimmed over in most public accounts of his story told on Black Consciousness Day, or in the space of the *terreiro*. Black groups commonly retell Zumbí's story entirely as one of an African in Brazil – not as a creolized Afro-Brazilian. Similarly, a number of scholars, most notably Freitas (1973), have contributed to the belief that Palmares was, ethnically, composed almost entirely of individuals from one area of central Africa. R.N. Anderson (1996) attributes much of the reimagining of Palmares to political and social movements in Brazil pertaining to Black society and racism: "Whatever the Central African presence in Palmares, by the second half of the seventeenth century it was clearly a multiethnic and mostly creole community ... The population of Palmares in the 1670s appears to have been largely native-born and of African descent ... The historiography of Palmares is necessarily elite historiography"

(559–65). Palmares has become firmly ingrained in the popular consciousness of Brazil and in the array of key symbols employed by the Black movement. Moreover, Palmares and Zumbí have also become important rallying points for fundamental changes in the way the Brazilian government deals with rural communities.

In 1988, after more than twenty years of military rule, Brazil came under the legislation of a new democratic constitution that included a clause, article 68, which granted land rights to descendants of runaway slave communities known as *quilombos*. In that same year, members of *Movimento Negro Unificado* (MNU), along with other Black movements, chose to boycott the centennial abolition celebrations in favour of marking a day that they felt better represented a militant and empowered opposition to slavery as opposed to grateful thanks for manumission. The 20th of November, the anniversary of Zumbí's death in 1695, became known throughout Brazil as the *Dia Nacional da Consciência Negra*, the Day of Black Consciousness, and is now the centrepiece event of an entire month devoted to Black and Afro-Brazilian issues. For the *Movimento Negro Unificado*, the new constitution meant that the descendants of the *quilombos*, many of whom still occupied the rural settlements staked out by their maroon ancestors, would finally be given the right to hold title to their lands. However, after years of legal equivocating on the part of the Brazilian government, actual land titles granted have been few and far between. The problem emerged from the criteria used to define whether rural Black communities were *actually* descended from *quilombos* and not simply self-identified as such. One such community is the *quilombo* of Rio da Rãs, very close to the town of Bom Jesus da Lapa.

Bom Jesus da Lapa and Rio das Rãs

The town of Bom Jesus da Lapa was established in 1691 by Francisco de Mendonça Mar. As the story is told by locals, Mendonça Mar was born in Lisbon in 1657 and left for Salvador when he was twenty-two to undertake the job of painting the government palace in colonial Brazil's capital at the time. After finding success in Salvador, he left the city and began wandering the lands of the interior. Upon arrival at the banks of the Rio São Francisco he discovered a grotto within the *morro* or rocky outcrop that dominates the town of Bom Jesus da Lapa. Here he began a monastic life, serving a small community of religious pilgrims that

Figure 4.1 Bom Jesus da Lapa.

grew up around his sanctuary – these included small numbers of hard-scrabble settlers, local Amerindian groups looking to escape the preda-tions of slave traders, and a growing community of runaway slaves.

Now, every year, thousands of people make a pilgrimage or *romaria* to the grotto of Bom Jesus. The pilgrims come to ask for divine inter-vention, for healing, and for miracles, and will often leave bandages, crutches, or prosthetics in the hopes that their devotions will help to cure a beloved family member of an ailment or disability. Consequent-ly, thousands of crutches, walking sticks, and prosthetic limbs can now be found adorning the sheer cliff faces of the *morro* near the entrance to the chapel. The grotto contains a functioning chapel with pews, altar, and electric lighting, all located within a cave replete with stalactites that descend from the rocky ceiling and continually drip calcified water on mass-goers. In the neighbourhood surrounding the grotto, a thriv-ing cottage industry has developed in the sale of plaster effigies of

Catholic saints, Maria de Soledade (Mary of Solitude, the local iteration of Nossa Senhora da Aparecida), Jesus, and also *Candomblé orixás*, to be used in the pilgrim's novenas or petitions at the grotto.

Approximately 80 kilometres from and within the municipal district of the town of Bom Jesus da Lapa, on the banks of the Rio das Rãs, a tributary of the São Francisco and part of the overall São Francisco drainage system, is a small community of farmers and herders who live in some of the most inhospitable terrain in the *sertão*. While there is little archival or documentary evidence pertaining to the community's history, anthropologist Jean François Véran (2000) has conducted some of the only comprehensive ethnographic research on the area. The community is composed of four small hamlets with about 210 families that make a living, like many in the *sertão*, through cassava cultivation, small-stock holdings, labour on large *fazendas*, and sale of agricultural surplus. Throughout much of the twentieth century, the community has been and continues to be embroiled in an ongoing cycle of violence and land wars with neighbouring *fazendeiros* (land-owning farmers or ranchers). These four small hamlets, each composed primarily of individuals related to each other through marriage or through third- or fourth-level kinship attachments, are all that is left of a maroon community called Mucambo (Véran 2000). The *quilombo* status of the community is a contested one as there appears to be a great deal of confusion about when members of the community of families stopped recognizing themselves as an actual maroon settlement – a community formed by runaway slaves – and simply became a network of related groups living roughly in the same area of the Rio das Rãs (296). Véran asserts that many of the residents had long heard talk of Mucambo, but none had ever been there – it was a place where the "forest was so thick, it only held jaguars" (295). Mucambo itself no longer exists as a real community, and for many of the residents around the Rio das Rãs, there exists only an ambiguous social memory of the place and little concrete awareness that it may have been a refuge for escaped slaves. Access to the actual geographical location where the *quilombo* allegedly once existed has been blocked by the neighbouring *fazendeiro* for almost twenty years and, consequently, an entire generation of residents has no idea about the actual physical location of their ancestors' supposed former home and possess only the second-hand recollections of grandparents, aunts, and uncles.

However, for the Black movements from Salvador, many of whom are funded by Fundação Palmares and the Ministry of Culture, there appears to be no doubt whatsoever that Mucambo was once a thriving maroon slave community. Indeed, before the word *quilombo* became the more popularly used term to describe maroon societies in Brazil, *mucambo* was the generally accepted descriptor for such a maroon community. The question of what indeed constitutes a *quilombo* has been one that has, since the drafting of the new constitution and the inclusion of article 68, continued to place the government and the Black movements in opposition. For the Black movements in Salvador, where the political solidarity of the *terreiros*, *blocos afros*, and community groups along with their academic patrons is powerful, the *quilombos* are potent symbols of active Black and African resistance to oppression and enslavement. Consequently, there is much at stake for these groups in ensuring that "*comunidades remanescentes de quilombo*" (remnant *quilombo* communities) are guaranteed title to the land that their maroon ancestors once occupied.

The vast majority of Black *sertão* communities that have sought protection from article 68 have been ones that have long been under pressure of eviction from neighbouring landowners, typically cattle ranchers. Their closest and most vociferous allies have now become anthropologists, lawyers, and other activists. The media in Brazil have grabbed hold of these stories and presented the interior communities and their daily fight against drought, desert, and debt as part of a hard-fought quest for survival by the remnants of "African tribes" still living in the backlands of Brazil. Véran (2002), writing in *Cultural Survival Quarterly*, notes:

> Considered by the state simply as objects of the nation's cultural and historical patrimony, and presented by the mass media as authentic and archaic African tribes in the midst of contemporary Brazil, the remnant *quilombo* communities briefly mentioned in the constitution were now taking on a new shape within a modernity framed by urgent issues of rights and citizenship, cultural minorities, racism, and agrarian reform ... Even if, so far, only a small minority have received their land titles, the ongoing process has gained a rather unexpected magnitude. (20)

Véran (2002) suggests that few in the community understood the "*quilombo* story" and that, for the local population, what mattered was not the restoration of a Black, African, or slave identity, but rather an end to a land conflict that had meant ongoing harassment and eviction by rich landowners (20). For the Black groups in Salvador, however, the

success of the Rio das Rãs case has become a rallying cry for the continued fight to restore the African and slave past of Bahia's Black community. The Rio das Rãs community became symbolic of the ongoing
legacy of Zumbí's aggressive and rebellious confrontation with colonialism and slavery. Now, a whole array of anthropologists, historians,
other social scientists, lawyers, and NGOs, many of them funded by
Fundação Palmares, are involved in fighting for the rights of what once
were settlements of Black rural peasants but that are now symbols of an
African past that was lost to the wilderness in a fight for survival. Cur-
rently, a number of other predominantly Black communities in the
sertão are still in the process of making their case for quilombo remnant
status.

Richard Price (1999, 247) has criticized a number of the anthropological
studies that first identified quilombo remnant communities in Brazil,
asserting that many ethnographic accounts of rural hamlets or towns as
remnant maroon settlements were overly romanticized conflations of
the historical record with political agendas. Price then turns his attention specifically to the case of Rio das Rãs and the work of Carvalho
(1996b) and Doria (1996). Carvalho, Price claims (1999, 249), draws
heavily on Price's own work on Saramaka maroons in Suriname, while
also suggesting that a fundamental difference exists between the Saramaka and the communities of the sertão like Rio das Rãs. This distinction lies, according to Carvalho (1996b), in the kind of resistance offered
by many of the communities of the interior like Rio das Rãs – one that
consisted of a "dignified," "democratic," and non-racially exclusive
approach to their new sertanejo neighbours, including white farmers,
Amerindian populations, and other Black communities (154–7). Further, Carvalho believes that these backland communities also incorporated the religious practices of their neighbours, making for more
eclectic and diverse forms of Candomblé and other forms not found
in Salvador.

Carvalho's work provides an explanation for why these maroon
communities lost their African practices. His assertion is curiously dissonant with an evocation of Price's work on Saramaka maroons. Those
communities of the Suriname bush, released from the torturous life of
the plantation, were able to create rich and innovative forms of Black
culture that drew upon a diversity of African traditions (Price 1983),
but, according to Carvalho (1996b), similarly liberated former or escaped slaves in Brazil quickly lost or diluted their African practices.
Due to the continual harassment, killing of animals, destruction of

houses and of fields and general marginalization the community member experienced at the hands the neighbouring by a *fazendeiro* and documented by Doria (1996),[1] Price believes many of the ethnographers and historians have become motivated to be actively committed to legitimizing the residents of Rio das Rãs' legal claims. He believes that the research carried out by Carvalho and Doria was of very short duration, unlike that conducted by himself and other scholars of maroon societies, and lacks the kind of detailed oral testimony and "ethnographic texture" that any study of a community whose origins are uncertain would require (Price 1999, 251–3). This is particularly problematic, believes Price, when not one member of the community can remember any story about the founding of their settlement beyond the generation of their grandparents and when those stories appear to be, in part, directed and biased by the interview techniques of the researchers (253). This bias needs to be understood in the context of what the idea of *quilombo* now means for the Black movements in Salvador and elsewhere in Brazil.

From the music of Gilberto Gil and Caetano Veloso, to films about Palmares like *Quilombo* (1984) by Carlos Diegues, to stores and restaurants in Salvador that incorporate the word into their names, even to attempts to recognize Pelourinho as a maroon remnant community, *quilombo* as an idea carries almost as much symbolic clout for the Black movements as do concepts such as *Candomblé* and *orixás*. The *quilombo* has become one of the key symbols mobilized by groups such as Ilê Aiyê and the *terreiros*. It represents a social and military analogue to the kind of resistance offered by the religious centres of Salvador and valorization of this maroon space – not just in Brazil, but throughout the Afro-American world – and forms an important part of the Africanized identity they wish to activate and deploy. The value that many leaders in Salvador attach to the resuscitation of the *quilombo* has been discussed extensively by venerated Rio de Janeiro–based Black activist Abdias do Nascimento (1980). Writing from a distinctively Afrocentric perspective that even goes so far as to suggest that Africa had contact with the Americas prior to the arrival of Columbus, Do Nascimento (1980) suggests that "quilomboist society represents an advanced stage in socio-political and human progress in terms of economic egalitarianism" and that "it is for the Black people of today to sustain and amplify the Afro-Brazilian culture of resistance and affirmation of our truth" (161). So, on the one hand, we have the assertion from anthropologists such as Carvalho and Doria that the *quilombos* represent a kind of resistance to slavery that is not only unlike that of the Suriname or Jamaica maroons but also one whose African traditions have been lost to oblivion and need to be restored. Abdias do Nascimento and other activists, on the other hand, suggests that *quilombos* are far more than just remnant communities – they represent a way of life, an African communal way of life that all Black Brazilians must rediscover as an alternative to the status quo of Brazilian racial oppression. Further, even Price (1999), despite his misgivings about some of the research conducted in the area of Rio das Rãs and other alleged *quilombo* remnants, suggests that obtaining title to these lands is vital for both residents and for the Black movement.

For the residents of Rio das Rãs and for the activists from Fundação Palmares, the use of article 68 has been, for both communities, an extremely fortuitous marriage of intentions. Rio das Rãs inhabitants have finally found a successful legal avenue to achieve their land rights claims and the Black movements have gained added symbolic collateral for their assertions that Bahia's interior is full of the remnants of escaped slave societies. Although Rio das Rãs residents have won a first victory against the *fazendeiro* through the use of article 68, the legitimacy of many rural communities' status as *quilombo* remnants remain uncertain as cases still wend their way through the Brazilian courts (Scolese 2008).

Now, to be sure, it is quite likely that many of the settlements in the *sertão* contain the descendants of slaves who made their way into this part of the interior in search of a better life and a new homestead because of land donations, or for any of the host of reasons suggested by Price (1999). However, whether or not they are the descendants of a community of slaves who came to *sertão* to escape and resist enslavement remains less than certain. But does it really matter? Most communities in the *sertão* are marginalized, impoverished settlements of people, many of whom are likely of slave descent. Should their status as individuals who might be eligible for land rights hinge upon whether or not their ancestors actively rebelled against enslavement to form a new society in the wilderness? Certainly, there are many legal implications to be considered. If Rio das Rãs were merely a community of Black rural peasants descended from slaves who formed a new settlement on the periphery of Brazilian society and then granted land title, would that imply that all communities of predominantly Black Brazilians should be entitled to government guaranteed land title? Clearly, for this legislation to work the definition and the criteria used to circumscribe what counts as a *quilombo* must be, as Price (1999) suggests, precise. Does Rio das Rãs qualify? It is not entirely certain. But I return to my original question – does it really matter?

Contained in the legal arguments over the definition of a maroon remainder community are again, shades of the perennial Herskovits–Frazier debate. As I have reiterated throughout the present work, my goal is not to try and contribute to one side of this debate or the other. Rather, within the context of this debate, my intent is to try and understand how an Africanized idea of what it means to be Black in Brazil is used and manipulated in order to mobilize the Afro-Brazilian community in Brazil and specifically in Bahia. This same approach to understanding Black identity can also be located within the confines of the *quilombo* debate. Indeed, many of the players and stakeholders are the same, including anthropologists and academics who are committed advocates of the Black community; *terreiros, blocos afros,* and other associations within Salvador's Black movement who actively support the granting of *quilombo* status to a wide range of rural Black communities; government agencies such as the Ministry of Culture and Fundação Palmares; and, finally, a community of predominantly Black individuals in which there is mixed and sometimes ambivalent support for such identity-oriented initiatives.

For the purposes of a study that seeks to understand how concepts such as "slave," "Africa," and also "maroon," or "*quilombo*" are used in Brazil, the "truth" of the settlement's origins are not particularly relevant. But, even from this perspective, one of discourse and dialogue, the answer to my question is that, yes, it does matter – politically and in terms of Black identities – for some stakeholders. Debates about the ethnic composition of the plantation are, ultimately, futile, as the historical record is simply insufficient to accurately determine the percentages of African ethnic groups. However, *quilombo* remnant communities do exist today – they are living, breathing societies that are part of the ethnic landscape of the *sertão,* and determining their origins entails powerful repercussions for the Black movements in Brazil and for the residents of these communities. For Black groups in Salvador and for agencies like Fundação Palmares, identifying communities such as Rio das Rãs as *quilombos* contributes significantly to the symbolic capital they accrue by fighting on the side of a people that, historically, also fought against slavery and racism. For the government and for state agencies it is vitally important to ascertain a plaintiff community's origins in order to prevent a free-for-all in terms of land claims.

Blackness in the *Sertão*

In the town of Bom Jesus da Lapa, there appears to be general acceptance that the community of Rio das Rãs is comprised of descendants of
an ancient *quilombo*. People in Bom Jesus da Lapa with whom I spoke
are aware of the community, are familiar with the legal issues pertaining to the community's status, and have much to say about the aid sup-
plied by Black organizations from Salvador, about Black society in the
interior, and about the history of slavery in the *sertão*.

However, before I turn to these individuals, I wish to return briefly to
the city of Salvador. In interviews conducted with members of the *blocos
afros* in Salvador about people of the *sertão* and specifically about the
town of Bom Jesus da Lapa, two dominant themes emerged. Whenever
I introduced the topic of this small town, responses focused on the
Catholic pilgrimages made to the grotto and the battle to obtain legal
status for Rio das Rãs. I recount here an interview with Marcelo, a forty-
five-year-old man from the town of Jacobina and a member of Ilê Aiyê
whom I met in the famed Pelourinho *cachaça* bar O Cravinho:

AD: Marcelo, you're from the interior. Tell me about Bom Jesus da Lapa.
I'm going there in a week or so.[2]

MARCELO: You know, Bom Jesus is famous all around Brazil, because of
the chapel and grotto inside the *morro*. They say it has healing powers.
I don't disbelieve such things, but I don't put much stock in them
either. Ilê Aiyê is also a sponsor of a *quilombo* out there. It's called Rio
das Rãs and it is just outside of Bom Jesus da Lapa. They are the
descendants of slaves who fought against the slave-owners and ran
away to the interior. Now, with the new constitution, we've been
assisting them to get title for their land. During the last *dia da
consciência negra*, we had T-shirts that said *Rio das Rãs*, and we
contributed some of the profits to the community's defense.

AD: What do you think of article 68 and the so-called *quilombos* in the
sertão?

MARCELO: Why do you say "so-called"? The *quilombos* are like
Pelourinho, they are places of resistance. They practise *Candomblé* like
us, some of them still have some African words in how they speak
Portuguese, more than we do, I think ... But towns like Bom Jesus are
totally Christianized and agricultural. Everyone out there listens to
forro (Brazilian country music) and works on the farms. The life is hard
out there, I know this, but the Black people in heavily Christianized

towns like Bom Jesus, where the Catholic Church is so powerful, they've forgotten their Black traditions, their African traditions – not like us in Salvador. Some of them do practise *Candomblé* in towns like that, but it is polluted and more like *Umbanda* now than real *Candomblé*. They have what we call *Candomblé de Caboclos*, which is like our religion, but with the *caboclo* spirits that *Umbanda* has. Here in this city, we have so many reminders, in our food, in our music, our religion.

.Members of MNU in Salvador like Marcelo often regard the "Black" citizenry of the *sertão*, who are not actively involved in radicalizing their communities against white oppression, as not fully cognizant of their Blackness and of what such an identity should entail. This sentiment is echoed by Abdias do Nascimento (1980): "Each and every Black or mulatto who accepts 'racial democracy' as a reality, and miscegenation in the form it takes today as a positive phenomenon, is a traitor to himself and considers himself inferior" (167). Many leaders in Salvador also regard the residents of the Bahian backcountry as somewhat religious apostates. There are forms of *Candomblé* that are widely practised in the towns of the *sertão*, but for the most part they are far more heterodox forms of the *orixá* tradition than the kind practised and promoted by the powerful *terreiros* in Salvador such as Opô Afonjá and Casa Branca. The *Candomblé* found in the *sertão* does worship the *orixás* of the Yoruba, but also includes other deities such as Amerindian spirits. These heterodox forms include the *Candomblé de Caboclos* mentioned by Marcelo, another *orixá* tradition called *Jarê*,[3] along with actual *Umbanda* and spiritist centres. These alternatives to so-called pure *Candomblé* place the spirits of the forest and those of Amerindian warriors in the *orixá* pantheon alongside those of Yoruba deities. To the famous and affluent leaders of *terreiros* in Salvador such as Ilê Axé Opô Afonjá, this is a heresy which, in the words of one devotee, "dilutes" the most purely African religion of Brazil – *Candomblé*.[4]

However, there exists a very different perspective in the towns of the *sertão* like Bom Jesus da Lapa about the place of Black activist groups such as *Movimento Negro Unificado*, the *Candomblé terreiros*, *quilombismo* and *blocos afros* in the fight against racism in Brazil. In Bom Jesus da Lapa and other small towns of the Bahian interior, there grows a palpable cynicism among individuals who are visibly *Afro-Brasileiro* towards the work of Black activists in Salvador. Additionally, the enthusiasm with which government agencies such as the ministries of culture, tourism, education, and others have engaged the agenda of celebrating

Afro-Brazilian patrimony is also eyed with some scepticism. This concern seems to go beyond the usual suspicion of elites from the city – Black or white – and government representatives found in rural areas. Many residents of Bom Jesus da Lapa with whom I spoke are not, on the whole, interested in engaging in identity-based discussions of Blackness, let alone African-oriented ideas of Blackness, despite the fact that a symbolic focal point for this discourse – the *quilombo* remnant community of Rio das Rãs – is, quite literally, right in their backyard.

A profound difference appears to exist in the ways in which rural Bahians construct ethnic categories such as Black and Afro-Brazilian and in the ways in which the slave past is used to talk about social conditions in the present. In nearly all of my interviews with residents of Bom Jesus da Lapa, individuals identified themselves as Brazilians and *Sertanejos* – people of the *sertão*.

Most informants that I spoke to in Bom Jesus da Lapa were perfectly willing to identify themselves as possessing some degree or another of Afro-Brazilian heritage, except for a few wealthy and affluent hotel managers, restaurateurs, and visiting engineers. But the language they used was subtle and carefully chosen. Very few seemed willing to outright use the word *negro* to describe their Black skin colour, and most resorted to the term *preto* or *morena* to describe their Blackness. Indeed, throughout my time in Bom Jesus da Lapa, only one informant seemed to articulate the philosophy of the Black movements of Salvador. He was a young man who worked in one of the stores that sells religious effigies made for petitions and venerations at the grotto. He had spent six months living in Salvador with an aunt in Curuzu-Liberdade, where he had started attending a *terreiro* and occasionally visiting Ilê Aiyê. He said he was forced to come back to Bom Jesus da Lapa because his family's business – the *artigos religiosos* shop – was floundering and his father needed help. However, he informed me that he views the *sertão* differently now. He believes that the interior is a place where slaves fled in order to escape the hardship of the plantation even though they knew that life in this part of Brazil would be different. He believes that all residents of Bom Jesus da Lapa and of the *sertão* in general are, in some way, descended from the slaves that came to the interior. In his words: "*Todos os sertanejos são negros*" (All people of the *sertão* are Black).[5]

These are not sentiments shared by most informants. Indeed, most individuals who chose to identify themselves ethnically did so as either *pretos* or *morenas* or simply as *Afro-Brasileiro*.[6] Most individuals with whom I spoke saw their hard life in the interior not as a product of racism and prejudice towards Black culture – though racism exists here as much as elsewhere in Brazil – but rather as a consequence of the deeply entrenched class divisions in rural Brazilian society and because they didn't own any land. Very few people in either the town of Bom Jesus da Lapa or in the surrounding rural environs own title to the land on which they live. Most of them pay rent to a landlord or *patrão* (patron) or to a local *fazendeiro*. Indeed, the long-running fight over the land occupied by the residents of Rio das Rãs did not become truly racialized until the introduction of article 68 in the new constitution and the activation of the Black movement for the settlement's claims. Prior to this, throughout most of the twentieth century, the struggle was one between a wealthy landowner and a group of landless peasants – a scenario that is played out again and again, from the southern *gaúcho* lands of Paraná to the Amazon basin.

Edson, Carlos, and Antônio

Edson makes *jenipapo* in a small shed behind his home. It is seasonal country liquor, common in the interior of Bahia, made from macerating the jenipapo fruit with *cachaça*, Brazil's form of sugarcane spirit. Edson has a small grove of *jenipapo* trees surrounding his two-room, zinc roofed house on the outskirts of Bom Jesus da Lapa. I met Edson in search of a bottle of *jenipapo* to take back to a friend in Salvador. When I first arrived in town, I was told that it was not the right season and that I would have a hard time finding a bottle. Finally, though, I encountered Edson who made the liquor each year and still had some bottles left from the previous season. He told me that it wouldn't taste as good as it had been sitting for too long, but I bought them regardless and asked if I might stay and chat for a while.

Selling this sweet spirit is only one of the many trades that Edson plies in order to make ends meet in the dry, hot, and hard climate of Bahia's interior. He has worked for a mobile phone company – assisting in the erection of signal towers – as a policeman, as a bus driver and, each year, as a ranch hand on a nearby *fazenda*. Edson is married with two children and is every bit the typical *sertanejo*. We start talking about how people in Salvador view the *sertão*, people of the interior, and issues of *quilombismo*:

> Salvador used to be the capital of Brazil in the colonial period and today, it is one of contemporary Brazil's great cities. But, I say to you, Bahians in

Salvador know nothing about the life of the interior, life in the interior is very hard ... the land doesn't have enough water and now the officials in Salvador and Brasilia want to change the path of the São Francisco River. Yes, racism exists out here, but Salvador is disconnected from the life of the interior.[7]

I told Edson that he was forgetting the staunch defence of many of the *quilombo* remnant communities in the interior and that many of the *terreiros, blocos afros,* and other Black political organizations were fighting for the rights of these rural communities. He admits that such movements are good and helpful to many of the poor Black communities in the *sertão*. But, he asks plaintively, "What about me?" He claims that he, too, has Afro-Brazilian ancestry and that one of his grandparents came from the Rio das Rãs area and so he, too, is a descendant of slaves. This should mean, Edson believes, that he should also enjoy title to land. However, his situation, he tells me, does not fit within the parameters of what others have determined defines a *quilombola* – a descendent of maroons.

Edson tells me that he knows many residents of Rio das Rãs and has worked with them on the cattle ranch. Further, he believes that many of the residents of Rio das Rãs are not committed to the same agenda as their supporters in Salvador but, in his words, "mimic" the language of the lawyers and anthropologists. He doesn't blame them for this, indeed, he tells me he would do the same if he was in their position, but he also does not believe it is fair. Edson suspects that some from Salvador are using the people of Rio das Rãs more than the residents of that community are using the movements. He believes that, ultimately, the groups in Salvador will get more out of the deal and that even if the residents get their land title, they will still be harassed by the *fazendeiro*. He asserts that if his ancestors had stayed out on a rural settlement instead of coming into the town of Bom Jesus da Lapa, then he, too, could have had access to land. As it is, he is forced to rent a plot of land from a *patrão* to keep his small herd of goats. Life is hard for him and for many of his fellows and he tells me that his wife is always urging him to pack up and move to Rio de Janeiro with his family.

The swollen mega-cities of the Southeast, Salvador, and even Brasilia offer many advantages to life in the *sertão*, both real and illusory, and migration from the interior to these centres has continued unabated through the twentieth century and into the twenty-first century. However, the reason why Edson and so many others have not abandoned this country in favour of a life in Salvador or Rio or São Paulo has much to do with a belief common to many *sertanejos:* that they can make it in the *sertão,* if they work hard enough. To be sure, money and opportunity are also impediments to escape from life in the Brazilian outback, but many, like Edson, want to stay: "Sure, life in the *sertão* is difficult. But, I couldn't survive in a city like Salvador. At least, this house belongs to me; more or less ... these goats are mine, more or less! The problem is that Brazilian society has no respect for the people of the *sertão* and the history of our country. The history of the *sertão* is the history of Brazil."

After spending some time in the company of Edson, I feel that we have developed a sufficient rapport to broach a particularly sensitive subject. The category of *negro* has long been considered something of a slur in the interior – used primarily as a pejorative for truly down-and-out individuals who were clearly of Afro-Brazilian background, and so I wanted to wait a little while before touching on the subject. One evening, on the main town square, Edson invited two of his workmates to join us for dinner and we talked about this word and what it means to *sertanejos.*

AD: Walking around, talking to people in Bom Jesus da Lapa, people don't use the word *negro* to describe themselves. In Salvador you hear it frequently. One hears it on the streets, at public demonstrations, scrawled on the wall as graffiti. But here it is absent. Why do you think this is so?[8]

EDSON: We are not blind to Brazil's racism. But we have other concerns out here. Concerns that people in Salvador don't understand. Out here, *negro* was not a word you used to describe someone and it is still considered rude. When people say it, they spit it out "*Porra, negro!*" I think that the people in Rio das Rãs have embraced the word because it helps them politically.

French's (2006) work on another *quilombo* community along the Rio São Francisco in Bahia would seem to parallel Edson's assertion. He writes that members of this community willingly took on the "much-derided" category of *negro* and its concomitant associations of oppression and slavery because it meant that they would be able to gain title to their land (340). Adopting this category implied a restructuring of the founding myths of the community to include – with the aid of anthropologists from Fundação Palmares – flight from slavery, although prior to the claim for *quilombo* status no such story or narrative had existed (345–50). The founding story is now acted out twice a year on special occasions and, according to French, represents a public performance of social categories that causes participants and observers alike to ritualize and talk about a new ethnic identity (353).

In a conversation with my three informants in Bom Jesus da Lapa – Edson, Carlos, and Antônio – I discussed these issues and specifically how they interpret the interplay of Black identity, the appellation *negro*, *quilombos*, *Candomblé* in the interior, and the role of important identity stakeholders and activists from Salvador, Brasilia, and elsewhere in Brazil.

ANTÔNIO: My family comes from a small rural community just north of Bom Jesus da Lapa. We were mostly what people in Brazil would call *preto*, and I heard stories when I was a child that former slaves founded our town or sometimes that we were taken in by the indigenous people. We had some people who practised *Candomblé de Caboclos*, but we didn't talk about these things. It was just a vague idea that used to be mentioned now and again. I think part of the reason why so many small communities in the interior look and sound the same in the *sertão* [is that] everyone is mixed and everyone is Black and everyone is white. If all one has to do is call themselves *negro* and talk about Africa, then why not?

AD: Do you think that your home village will do this?

ANTÔNIO: No, I don't think so. Like I said, this was only a rumour. We have no proof. I think Rio das Rãs had proof and some historian came from Salvador, from UFBa I think, and proved that they were *quilombolas*. I think that they wouldn't lie about such things. If they are *quilombolas*, then I say let them have the land. It doesn't matter. They'll have a hard time wresting it from that *fazendeiro*.

EDSON: Look, all of us sitting here have *sangue preto* (Black blood). Where do you think it came from? Just because some slaves rebelled and others didn't, does that mean we are not entitled to land? In that sense, all Brazilians are victims of slavery.

AD: What do you mean by that?

CARLOS: Look at my skin; it is darker than yours, but lighter than Edson's. Antônio has the darkest skin of all. What am I to do? Say that his hometown is a *quilombo* and mine isn't? That he has rights to his land, but in my community it is okay if the landlord burns out my mother and father, uncles and aunts, cousins and friends? Listen,

I don't want to be *negro, preto, quilombola*, whatever! I just want my
rights as a citizen of this country.
AD: But saying they are *negro* has helped the people of Rio das Rãs, no?
CARLOS: We'll see.

Carlos is the most cynical and sceptical informant that I interviewed
in Bom Jesus da Lapa. He is scornful of the Black movements and seems
to be quite hostile to any suggestion that he should call himself *negro*.
But contained in Edson's, Carlos', and Antônio's words and in the responses of many whom I spoke to in Bom Jesus da Lapa are, in some
small measure, the last hurrahs of "racial democracy" as an ideology in
Brazil. The ideology itself has been torn apart and decimated over the
last few decades – in no small measure thanks to the efforts of Brazilian
anthropologists and sociologists, affirmative action in governmental
hiring and post-secondary education designed to combat racial discrimination that "never really existed," and by the vigorous Black
movements in Salvador and Rio de Janeiro (Sheriff 2001). For these
three men and for many individuals like them in towns like Bom Jesus
da Lapa, racial categories and ethnic identities that correspond to an
idealized image of Blackness and Africanity do not appear to be viable
options. They are aware of their *mestiço* descent and the likely predominance of African slave ancestors in their background but choose not to
emphasize such elements. Rather, they adhere to the belief that they are
as Brazilian as anybody else, more so in fact, as they openly reject the
racialized language of the Black movements.
    As to racism, they believe it exists, but not to the same degree that it
does in the big cities of Brazil. All three of these men, if they were placed
on a street in Chicago, New York, Toronto, London, Kingston, or Cape
Town, would likely be categorized, quickly and without hesitation, as
Black. But in Brazil's interior, in the midst of a debate about the veracity
of slave origins for neighbouring remnant maroon communities, they
are able to engage in discourse about the relative benefits and pitfalls of
accepting that very category as a personal and ethnic identity for themselves and for those whom they reckon as family and community. Ultimately, though, both Edson and Antônio admitted to me that if they
could somehow appeal to the *quilombo* clause and get land title for their
families in their home communities they would happily do so – even if
it meant self-identifying as *negro*. Carlos, however, asserted that he
would never do such a thing, that he was a Brazilian, "*primeiro e ultimo*"
(first and last). At the intersection of these men's remarks, however, lies

more than just the rote recitation of the precepts of racial democracy. There also exists a clear idea about *sertão* and peasant identity and the curious dual nature of *quilombos* as communities that have lost their African heritage, but that are also – for Salvador's Black movements – emblematic of this heritage. Karina Baptista (2003), as part of an oral history project, has covered some similar terrain with her informants. Like Edson, Carlos, and Antônio, her interviewees seemed reluctant to broach the topic of racial identity, instead asserting that they were merely peasants. Baptista, however, concludes that Black or, indeed, ethnic identity of any sort had become diminished because of a lack of contact with "African" practices and so, consequently, a peasant identity became the principal identifier for the social group and informants fell back on the ideology of "racial democracy" (13–14).

The reduction of peasant or *sertão* identity to merely an articulation of the "myth" of racial democracy does the logically reasoned and well-thought arguments of men like Edson, Antônio, and especially Carlos a great injustice. To assert that they are just "falling back" on the ideology of "racial democracy" is to miss the point that the life of a rural peasant most accurately defines – at the level of collective identity – who these men are. In the workaday lives of these men and thousands of other men and women like them in the interior, the hard labour and scorched environment that defines their lives are not confined to people who, for all intents and purposes, look like them. All, not just those who obviously possess some degree of slave heritage, must confront the adversities of the interior, and peasant identity is not something that these individuals have resorted to because of a lack of Black or African cultural practices.

Edson does not define himself as a *sertanejo* merely because he is apprehensive of racial definitions such as *negro* or even *quilombola* and its concomitant slave associations. He and his fellows do so because the *life* of a rural peasant is one that best defines who they are and what they do. The sphere of social action and interaction within which these individuals dwell is one in which ethnic categories such as Black and white or European and African have little relevance – for them, economic identities invariably trump ethnic ones. Further, there exists little real difference in the daily lives of people who live in communities like Rio das Rãs and those who live in other rural settings on the outskirts of Bom Jesus da Lapa: they farm the same crops – cassava and maize – and they all keep small stock such as goats, sheep, and poultry. From a religious perspective, members of Rio das Rãs have also not completely adopted the spiritual orthodoxy of Salvador's African-oriented movements – *Candomblé*. Edson tells me that he knows a number of people from Rio das Rãs who occasionally attend, along with him, the congregation hall of the *Primeira Igreja Batista* (First Baptist Church) in the centre of Bom Jesus da Lapa, and knows others in the community who are Catholics and others who are evangelicals.

Finally, and perhaps most importantly, the people of communities like Rio das Rãs and Bom Jesus da Lapa are descended from the same people – a mixture of former slaves, Amerindian groups drawn into the social sphere of backland settlements, and white farmers. What truly makes one a *quilombola* and the other a rural peasant when members of the maroon community themselves are unsure of their origins and require the category of *"negro"* to be imposed upon them from without?

Creolization and the Folklorization of Blackness in the Sertão

The residents of Rio das Rãs, through their use of the *quilombo* clause in the new constitution, have begun to reinvent themselves not only in the context of, as French (2006) puts it, "representations of an imagined African past" (341). They have also, through their associations with academic and legal interlocutors from Salvador, associated themselves with the representatives, inventors, and agents of that imagined past. It is indeed an irony that a maroon remnant community should need the aid of anthropologists and attorneys to "remember" Africa. Maroons, assert Price and Price (1997), are most representative of creolization not because they have "forgotten" Africa, but rather because within these communities diverse African traditions truly came to the forefront, without a European voice imposed upon the dialogue. Without the overpowering authority of a European linguistic and cultural trope intruding in quotidian life, the African practices and traditions of different cultures could find new ways to interact, coexist, cross-pollinate, and co-mingle. In this setting, then, the maroon becomes perhaps the most fully creolized in that no one voice of the "Old World" takes precedence; no particular European language, cultural practice, or religious form dominates the process of ethnogenesis. Yet maroon communities "remember" the African past, not as intact or replicated cultural forms, but in eclectic and sophisticated ways that invoke multiple African histories and multiplex African identities (Price 2008) – not at all like the ethnically monolithic assertions of Yoruba or Akan origin found in many movements in Brazil and the United States.

That the "true" histories of these communities may have been lost due to the vicissitudes of time, oppression, eviction, harassment, and the hard-fought life of the interior is perfectly reasonable. But it is a strange turnaround indeed that the agencies and stakeholders responsible for helping to recover and, for some groups, reimagine, their "African" heritage also articulate, within the context of Salvador and its Black movements, the belief that Black communities were never, in fact, creolized and maintained their "proud" Yoruba origins throughout the colonial era. Let us accept, then, that at least some of the communities of the interior founded during the years of slavery were indeed formed by bands of runaway slaves – maroons. Let us also accept that, in the years after abolition in Brazil, many other similar rural communities were formed due to land donations, labour migration, and settlement around important Catholic pilgrimage sites such as Bom Jesus da Lapa. Finally, let us also accept that many of these communities held numbers of impoverished Europeans and Amerindians who had come to find work on the growing estates of rich landlords. In the context of this creolized milieu, is it not understandable that any African culture, traditions, or practices that might have been a part of those maroon societies gave way to a broader and more unified idea of shared *sertão* identity? As Baptista (2003) puts it, *sertão* or peasant identity may not have diminished African identities because such categories had no cultural reservoir upon which to draw. Rather, the nature of maroon societies, formed as they often are of *diverse* African practices, may have encouraged precisely the kind of cross-cultural borrowing and mingling that defines the culture and populace of the *sertão*.

I am not suggesting views held by Edson and his comrades are not, in some way, indebted to the dominant assimilationist ideologies of Brazil. However, they are also part of the cultural and identarian world view of the *sertão*. This world view was built not on the nationalist writings of Freyre or the pseudoscientific racist ponderings of Da Cunha, but was born out of a past in which new ethnic identities were generated and mobilized within the frameworks provided by previous social categories and past experience. Hanchard (1994, 164) believes that attempts to sacralize and elevate the *quilombos* – along with the space of the *terreiro* – as representative of bold manifestations of Black power, as symbolic reference points, and as a source of strength for their political and social initiatives is to look to the past. It is akin, as he puts it in his analogy that references both classical Greek mythology and a classic of Brazilian cinema,[9] to Orpheus' glance back at Eurydice as they emerged from the underworld, thus condemning her permanently to Hades and to the oblivion of history. Perhaps, not quite. The *quilombos* are important for two very important, contemporary reasons.

First of all, although the "true" history of the *quilombo* remnant communities is important for the Black movements, their funders, and stakeholders, it is a history that they themselves have constructed and that fits the political agenda of a globalized notion of Blackness – what matters most here is the creation of a symbol of Africanized Black resistance in the heart of the Bahian backlands. For the organizations in Salvador, it rounds out and completes Bahia's place as the epicentre and nexus of all things African in Brazil. Scholars who have focused on the construction of nations and national identities have suggested that the restoration and rescuing of traditions, whether real or invented, is a common practice (Hobsbawm and Ranger 1983). For the Black movements in Salvador, any community that can potentially contribute to the founding myth of an emergent Black or *negro* idea of African Brazilian citizenship is seized upon with great fervour. That incorporation in the "Africanizing" program requires the forgetting of a multifaceted and potentially diverse past in which African slaves from different backgrounds may have come together with white settlers and Amerindian populations to form a unique community represents a clear political desire within a particular identity project to consume and disseminate a re-Africanized idea of what Africanity can mean to Blackness. However, most *quilombos* represent a connection to a slave past quite dissimilar from the potently Yoruba-oriented spaces of the "pure" *terreiro*; they bear little or no resemblance to what they assert was the bastion of Africanity in Brazil – Palmares – and, most importantly, they contain populations that need to be *convinced* of their Blackness.

Informants in Bom Jesus da Lapa and in some of the surrounding rural communities that I visited frequently told me a story not dissimilar from the one I heard from Edson, Antônio, and Carlos. "What makes them so different from us?" was a common refrain, along with "They are no darker-skinned than we are, so why can't we get special status?" It is notable, however, that few informants seemed to begrudge the residents of Rio das Rãs the success they have enjoyed. For success, in the modest context of the *sertão*, is precisely what the community has enjoyed since receiving article 68 recognition. The settlement is now in the range of mobile phone towers, they have received monies from the federal government to improve schools and literacy levels, and a recent World Bank donation has now allowed for upgrades to the settlement's water and sanitation system (FUNASA 2008). Instead of resentment, there exists the glimmer of hope in many of these outlying hamlets that they, too, might be able to obtain some kind of special dispensation or title to land, because they, too, are descended from enslaved Africans.

Choosing to adopt the kind of Black identity that leaders and activist scholars would have members of predominantly Black, rural, peasant communities assume is not about rediscovering the Africanity or Black history of resistance. As Edson tells me, choosing to be *negro* in the *sertão* is not about becoming African, it is about gaining guaranteed access to what matters most to a *sertanejo* – land. Therefore, the choice to embrace article 68 is not, ultimately, an acceptance of a new form of Blackness, but rather the means to express an older identity, rooted in connectedness to land and the common aspirations of all people of the interior. But, contained within this act is the very heart of what Gramsci understood as the power of identarian intellectuals to control the discourse surrounding the ideology of culture, of conceptions of the world, and of collective identity – race – with the ultimate goal of changing power relationships with land, landowners – *fazendeiros* – and the ability to create economically viable communities. Gramsci (1971, 97) places enormous import on the inability of subaltern groups' to organize around ideas of solidarity and collectivity and this, he believes, was their greatest weakness. He argues that cultural elites control the ideological sectors of society and serve to organize the oppressed around common ideologies of opposition. Ideologies, however, that have largely been co-opted by intellectuals of the dominant class and thus, ultimately, betrayed by a unified enlightenment-rooted emphasis on progress. Such non-organic or non-working class intellectuals serve to produce cultural, intellectual, and symbolic hegemony through education or through popular manifestations and folklorization of culture such as religion, *quilombo* identity, and other African-oriented practices. I would suggest that the attitude that some of the leaders in Salvador have towards the people of the *sertão* is one that appears to be vaguely reminiscent of the paternalistic writings of Da Cunha. They profoundly believe that the people and communities of the interior like Rio das Rãs are, to use Da Cunha's (1902) words, the "bedrock" of the Black movement and of Black resistance. Yet they are also communities that need to be reminded and educated on what it means to truly be Black and "African" in Brazil, much as Da Cunha saw a need to "civilize" the people of the *sertão*.

Chapter Five

Conclusions

This work and the research upon which it is based have sought to show how Afro-Brazilians in the northeastern state of Bahia use the idea of Africa to redefine and reinvent meanings of Blackness. It has explored how Black communities in Bahia have attempted to engage Africa, both as an ideal and as a real place, in a active dialogue about what African cultures mean to Black society in Bahia and, more generally, in Brazil. From the early days of the plantation, through decades of slave revolt and "return" to the West African coast, to abolition and the foundation of the Brazilian Republic, Africa has always been woven into the fabric of Brazilian society. Whether through its diverse musical forms, the culinary traditions of Bahia and much of the Northeast, or through the varied possession religions found throughout the country, Africa has *always* been a part of Brazilian identity. However, it is only really in the last thirty to forty years that Afro-Brazilians, particularly in the northeastern state of Bahia, have started to consciously refer to Africa as a cultural and symbolic resource for manifestations of personal and collective identity. Africa, here, is seen not as a vague notion or distant remembrance that seems connected, in some small way, with cultural practice, sights, sounds, or smells, but rather as a place with whom everyday Brazilians can interact and from whom they can learn.

Black communities in Bahia that seek to incorporate elements of African culture, specifically Yoruba culture, into expressions of Blackness – that is, into more than just aspects of religious practice but into a fully developed ethnic identity for those Afro-Brazilians who choose to embrace it – use, as we have seen, a variety of approaches in order to further their goal of Africanizing definitions of what it means to be Black in Bahia. This exchange occurs in a varied assortment of locales, including the different religious centres – both Afro-Brazilian and Christian – of Salvador; in "Afrobeat-roots-reggae" bars managed by African cultural brokers from cities like Cape Coast in Ghana; in classrooms at state universities where the Yoruba language is taught; in shops that sell African handicrafts in the old city of Salvador; and also in tourist nexuses like the slave fort of Elmina, the *route des esclaves* in Ouidah, or at similar sites in other major cities of the West African coast.

We met Georgia, a young man from the Ghanaian city of Cape Coast who now lives and works in Salvador. Georgia has become a consummate storyteller and possesses an incredibly canny sense for knowing exactly what his audience wants to hear. Georgia arrived in Salvador through an extraordinary contrivance of circumstances that took him from his hometown in Ghana's Central Region to the heart of Yorubaland in the city of Lagos, Nigeria, thereafter, to a variety of ports of call in the merchant marine, and finally to the so-called Black Rome of Brazil. In Salvador, as we saw, Georgia is engaged in a variety of occupations, but most of his regular income comes from leading groups of travelers to important "African" sites in Salvador; from making contacts with Africa-centric community groups who then hire him to play "African" music and participate at public events; and now from working as a guide for Brazilians looking to travel to and connect with Africa. Georgia is not the only West African in Salvador. He is a member of a small, but growing community of students, merchants, priests, entrepreneurs, and academics who provide clear and distinct ideas about what African *can* mean to Black communities in Salvador and the interior *and* to those intellectuals and elites involved in organizing Black communities around a singular notion of what Blackness should mean as an identity. The majority of West Africans who reside in Salvador are Nigerians. This is unsurprising considering that the primary ethnic and cultural focus of Afro-Brazilian community groups who are engaged in Africanizing their identity discourse look primarily to the Yoruba society of southwestern Nigeria for inspiration and legitimacy.

Of all of the Nigerians living, working, and regularly frequenting Salvador, one of the most important and influential in recent years has been the professor of the Yoruba language, Félix Ayoh'Omidire who studied and taught at the Universidade Federal da Bahia (UFBa), and continues his affiliation with this university through regular visits and the sponsorship of students and other lecturers of Yoruba language and culture to the Centro de Estudos Afro-Orientais (CEAO). Félix is the most recent in a long line of Nigerians who have been involved in representing the Yoruba culture in Brazil and with strengthening the ongoing dialogue between Brazil and West Africa.

Other Nigerians are also present in Salvador. Some work at selling West African handicrafts in the city's old quarter, Pelourinho; others study at UFBa as part of an exchange program with a Nigerian university; some present themselves as Yoruba priests and offer their skills and knowledge to small and startup *terreiros*; and others are like Georgia – making ends meet through a variety of means. All of them, however, have become part of an ongoing process of emphasizing elements of Yoruba culture – specifically, knowledge about the *orixás*, the deities that populate the Yoruba cosmological universe, and knowledge of the Yoruba language – into Africanized expressions of Black identity. To be sure, not all of these individuals actively seek out work in the community organizations and religious centres of the Afro-Brazilian community or work as tour guides to "roots" travellers. Many of the students have come to Salvador simply to take advantage of a wonderful opportunity for education and travel. However, the very exchange program that facilitates their transfer is steeped in the history of Nigerian connections with the religious centres of Salvador and their Africanizing project. Simply by virtue of the fact that many of these individuals have come from Nigeria and may very well speak the Yoruba language – even if they are not themselves Yoruba – they are immediately individuals of importance in the dominantly Africa-centric culture of Black identity projects in Salvador. Many of these young individuals are able to work as Yoruba instructors outside of the main UFBa curriculum, become involved with organizations like the *blocos afros* (Black *carnaval* associations), and typically become associated with UFBa's Centro de Estudos Afro-Orientais (CEAO) – a major source of intellectual and academic support of the Africanizing efforts of the *Candomblé terreiros* and *blocos afros*.

Black travellers from both Brazil and West Africa have been and continue to be responsible for transacting ideas of Africanized Blackness in the space of the Black Atlantic – a symbolic space that contains far more than Gilroy (1993) ever imagined when he first proposed the idea. Their collaborators in this ongoing transatlantic dialogue between areas of Blackness are the anthropologists and other social scientists involved in exploring the Afro-American *problématique* – that is to say, those scholars concerned with unravelling the extent to which representatives of different African cultures in slave populations affected the emergence of unique Black cultures in the Americas. A number of debates, some of which continue to this day, have influenced the way in which different scholars have approached the Black culture of northeastern Brazil. Some have seen Afro-Brazilian society in Bahia as a culture that still retains a large number of Yoruba cultural elements that have "survived" the depredations of slavery and have been passed down from generation to generation. Other scholars assert that the manifestations of Africanity that exist in Bahia are a product of the blending and mixing of different African cultural patterns in the great sugar plantations surrounding Salvador in the eighteenth and nineteenth centuries. Still others declare that the emphasis on African religious practice and Yoruba traditions in Bahia are more a product of academic inventions and assertions of religious purity motivated by scholarly interest in "Africa in Brazil."

Reputations in academia are rarely built by suggesting middle ways or compromises between empathically asserted and dogmatically believed theoretical explain-it-all models. In the scholarship surrounding the Black societies of the Americas, two models hold sway in the study of African presence in the slave plantations and their respective adherents are often embroiled in fierce academic debates with each other. The first of these is often associated with the work of Melville Herskovits and his insistence that elements of African culture "survived" the Middle Passage and enslavement in the plantations and came to form an important part of the cultural praxis of Black communities throughout the Americas. This perspective has come to be a crucial part of the agenda of scholars that seek to show that saltwater Africans transported to the shores of the United States, Cuba, Jamaica, Haiti, Colombia, Brazil, and all of the other colonies of the New World that received slaves were able to, proudly, nobly, fearlessly, hold on to their own cultures. Herskovits' scholarship and the work that it prompted was inspired by the groundswell of anti-racist thought that arose from the revolutionary ideas of Franz Boas and the fluorescence of Black art, speech, and writing that was the Harlem Renaissance. Therefore, it is understandable that the work of those scholars, particularly Black scholars, who have inherited the mantle of Herskovits, would be driven by a similar goal of reclaiming the African past. The work of these historians, anthropologists, sociologists, and other social scientists needs to be understood and respected within the context of societies and academies – in Brazil, the United States, and elsewhere – in which racist and colonial attitudes were pervasive for a very long time. Their ideas and contributions to knowledge on Afro-America attempted to serve as corrective to decades of oppression.

The theoretical model that is often presented in stark opposition to the ideas of the neo-Herskovitsians is the approach put forward by Sydney Mintz and Richard Price (1976). This model asserts that the ethnic composition of slave plantations, like those in Bahia, consisted of individuals from throughout the regions of sub-Saharan African from which slaves were drawn, living in close proximity. In this cheek-by-jowl existence only very fundamental notions of African culture were retained – what Mintz and Price called "grammatical principles" (1976, 5). Specific traditions, especially those embedded in kinship practices, were invariably lost or subsumed by the emergence of new Afro-American cultures. This perspective, dubbed "rapid creolization" by both adherents and opponents, suggests that the Black societies of the Americas were born in the social context of the plantation.

The search for meaning entailed in the Africanizing identity discourse presented to me during my time in Bahia was rooted in a desire to find an African experience or tradition that could help to redefine what it meant to be Black in the Americas. The two ethnic groups that have come to prominence in this process of globalizing constructions of African Blackness are the Yoruba of Nigeria and the Akan people of Ghana. The Akan monopolize images and ideas of the African in the United States. This is largely a result of the historical connections and ongoing dialogue between the writers of the Harlem Renaissance and the intelligentsia of the Ghanaian independence and Pan-African movement. This relationship grew and blossomed through the twentieth century and Ghana, home to the Akan chiefdoms, became the principal reference for African Americans seeking to orient a new Black identity towards Africa. For Brazilians and for other Caribbean societies, Nigeria, and specifically, the Yoruba culture, came to be seen as the wellspring of all that is African. To be sure, there are other African foci such as Angola and the Jeje or Ewe/Fon peoples of Ghana-Togo-Benin, but these are completely overshadowed by the emphasis placed on the Yoruba. Indeed, even elaborations of Jeje or Angolan culture in Salvador often include transposed elements of Yoruba practice – such as an emphasis on Yoruba *orixás*. Yoruba-centricity overwhelms all other aspects of African-oriented discourse in Bahia. Consequently, despite asserting that historical investigation into the ethnic makeup of the slave population is, ultimately, fruitless, this work has sought to undertake some historical sleuthing to suggest origins for the accentuation of Yoruba practice over all else.

Certainly, as Matory (2005), Nishida (2003), and Reis (2001) have all pointed out, large numbers of slaves in eighteenth- and nineteenth-century Bahia were shipped to Brazil from the West African ports of Ouidah, Porto Novo, and Lagos. Further, although African point of departure is a very poor metric for determining the percentages of different ethnic groups in any given slave population (Nishida 2003), we can be certain that at least some of the slaves shipped from these ports – especially during the height of the kingdom of Dahomey – were members of the inchoate Yoruba chiefdom. This means that there were individuals who worshipped the Yoruba pantheon of *orixás* in the slave community. However, this historical assumption – and it is an assumption, not a fact – is nowhere near sufficient to account for the ascendance of Yoruba cultural practices in Bahia. Another perspective, offered by Matory (1999, 2005), convincingly argues that the emphasis on Yoruba practice is a direct consequence of an ongoing dialogue between Lagos and Salvador in which ideas of Yoruba purity were cultivated through interaction about the nature of the coalescing Yoruba identity in Lagos and the prevalence of Yoruba traditions in some of the houses of Afro-Brazilian religious practice in Salvador. This back-and-forth between the West African littoral and northeastern Brazil made Yoruba the principal cultural trope within which all ideas of Africa were embedded.

A final point of view places Brazilian academics, U.S.-based anthropologists, and other scholars at the centre of a project to construct Afro-Brazilian religion and other Africanized elements of Bahian culture as representative of what these researchers asserted was a politically and cosmologically sophisticated African culture – the Yoruba (Fry 1982). In this model, academics and intellectuals sought to impose "invented" ideas of Yoruba purity upon those houses of Afro-Brazilian religious practice with whom they were affiliated. This manufactured form of Yoruba-centricity spread beyond the confines of a few select *terreiros* and came to be a dominant cultural force in expressions of Africanity in Bahia and throughout Brazil. Now, even if one adheres to the model of rapid creolization put forward by Mintz and Price, there remains room for the expression, in different circumstances and at different times, for singular African voices to sometimes rise above the multiplicity of African and European culture in creolized societies. Richard Price (1975, 1996, 2008) demonstrates this ably in his studies of maroon societies in Suriname and elsewhere. Maroon societies, Price believes, are most ideally representative of the process of creolization because these communities, often located in the bush or in the hinterlands, were able to forge new African American cultures out of a variety of different African sources. However, it appears that in some manifestations of maroon culture – specifically, Saramaka maroon culture – motifs from different African regions are more prominent. For example, the Saramaka's spiritual universe includes divine entities known as Wénti spirits (Price 2008). These are wholly Saramaka supernatural beings – not Akan, nor Yoruba, nor Mande. However, from an analytical perspective, the etymology of the Wénti concept likely owes something to vague Akan origins. That is about as far as Price, his key informant and interlocutor, Tooy, or we can take it. No other suppositions or assumptions about the origin of Wénti spirits or the importance of the Akan, according to Price, should be made. They need to be viewed, understood, and categorized entirely as Saramaka entities.

The perspective that the emphasis on Yoruba in Bahia is a product of dialogue and interaction between Africa and Brazil carried out by Black agents of identity and brokers of culture has much to recommend it. Matory (2005) draws on a vast array of historical and ethnographic data to construct a model that places the rise of the Yoruba – in both Brazil and Nigeria – in Black hands. One needs to look no further than contemporary cultural brokers, such as Georgia, Félix, and others presented earlier in this work, to understand why this perspective is so persuasive. The transmission of ideas about Africa by African entrepreneurs of identity has continued throughout the twentieth century and into the twenty-first. These individuals are active participants in helping to define Blackness for residents of Salvador, and are also contributing, through their participation in Black "roots" tourism and through the furthering of a Yoruba-centric discourse, in helping to globalize an idea of Africanized Blackness that is composed of key symbols such as "orixá," "slavery," "roots," "spirit," "possession," and others. Such key symbols, I have argued, are employed at a global level in the creation of a notion of globalized Blackness that makes a generic or largely homogenized idea of Africa the centrepiece of Black identity. Finally, Brazilian and foreign academics – especially anthropologists – were and continue to be important sources of legitimization for Black communities in Salvador. I suggest that this is the case because of the frequency and ubiquity with which members of Salvador's Black movements continually refer to the work of anthropologists such as Ruth Landes, Pierre Verger, and even Matory as individuals that have given the ethnographer's imprimatur of authenticity to Africanized Black culture in Bahia. The work of these and other scholars at UFBa's CEAO, and at the federally funded Fundação Palmares, continues to be used to advocate for the importance of recognizing and privileging African-derived practices in Bahia's Black community.

The goal in this work has been to try and find the middle ground between what practitioners of the perspectives presented here seem to eschew. Like M.G. Smith (1957), I believe that the academic wrangling over theoretical models that, ultimately, can work side-by-side in anthropological, sociological, and historical examinations of African American societies is of little benefit – neither to scholarship nor to the communities under research. In this work, I suggest that the creolization model best coincides with an interpretation of how Black communities use the idea of Africa in the *contemporary* setting. To be sure, its merits in explaining the history, composition, and culture of many American societies are powerful. However, this work is about Africa in the here and now in Brazil. In that context, the idea of a polyphonous and multiplex dialogue, contestation even, over the role Africa should play in forming Black identity is also assisted and made clearer – hopefully the goal of any theoretical model – by an appreciation of creolization-like process. However, this does not necessarily mean that an analysis of "survivals" cannot bear fruit. I suggest that those historians who seek to understand ethnic categories and the cultures with which they are associated in the slave plantation turn their attention away from the verification of the actual presence of members of those societies. Rather, what we should be concerned with is the way in which both slaves and masters used *ideas* and *discourse* about Yoruba, Hausa, Akan, or any other ethnic group in the plantation. This approach places Black societies in an American context, rather than an African one that cannot, ultimately, be authenticated. The use of African identities – whether generalized and essentialized notions of Africa or specific African ethnic categories – as a symbolic anchor for notions of Blackness is ultimately about the creation of *meaning* for historically marginalized communities. I contend that historical investigations into how categories such as Nagô (Yoruba), or Jeje (Fon), or Malê (Hausa) were used, manipulated, and constructed in the plantations of Bahia can, in the end, be of more contemporary anthropological and historical value than assertions that such ethnic groups were actually present in the slave communities of Brazil or, indeed, anywhere else in the Americas.

There remains considerable ambivalence in Bahia towards the Africanizing agenda of Black elites in the *terreiros* and *blocos afros* of Salvador and of their academic interlocutors at UFBa, Palmares, and elsewhere. Among Catholics who worship in the context of the Pastoral Afro and who frequent predominantly Afro-Brazilian churches in Salvador, alternative expressions of Blackness, such as reverence for the tortured slave Anastácia and participation in the inculturated mass, take precedence over Yoruba-centric religious forms or language instruction. Individuals such as Maria, a street-seller of one of the most iconic manifestations of Bahia's Africanity, *acarajé* – the West African-derived food made of bean flour, chilies, okra, and fried in palm oil, – admits that she uses the African symbols of Bahia, but does not really believe in them. Maria's life story is one in which a Black form of Catholicism that speaks directly to her experience as a Black woman in Salvador continues to be an important foundation for her life and for her identity. She admits that Brazil is a racist country, but also that Africanity or the Yoruba culture that underpins it in Bahia is of no immediate relevance to her daily life. Maria does not deny that being an *acarajé* vendor is hard work and that she makes a very meagre living from selling snacks on the street. But she seems resigned to her life – one of menial work and little hope for change in the future. Further, she does not believe that the African message of many of the the Black movements can help bring about much change for her or for her fellows.

Members of the evangelical churches, especially the large neo-Pentecostal megachurches, are more than ambivalent about the Africanizing project of the Black movements – they condemn the influence of African culture and the Afro-Brazilian possession religions as devil worship and as a source of spiritual corruption for Brazilian society. These churches continue to make significant inroads into the impoverished neighbourhoods of Brazil's towns and cities. They claim that they can offer real remedies and solutions to life's problems – that through prayer and devotion to Christ, through the intercession of flamboyant evangelical pastors, poor Black communities can be released from the cycle of poverty. In addition, the mode of worship that is practised in the neo-Pentecostal churches is one that appeals to many in the Black community, especially in Salvador, where emotive and exuberant forms of religious performance are the norm. Members of the evangelical churches, notably the large and incredibly influential Igreja Universal do Reino de Deus, who identify themselves as Afro-Brazilian, believe that the Black movement in Bahia is being led down the wrong path. They see this primarily as a result of the undue influence wielded by the *terreiros*, *blocos afros*, and other organizations involved with injecting ideas about Africa into constructions of Brazilian Blackness.

Finally, this volume explored how ideas of Africa and Africanized Black identity play in the hardscrabble interior of Bahia – the *sertão*. These backlands have long been an important part of the Brazilian imaginary, existing on a frontier that has helped to define much of what it means to be Brazilian. Here in the arid and remote Brazilian hinterland, the Black movements of Salvador have sought to preserve another important symbol of Africa and of the slave past. Throughout the colonial era, rebel and runaway slaves fled to the desolate and forbidding *sertão* and founded communities that came to be truly creolized settlements. In these *quilombos*, slaves from a variety of African backgrounds along with Amerindian groups, wandering interior missionaries, and European prospectors came together to found villages and towns in the desert – away from the prosperous and fertile land of the Bahian coast. In recent years, the Brazilian government, under pressure from scholars, community advocates, and anti-racism groups, has started to provide legal protection for *quilombo* remnant communities under a new provision in the Brazilian constitution. Many of these small rural communities typically face harassment and the threat of encroachment and eviction from their land by large cattle ranches in the interior. In response, the Black movements – aided by anthropologists and funded by groups such as Palmares – have become embroiled in helping to determine whether or not a rural community was, in fact, a *quilombo*. This has resulted in a number of legal victories for small communities in the interior who have now been granted, through use of the *quilombo* clause, title to the land on which their community rests.

However, those villages and settlements that have been declared *comunidade remanescente de quilombos* (maroon remnant communities) have had to change much about their founding narratives. Often this means that the place of African religious traditions is accentuated and any contributions made to a community by non-Black elements – such as Amerindian groups – are downplayed. This is all done to conform to the "official" criteria of what composed a *quilombo* during the colonial era – a definition created with the assistance of community groups and scholars committed to an Africa-centric ideal for the Black communities of Bahia. This definition casts Brazilian maroon communities as bastions of African cultural "survivals," where African rituals and African beliefs were preserved, unsullied by European cultures. This is ironic, in that most *quilombo* remnant communities in the interior are often only vaguely aware of descent from runaway slaves and are, for the most part, small rural communities where *sertão* or peasant identities supersede or completely eclipse notions of Blackness or Africanity. The origin and status of these communities has also become a contested issue for *sertanejos* (residents of the *sertão*) who live on the outskirts of larger towns in the interior. Many of these individuals claim to have Black ancestry and plaintively remark that they, too, should be entitled to land and that the inhabitants of communities granted *quilombo* status are no more ethnically or culturally "Black," no more in-tune with their slave roots, than anybody else in the *sertão*.

Luiza Bairros' (2008) ideal of Afro-Brazilian society as "a community of destiny" (50) can only be achieved if, as she puts it, "the myth of racial democracy" is once and for all obliterated (51). However, she sees one problem that still remains: the fragmentation of the Black community into segments or interest groups. She continues: "A major tendency within the Black population has been the propensity to organize in segments – as women, as lesbians, as rural residents of *quilombos*, as youth, by arenas of social life" (51). This kind of fractured response to racism, she asserts, prevents consensus and, consequently, the ability to mobilize action and ideology in terms of what Blackness means to all Afro-Brazilians. But there's the rub – many Afro-Brazilians do not *want* to conceive of Blackness in the same terms as those laid down by the Black movements, by the *terreiros*, by scholars, or by *blocos afros*. There is great diversity in the Black communities of Brazil and not all of them are interested in articulating an African-oriented identity or, for the matter, a Black identity. Many "segments" of the Black community are not interested in participating in an Africa-centric discourse of certain Black movements – even though that identity seeks to topple and counter centuries of oppression and hegemony by a predominantly white, European settler society. However, they are also not blinded by the distortions of racial democracy or by faith in a non-African religious form. They simply find that identities that speak to African formulations of Blackness do not resonate or speak to their lives and their realities. For many groups in Bahia, African-oriented notions of Blackness have powerful symbolic relevance, but they are not, as emphasized throughout this volume, always the most important identity in their cultural repertoire. Once again, I recall the case of Maria – she is a Black, Catholic woman, but she also, through her work as an *acarajé* seller, represents all that is African about Bahia. For, although she claims the image of the *Baiana* selling her African "food of the *orixás*" is merely a role she plays, it is an identity that she participates in and helps to propagate – thus perpetuating the image of Salvador as quintessentially African.

This study has attempted to show the different ways in which Africa has been and continues to be used and manipulated in order to under-pin what is, in essence, a Brazilian ethnic identity. Over the past century, Africa has come to mean many things to the Afro-Brazilian community and to Brazilian society in general. In the language of Da Cunha (1902), Calógeras (1930), and Nina Rodrigues (1932), the "African" elements in Brazilian society were a problem that had to be eradicated through con-tinued racial mixing and miscegenation. Now, however, Africa has be-come a cultural trope that has acquired significant cultural and political capital in the context of a state – Bahia – where Afro-Brazilian practices and traditions are placed front and centre in the public consciousness. My argument in this work has been twofold: that scholarship on Afro-Brazilian identities needs to be relocated away from attempts to au-thenticate the past and that, even though explorations of Black identity in Bahia privilege the dominant African-oriented articulations of the Black movements, Afro-Brazilian identities are, in fact, incredibly var-ied and contested. Selka (2007, 151) notes, quite poignantly, that this diversity and complexity presents the same challenge to theory as it does to the kind of Black mobilization suggested by Bairros. However, I believe that this kind of heteroglossia, this multiplicity of perspec-tives, defines the very nature of identity. Throughout the human lifes-pan we are all forced to make ongoing choices about who we are as individuals, as members of society, of cultural groups, of institutions, and of nations. Perspectives on identity that seek to essentialize indi-viduals, regardless of origin or destiny, can ultimately serve to contrib-ute to racism and intolerance and create new hegemonies.

All of us possess the ability to reshape and redefine ourselves, de-pending on context and circumstance, and this is certainly true of the Black communities of Bahia. There are many individuals in Salvador who believe that greater incorporation of African cultural elements is essential to redefinitions of Black identity. There are those who wish to embrace the idea of Africa in more subtle and nuanced ways, in modes that speak more to Brazilian realities than to African ones. Still others seek to completely reject the idea that Africa should have anything to do with Afro-Brazilian culture or identity.

On the first page of this volume I quoted the Harlem Renaissance poet Countee Cullen. In his classic poem, "Heritage," Cullen (1925, 36) asked "What is Africa to me?" If Cullen were a resident of Salvador, living in a community like Curuzu-Liberdade, one would be forced to reply, "many different things." Africa is of vital importance to the identities mobilized by members of *terreiros* like Casa Branca and to groups like Ilê Aiyê, but to individuals like Maria or Edson in Bom Jesus da Lapa, Africa means something quite different. Even individuals like Georgia and Félix, two *Africans*, must grapple with what the idea of Africa means to them as they engage in composing representations of their homeland that speak to varied expectations and beliefs. I wish to suggest that continued study of the ways in which the *idea* of Africa is understood, used, constructed, and deconstructed by Black populations in the Americas is a field of research rife with opportunity for anthropologists, historians, sociologists, and other social scientists. This is the path that I believe investigation of Afro-America must follow in order to fully understand how Black communities in an ever more connected and networked world relate to and incorporate Africa into definitions of self and community.

Notes

1. Blackness and Africanity in Brazil and Elsewhere

1 Comments recorded during participation in a tour led by Georgia for a group of African-American travellers from Atlanta, 13 September 2005.

2 Georgia is referring to Robert Sutherland Rattray, an early Africanist ethnographer and author of *Tribes of the Ashanti Hinterland*, an important two-volume monograph about cultures that lived in the orbit of the Asante chiefdom in Ghana.

3 Interview with Georgia, Salvador, Bahia, Brazil, 21 September 2005.

4 See Ross' volume *Wrapped in Pride: Ghanaian Kente and African American Identity* (1998) for excellent coverage of this topic.

5 Interview with Ama N, Elmina, Ghana, 11 March 2003.

6 This initiative, proposed by Haiti and supported by the African Union and UNESCO, claims as its principal objective the global acceptance of the horrors of the Atlantic slave trade and slavery in general, and an awareness of the historical consequences and interactions that have resulted from the slave trade (UNESCO 2008).

7 During this fieldwork, I was able to speak to four tourist groups from Brazil involved in activities oriented towards slave history, what the groups generally called "religious, cultural, and historical rediscovery." In total I conducted nineteen unstructured interviews with travellers who identified themselves as Brazilians and who were members of an Afro-Brazilian religious congregation. Two of the groups were entirely composed of members from Salvador in Bahia. The other two groups were more diverse, containing members from Salvador, São Paulo, and Rio de Janeiro. I also participated in the "slave walk" in Ouidah where I met two

other groups of tourists that contained participants from Brazil and conducted an additional four unstructured interviews. I was also able to interview a number of hoteliers, tour guides, and restaurateurs in Benin, Ghana, and Nigeria. These unstructured interviews primarily covered perceptions of "roots"' tourism and what kind of services and information they offer to travellers and tourists from Brazil, the U.S., and other places in the Americas.

8 Over the eighteen months spent in Bahia from 2004 to 2006, I conducted a total of 211 unstructured interviews: 141 of these interviews were conducted in the city of Salvador, 28 were conducted in the city of Ilhéus, 27 in the town of Bom Jesus da Lapa, and 15 in the town of Jacobina. Eighty-nine interviews were conducted with women informants and 122 with men. In 2011, an additional 30 interviews were conducted, almost exclusively with the women and few men who sell *acarajé* on the streets of Salvador.

2. West African Cultural Brokers in Northeast Brazil

1 Interview with Georgia, Salvador, Bahia, Brazil, 5 April 2005.
2 Interview with Georgia, Salvador, Bahia, Brazil, 7 May 2005.
3 See Parés' (2001) work on the Jeje or Fon presence in the *Candomblés* of Bahia.
4 In 2004, TV Record, fighting back against Globo's domination of the *telenovela* format, produced a remake of *A Escrava Isaura* that did extremely well in the ratings.
5 Email correspondence with a former teacher from a community group in Salvador, 14 September 2007.
6 *Afoxé* is a secular manifestation of the music typically played in *Candomblé terreiros*. The basic rhythm of the *terreiro* chant is called *ijexá*, and this backbeat now serves as an underlying rhythm for much popular music in Brazil, including *Afoxé*. Interview with Georgia, Salvador, Bahia, Brazil, 14 November 2005.
7 Interview with the *mãe* of a small *terreiro* in the Saúde neighborhood of Salvador, Bahia, Brazil, 16 November 2005. The *mãe* requested anonymity for herself and the *terreiro* because of her critical stance towards the larger and richer *terreiros* in Salvador and their leaders.
8 Interview with Georgia, Salvador, Bahia, Brazil, March 2006.
9 Interview with Nwafor, Salvador, Bahia, Brazil, September 2005.
10 Interview with Adebola, Salvador, Bahia, Brazil, August 2011.

11 Section 419 is the portion of the Nigerian penal code that deals specifically with fraud and counterfeiting, and so the term "419er" has become a popular slang term for con artists and swindlers of all sorts.

12 Interviews with Félix, Salvador, Bahia, Brazil, January 2006.

13 Abitoks specializes in selling West African handicrafts from Senegal, Ghana, and Nigeria. They usually stock a large array of drums, hand-woven and printed cloth, imitation *kente* cloth, and most importantly, Yoruba smocks or *gbariye*. The store prides itself on supplying smocks to a number of important *babalaôs* throughout the city who have been unable to make a trip to Nigeria to purchase their own.

3. Manifestations of Afro-Brazilian Blackness

1 "Reconnecting with Africa Forum," entitled "A África na visão dos Africanos e a África na visão dos Afro-Baianos,"Bloco Afro Ilê Aiyê, Salvador, Bahia, Brazil, November 2005.

2 Interview with A.C.A. and B.R., Salvador, Bahia, Brazil, November 2004. This history of club-membership criteria was confirmed to me in a number of conversations that I had with Ilê Aiyê members and is confirmed by Matory's (2005, 255) personal communication with Antônio Carlos dos Santos Vovô.

3 Presentation held in English for a visiting Nigerian journalist celebrating the music of Fela Kuti, Salvador, Bahia, Brazil, March 2005.

4 The February festival has become big business in Salvador and is considered by many in Brazil to be the "real" *carnaval* to attend in order to avoid the commercialism of Rio – many of the *blocos afros* in Salvador will charge locals and tourists alike upwards of one thousand dollars to participate in the street parade as a dancer or reveler.

5 Interview with Waldemar, drummer for Olodum, Salvador, Bahia, Brazil, November, 2004.

6 Interview with Francesca, drummer for Olodum, Salvador, Bahia, Brazil, November, 2004.

7 See http://www.ileaiyeoficial.com/acoes-sociais/escola-mae-hilda/

8 Interview with G.C.N, a former part-time teacher at Escola Ilê Aiyê, Salvador, Bahia, Brazil, October, 2004.

9 See http://www.ileaiyeoficial.com

10 During *carnaval*, Brahma, the largest producer of beer in Brazil, proudly advertises itself as the official beer of Ilê Aiyê and includes African imagery, pan-African colours, and cowrie shells in its advertisements.

11 Interview with Maria, a former member of the Opô Afonjá *terreiro* who has now left to start her own small *terreiro* in the neighbourhood of Brotas, Salvador, Bahia, Brazil, 25 September 2005.

12 Interview with Maria in the neighbourhood of Brotas, Salvador, Bahia, Brazil, 12 November 2005. Maria asked for anonymity for her *terreiro*.

13 Lebanese diaspora businesspeople have come to dominate much of the hotel, restaurant, and hospitality industry along the West African coast.

14 Interview with Emmanuel, Ouidah, Benin, 1 February 2003.

15 Interview with Anna, Ouidah, Benin, 1 February 2003.

16 Interview with Gregório, Salvador, Bahia, Brazil, 12 August 2005.

17 Ubiratan Castro de Araújo speaking at the África seminar, Teatro Vila Velha, Salvador, Bahia, Brazil, 16 November 2005.

18 Interview with Nelson, Campo Grande, Salvador, Bahia, Brazil, 16 November 2005.

19 Interview with Nelson, Marco, Paulinha and Denílson, Campo Grande, Salvador, Bahia, Brazil, 16 November 2005.

20 Interview with Nelson, Marco, and Denílson, Campo Grande, Salvador, Bahia, Brazil, 16 November 2005.

21 Discussant comments by Stephan Palmié at the 2007 Meeting of the Society for the Anthropology of Religion, 13–16 April, Phoenix, Arizona, for the panel "African Diasporic Religions: Tradition, Modernity and Post-Modernity." The improvised kind of "cooking" of cultural symbols and ideas that Palmié suggests would appear to be indebted, at least nominally, from one of Palmié's own intellectual antecedents in the area of Cuban Black studies: Fernando Ortiz and the notion of an *ajiaco cultural* or cultural stew.

22 There is an irony here, in that, from the perspective of an Africanist, *Umbanda* appears, in many ways, to be ontologically and epistemologically more "African." Although *Candomblé* – especially Mãe Stella's and Mestre Didi's so-called pure Nagô form – claims to be more authentically African in practice and in belief, its rigidity and emphasis on what they perceive as strict Yoruba dogma very much goes against the kind of flexible and dynamic nature found in many West African religious traditions. In its cultural permeability and heteroglossia of voices, *Umbanda*, it can be argued, is the more African form. Purity, as a concept, is anathema to most West African religious traditions.

23 Interview with schoolchildren outside Galeria Pierre Verger, Pelourinho, Salvador, Bahia, Brazil, December 2005. Conversation format of this interview does not facilitate presentation of original Portuguese.

24 ErêGege (Espaço de Reflexão Étnica e de Gênero) Religious tolerance seminar, Salvador, Bahia, Brazil, 8 October 2004.

25 Patrimônio da Bahia event at Ilê Axe Opô Aganjú, Lauro de Freitas, Bahia, Brazil, November, 2005.
26 Interview with G.C.N, a former part-time teacher at Escola Ilê Aiyê, Salvador, Bahia, Brazil, October 2004.
27 Interview with Aninha, member of *terreiro* Casa Branca, Salvador, Bahia, Brazil, December 2005.
28 *Acarajé* is an Afro-Brazilian culinary specialty made of a bean flour fritter, deep fried in palm oil, and served with shrimp, chili, cilantro, and other condiments. Most Brazilians see it as the food that best represents the cuisine of the Northeast state of Bahia, as it is commonly believed to be African in origin. Indeed, *acarajé* does owe much to the West African dish of *àkàrà*, a similar form of fritter common in Nigeria and a likely precursor to the *acarajé* of the slave period. Because of its African origins, *acarajé* is typically presented as an offering to the *orixás* in *terreiros*. Beyond the religious space of the *terreiro*, *acarajé* is sold on almost every street corner in Bahia by working-class women of all ages as quick street food, and it is consumed in large amounts by locals and tourists alike. The image of the *acarajé* seller – dressed in a flowing white dress elaborated with lace and beads – selling this so-called food of the gods is one of the most iconic images of Salvador. It is often used by tourist agencies and travel companies to depict the city as Black and African.
29 Interview with Maria, Pelourinho, Salvador, Bahia, Brazil, 30 March 2006.
30 The Centro Arquidiocesano de Articulação da Pastoral Afro (Archdiocese Center for the African Pastoral) or Pastoral Afro is an important outreach project of the Catholic Church that ministers specifically to Black communities and deals with Black issues. The Pastoral Afro is very much concerned with racism and fighting poverty in Black communities and has grown out of Brazil's liberation theology movement.
31 Interview with Maria, Salvador, Bahia, Brazil, 9 January 2006.
32 Group interview with associates of Ilê Aiyê, Salvador, Bahia, Brazil, 10 October 2005.
33 Interview with Georgia through email, 14 June 2007.
34 Interviews with Edmar, Salvador, Bahia, Brazil, 14 February 2006.
35 Interview with Marisol, Rodoviário, Salvador, Bahia, Brazil, 1 February 2006.

4. Blackness in the Bahaian Sertão

1 Incidentally, this *fazendeiro* had received money from the Interamerican Development Bank for protection of these very lands (Carvalho 1996a, 428).

2 Interview with Marcelo, Pelourinho, Salvador, Bahia, Brazil, December 2005.
3 *Jarê* is a form of Afro-Brazilian *orixá* religious practice that includes the veneration of Amerindian deities. *Jarê's* ritual style, Senna (1984, 2004) asserts, speaks more to the rough and hardscrabble life of the interior in that it elevates the Indian or *caboclo* spirits to the same level as African spirits.
4 Interview with Raimundo in Curuzu-Liberdade, Salvador, Bahia, Brazil, April 2005.
5 Interview with Carlos, Bom Jesus da Lapa, Bahia, Brazil, 9 January 2006.
6 These self-identified characteristics were provided in response to the question "How would you describe your racial background?"
7 Interview with Edson Dos Santos Ferreira about the Black community movements of Salvador, Bom Jesus da Lapa, Bahia, Brazil, 7 February 2006.
8 Interview with Edson, Carlos, and Antônio, Bom Jesus da Lapa, Bahia, Brazil, February 2006. Conversation format of this interview does not facilitate presentation of original Portuguese.
9 *Orfeu Negro* (1959), directed by Marcel Camus.

Bibliography

Amos, Alcione M., and Ebenezer Ayesu. 2002. "'I Am Brazilian': History of the Tabon, Afro-Brazilians in Accra, Ghana." *Transactions of the Historical Society of Ghana* 6: 35–58.

Anderson, Benedict. 2006. *Imagined Communities: Reflections on the Origin and Spread of Nationalism*. London: Verso. Original edition, 1983.

Anderson, Robert Nelson. 1996. "The Quilombo of Palmares: A New Overview of a Maroon State in Seventeenth-Century Brazil." *Journal of Latin American Studies* no. 28 (3): 545–66.

Andrews, George Reid. 2004. *Afro-Latin America, 1800–2000*. Oxford: Oxford University Press.

Anonymous. 1998. "The War against Palmares." In *The Brazil Reader*, edited by Robert M. Levine and John J. Crocitti, 125–30. Durham: Duke University Press. Original edition, 1675–78.

Asante, Molefi K. 1988. *Afrocentricity*. Trenton: Africa World Press.

Ayoh'Omidire, Félix. 2005. *Yorubanidade Mundializada: o Reinado da Oralitura Em Textos Yorubá – Nigerianos e Afro-Baianos Contemporâneos*. PhD Dissertation, Letters, Universidade Federal da Bahia, Salvador.

Babalola Yaï, Olabiyi. 1997. "Les 'Aguda' (Afro-Brésiliens) Du Golfe Du Bénin." *Lusotopie* (4): 275–84.

Bacelar, Jeferson. 2001. *A Hierarquia da Raças: Negroes e Brancos Em Salvador*. Rio de Janeiro: Pallas.

Bair, Barbara. 1994. "Pan-Africanism as Process: Adelaide Casely Hayford, Garveyism, and the Cultural Roots of Nationalism." In *Imagining Home: Class, Culture and Nationalism in the African Diaspora*, edited by Sidney J. Lemelle and Robin D. G. Kelley, 121–44. London: Verso.

Bairros, Luiza. 2008. "A Community of Destiny: New Configurations of Racial Politics in Brazil." *Souls* 10 (1): 50–3.

Bakhtin, M.M. 1981. "Discourse in the Novel." In *The Dialogic Imagination*, edited by Michael Holquist, 259–422. Austin: University of Texas Press.

Baptista, Karina Cunha. 2003. "O Diálogo dos Temps: História, Memória e Identidade nos Depoimentos Orais de Descendentes de Escravos Brasileiros." *Primeiros Escritos de Laboritório de História Oral e Imagem* 11: 1–23.

Barth, Fredrik. 1969. "Introduction." In *Ethnic Groups and Boundaries*, edited by Fredrik Barth, 9–38. Oslo: Universitetsforlaget.

Bastide, Roger. 1971. *African Civilizations in the New World*. New York: Harper and Row.

Beate de Yemonja, Mãe. 1996. *Caroço de Dendê: A Sabedoria de Terreiros*. Rio de Janeiro: Pallas.

Berlin, Ira. 1998. *Many Thousands Gone: The First Two Centuries of Slavery in North America*. Cambridge, MA: Belknap Press of Harvard University Press.

Birman, Patricia, and David Lehmann. 1999. "Religion and the Media in a Battle for Ideological Hegemony: The Universal Church of God and TV Globo in Brazil." *Bulletin of Latin American Research* 18 (2): 145–64.

Boddy, Janice Patricia. 1988. "Spirits and Selves in Northern Sudan: The Cultural Therapeutics of Possession and Trance." *American Ethnologist* 15 (1): 4–27.

Boddy, Janice Patricia. 1989. *Wombs and Alien Spirits: Women, Men, and the Zar Cult in Northern Sudan, New Directions in Anthropological Writing*. Madison: University of Wisconsin Press.

Bourguignon, Erika. 2004. "Suffering and Healing, Subordination and Power: Women and Possession Trance." *Ethos* 32 (4): 557–74.

Boyer-Araújo, Véronique. 1993. *Femmes et Cultes de Possession Au Brésil: Les Compagnons Invisibles, Connaissance Des Hommes*. Paris: Editions L'Harmattan.

Brown, Diana DeG. 1999. "Power, Invention, and the Politics of Race." In *Black Brazil: Culture, Identity, and Social Mobilsation*, edited by Larry Crook and Randal Johnson, 213–36. Los Angeles: UCLA Latin American Center Publications.

Bruner, Edward M. 1996. "Tourism in Ghana: The Representation of Slavery and the Return of the Black Diaspora." *American Anthropologist* 98 (2): 290–304.

Burdick, John. 1998a. *Blessed Anastácia: Women, Race, and Popular Christianity in Brazil*. New York: Routledge.

Burdick, John. 1998b. "The Lost Constituency of Brazil's Black Movements." *Latin American Perspectives* 25 (1): 136–55.

Butler, Kim D. 1998. "Afterword: Ginga Baiana – the Politics of Race, Class, Culture, and Power in Salvador, Bahia." In *Afro-Brazilian Culture and Politics: Bahia, 1790s–1990s*, edited by Hendrik Kraay, 158–76. Armonk: M.E. Sharpe.

Calógeras, João Pandiá. 1930. *A Formação Historica do Brasil*. Rio de Janeiro: Pimenta de Mello.

Capone, Stefania. 2004. *A Busca da África no Candomblé*. Translated by Procópio Abreu. Rio de Janeiro: Pallas Contra Capa. Original edition, 1999.

Capone, Stefania. 2010. *Searching for Africa in Brazil: Power and Tradition in Candomblé*. Durham: Duke University Press. http://dx.doi.org/10.1215/9780822392040

Carneiro, Edison. 1946. *Guerras de los Palmares. 1*. México: Fondo de Cultura Económica.

Carneiro, Edison. 1948. *Candomblés de Bahia*. Salvador: Secretaria de Educação e Saúde.

Carvalho, José Jorge. 1996a. "Globalization, Traditions and Simultaneity of Presences." In *Cultural Pluralism, Identity, and Globalization*, edited by Luiz E. Soares, 414–58. Rio de Janeiro: UNESCO/ISSC/EDUCAM.

Carvalho, José Jorge. 1996b. "Prefácio." In *Quilombo do Rio das Rãs: Historias, Tradições, Lutas*, edited by José Jorge Carvalho, 7–10. Salvador: EDUFBA.

Castro de Araújo, Ubiratan. 1992. *Le Politique Et L' Économique Dans Une Société Bahia, 1820 À 1889*. Lille: Université de Lille.

Castro de Araújo, Ubiratan. 1999. *Ii CentenáRio da Sedição de 1798 na Bahia*. Salvador: Academia de Letras da Bahia and O Governo da Bahia, Secretaria da Cultura e Turismo.

Castro de Araújo, Ubiratan. 2000. Reparação Moral, Responsabilidade Pública e Direito À Igualdade do Cidadão Negro no Brasil. Paper read at Seminário "Racismo, Xenofobia e Intolerância", 20/11/2000, at Salvador.

Castro de Araújo, Ubiratan. 2001. *A Guerra da Bahia*. Salvador: Centro de Estudos Afro-Orientais.

Castro de Araújo, Ubiratan. 2006. *Sete Histórias de Negro*. Salvador: Edufba.

Chapman, Charles E. 1918. "Palmares: The Negro Numantia." *The Journal of Negro History* 3 (1): 29–32.

Chaudenson, Robert, Salikoko S. Mufwene, and Sheri Pargman. 2001. *Creolization of Language and Culture*. London: Routledge.

Clarke, Kamari Maxine. 2002. "Governmentality, Modernity and the Historical Politics of Oyo-Hegemony in Yoruba Transnational Revivalism." *Anthropologica* 44 (2): 271–93.

Clifford, James. 1986. "Introduction: Partial Truths." In *Writing Culture: The Poetics and Politics of Ethnography*, edited by James Clifford and George E. Marcus, 1–26. Berkeley: University of California Press.

Clifford, James. 1992. "Travelling Cultures." In *Cultural Studies*, edited by Lawrence Grossberg, Cary Nelson, and Paula A. Treichler, 96–116. New York: Routledge.

Clifford, James. 1994. "Diasporas." *Cultural Anthropology* 9 (3): 302–38.

Clifford, James. 1997. *Routes: Travel and Translation in the Late Twentieth Century.* Cambridge: Harvard University Press.

Clifford, James, and George E. Marcus. 1986. *Writing Culture: The Poetics and Politics of Ethnography.* Berkeley: University of California Press.

Collins, John. 2008. "But What If I Should Need to Defecate in Your Neighborhood, Madame?: Empire, Redemption, and the Tradition of the Oppressed in a Brazilian World Heritage Site." *Cultural Anthropology* 23 (2): 279–328.

Corin, Ellen. 1979. "A Possession Psychotherapy in an Urban Setting: Zebola in Kinshasa." *Social Science and Medicine* 13B (4): 327–38.

Crehan, Kate A.F. 2002. *Gramsci, Culture and Anthropology.* London: Pluto.

Crist, Raymond E. 1944. "Cultural Crosscurrents in the Valley of the Rio Sao Francisco." *Geographical Review* 34 (4): 587–612.

Cullen, Countee. 1925. *Color.* New York: Harper and Brothers.

Da Cunha, Euclides. 1902. *Os Sertões: Campanha de Canudos.* Rio de Janeiro: Laemmert.

DaMatta, Roberto. 1984. "On Carnaval, Informality and Magic: A Point of View from Brazil." In *Text, Play and Story: The Construction and Reconstruction of Self and Society,* edited by Edward M. Bruner, 230–46. Washington, DC: American Ethnological Society.

Dantas, Beatriz Góis. 1988. *Vovó Nagô e Papai Branco: Usos e Abusos da Africa no Brasil.* Rio de Janeiro: Graal.

Dantas, Beatriz Góis. 2002. "Nanã de Aracaju: Trajetória de Uma Mãe Plural." In *Memória Afro-Brasileiro: Caminhos de Alma,* edited by Vagner Gonçalves da Silva, 89–131. São Paulo: Selo Negro.

Davis, Arthur P. 1953. "The Alien-and-Exile Theme in Countee Cullen's Racial Poems." *Phylon* 14 (4): 390–400.

De Santana Pinho, Patricia. 2005. "Descentrando os Estados Unidos nos Estudos Sobre Negritude no Brasil." *Revista Brasileira de Ciências Sociais* 20 (59): 37–50.

Diggs, Irene. 1953. "Zumbí and the Republic of Os Palmares." *Phylon* 14 (1): 62–70.

Do Amaral Lapa, José Roberto. 1980. *Modos de Produção e Realidade Brasileira.* Petropolis: Vozes.

Do Nascimento, Abdias. 1980. "Quilombismo: An Afro-Brazilian Political Alternative." *Journal of Black Studies* 11 (2): 141–78.

Doria, Siglia Z. 1996. "O Processo de Ocupação do da Região do Rio das Rãs." In *Quilombo do Rio das Rãs: Historias, Tradições, Lutas,* edited by José Jorge Carvalho, 83–114. Salvador: EDUFBA.

Dos Santos, M. Desoscordes. 2003. *Contos Negros da Bahia e Contos de Nagô.* Salvador: Corrupio.

Dzidzienyo, Anani. 1999. "Africa-Brazil: "Ex Africa Semper Aliquid Novi"?" In *Black Brazil: Culture, Identity, and Social Mobilization*, edited by Larry Crook and Randal Johnson, 105–42. Los Angeles: UCLA Latin American Center Publications.

Edge, Hoyt. 1996. "Possession in Two Balinese Trance Ceremonies." *Anthropology of Consciousness* 7 (4): 1–8.

Ferreira, Roquinaldo. 2007. "Atlantic Microhistories: Mobility, Personal Ties, and Slaving in the Black Atlantic World (Angola and Brazil)." In *Cultures of the Lusophone Black Atlantic*, edited by Nancy Priscilla Naro, Roger Sansi-Roca, and David H. Treece, 99–128. New York: Palgrave Macmillan.

Foucault, Michel. 1978. *The History of Sexuality*. 1st American ed. New York: Pantheon Books.

Foundation for Research in the Afro-American Creative Arts. 1977. "Festac '77." *The Black Perspective in Music* 5 (1): 104–17.

Fox, Richard G. 1991. "Introduction." In *Recapturing Anthropology: Working in the Present*, edited by Richard G. Fox, 1–16. Santa Fe: School of American Research Press.

Freitas, Décio. 1973. *Palmares: A Guerra dos Escravos*. Porto Alegre: Editora Movimento.

French, Jan Hoffman. 2006. "Buried Alive: Imagining Africa in the Brazilian Northeast." *American Ethnologist* 33 (3): 340–60.

Freyre, Gilberto.1933. *Casa-grande & Senzala: formação da família brasileira sob o regime de economia patriarchal*. Rio de Janeiro: Maia and Schmidt.

Fry, Peter. 1982. *Para Inglês Ver: Identidade e Política na Cultura Brasileira*. Rio de Janeiro: Zahar Editores.

FUNASA. 2008. *Quilombolas de Rio das Rãs Recebem Visita de Representantes do Banco Mundial*. FUNASA. Retrieved 14 April 2014 from http://www.funasa .gov.br/site/wp-content/files_mf/boletim_vale_javari.pdf

Geertz, Clifford. 1973. *The Interpretation of Cultures*. New York: Basic Books.

Gilroy, Paul. 1987. *"There Ain't No Black in the Union Jack": The Cultural Politics of Race and Nation*. London: Hutchinson.

Gilroy, Paul. 1993. *The Black Atlantic: Modernity and Double Consciousness*. Cambridge, MA: Harvard University Press.

Goffman, Erving. 1974. *Frame Analysis: An Essay on the Organization of Experience*. Cambridge, MA: Harvard University Press.

Gomez, Michael A. 1998. *Exchanging Our Country Marks: The Transformation of African Identities in the Colonial and Antebellum South*. Chapel Hill: University of North Carolina Press.

Gomez, Michael A. 2005. *Reversing Sail: A History of the African Diaspora, New Approaches to African History*. Cambridge: Cambridge University Press.

Gomez, Michael A. 2006. "Diasporic Africa: A View from History." In *Diasporic Africa: A Reader*, edited by Michael A. Gomez, 1–23. New York: New York University Press.

Gonçalves da Silva, Vagner. 1995. *Orixás da Metrópole*. Petrópolis: Vozes.

Gramsci, Antonio. 1971. *Selections from the Prison Notebooks of Antonio Gramsci*. New York: International Publishers.

Gramsci, Antonio. 1985. *Selections from Cultural Writings*. Cambridge, MA: Harvard University Press.

Greenfield, Gerald Michael. 1993. "Sertao and Sertanejo: An Interpretive Context for Canudos." *Luso-Brazilian Review* 30 (2): 35–46.

Hall, Gwendolyn Midlo. 2005. *Slavery and African Ethnicities in the Americas: Restoring the Links*. Chapel Hill: University of North Carolina Press.

Halperin, Daniel. 1995. "Memory and "Consciousness" in an Evolving Brazilian Possession Religion." *Anthropology of Consciousness* 6 (4): 1–17.

Hanchard, Michael George. 1993. "Racial Consciousness and Afro-Diasporic Experiences: Antonio Gramsci Reconsidered." *Socialism and Democracy* 7 (3): 83–106.

Hanchard, Michael George. 1994. *Orpheus and Power: The Movimento Negro of Rio de Janeiro and São Paulo, Brazil, 1945–1988*. Princeton: Princeton University Press.

Handler, Richard. 1993. "Fieldwork in Quebec: Scholarly Reviews, and Anthropological Dialogues." In *When They Read What We Write: The Politics of Ethnography*, edited by Caroline B. Brettell, 67–74. Westport: Bergin and Garvey.

Hannerz, Ulf. 1987. "The World in Creolisation." *Africa: Journal of the International African Institute* 57 (4): 546–59.

Hasty, Jennifer. 2002. "Rites of Passage, Routes of Redemption: Emancipation Tourism and the Wealth of Culture." *Africa Today* 49 (3): 47–76.

Hayes, Kelly E. 2007. "Black Magic and the Academy: Macumba and Afro-Brazilian "Orthodoxies"." *History of Religions* 46 (4): 283–315. http://dx.doi.org/10.1086/518811

Hennessy, C.A.M. 1978. *The Frontier in Latin American History*. London: E. Arnold.

Herskovits, Melville J. 1930. "The Negro in the New World: The Statement of a Problem." *American Anthropologist* 32 (1): 145–55.

Herskovits, Melville J. 1941. *The Myth of the Negro Past*. New York: Harper.

Hess, David J. 1989. "Disobsessing Disobsession: Religion, Ritual, and the Social Sciences in Brazil." *Cultural Anthropology* 4 (2): 183–92.

Hobsbawm, Eric, and Terence Ranger. 1983. *The Invention of Tradition*. Cambridge: Cambridge University Press.

Howard, Philip A. 1999. "Creolization and Integration: The Development of a Political Culture among the Pan-Afro-Cuban Benevolent Societies." In *Crossing Boundaries: Comparative History of Black People in Diaspora*, edited by Darlene Clark Hine and Jaqueline McLeod, 134–58. Bloomington: Indiana University Press.

Hymes, Dell H. 1971. *Pidginization and Creolization of Languages; Proceedings of a Conference Held at the University of the West Indies, Mona, Jamaica, April, 1968*. Cambridge: University Press.

Ilê Aiyê. 2001. *África: Ventre Fértil do Mundo (Caderno de Educação do Ilê Aiyê), Projeto de Extensão Pedagógica*. Salvador: Ilê Aiyê.

Instituto Brasileiro de Geografia e Estatística (IBGE). 2010. *Censo Demográfico 2010*. Rio de Janeiro: Instituto Brasileiro de Geografia e Estatística.

James, Preston E. 1948. "The Sao Francisco Basin: A Brazilian Sertao." *Geographical Review* 38 (4): 658–61.

Johnson, Paul C. 1997. "Kicking, Stripping, and Re-Dressing a Saint in Black: Vision of Public Space in Brazil's Holy War." *History of Religions* 37 (2): 122–40.

Jourdan, C. 1991. "Pidgins and Creoles: The Blurring of Categories." *Annual Review of Anthropology* 20 (1): 187–209.

Karasch, Mary C. 2002. "Zumbí of Palmares: Challenging the Portuguese Colonial Order." In *The Human Tradition in Latin Amerrica*, edited by Kenneth J. Andrien, 104–20. Wilmington: Scholarly Resources.

Knörr, Jacqueline. 2008. "Towards Conceptualizing Creolization and Creole-ness." *Max Plank Institute for Social Anthropology Working Papers* (100): 1–17.

Lake, Obiagele. 1995. "Toward a Pan-African Identity: Diaspora African Repatriates in Ghana." *Anthropological Quarterly* 68 (1): 21–36.

Lambek, Michael. 1980. "Spirits and Spouses: Possession as a System of Communication among the Malagasy Speakers of Mayotte." *American Ethnologist* 7 (2): 318–31.

Landes, Ruth. 1947. *The City of Women*. New York: Macmillan.

Leach, E.R. 1954. *Political Systems of Highland Burma: A Study of Kachin Social Structure*. London: The Athalone Press.

Lehmann, David. 1998. "Fundamentalism and Globalism." *Third World Quarterly* 19 (4): 607–34.

Lehmann, David. 2001. "Charisma and Possession in Africa and Brazil." *Theory, Culture & Society* 18 (5): 45–74.

Lewis, I.M. 1971. *Ecstatic Religion; an Anthropological Study of Spirit Possession and Shamanism, Pelican Anthropology Library*. Harmondsworth: Penguin Books. http://dx.doi.org/10.4324/9780203241080

Lewis, I.M. 2003. "Trance, Possession, Shamanism and Sex." *Anthropology of Consciousness* 14 (1): 20–39.

Lombardi, Mary. 1975. "The Frontier in Brazilian History: An Historiograph-
   ical Essay." *The Pacific Historical Review* 44 (4): 437–57.
Matory, J. Lorand. 1999. "The English Professors of Brazil: On the Diasporic
   Roots of the Yorùbá Nation." *Comparative Studies in Society and History* 41
   (1): 72–103.
Matory, J. Lorand. 2001. "The 'Cult of Nations' and the Ritualization of Their
   Purity." *The South Atlantic Quarterly* 100 (1): 171–214.
Matory, J. Lorand. 2005. *Black Atlantic Religion: Tradition, Transnationalism, and
   Matriarchy in the Afro-Brazilian Candomblé.* Princeton: Princeton University
   Press.
Matory, J. Lorand. 2006. "The 'New World' Surrounds an Ocean: Theorizing
   the Live Dialogue between African and African American Cultures." In
   Afro-Atlantic Dialogues: Anthropology in the Diaspora, edited by Kevin A.
   Yelvington, 151–93. Santa Fe: School of American Research Press.
McCreery, David. 2006. *Frontier Goiás, 1822–1889.* Stanford: Stanford Univer-
   sity Press.
Menchen, Denise. 2008. "Evangélicos São Acusados de Quebrar Centro de
   Umbanda no Rio." *Folha de São Paulo,* 6 March, 2.
Mintz, Sidney Wilfred. 1974. *Caribbean Transformations.* Chicago: Aldine.
Mintz, Sidney Wilfred, and Richard Price. 1976. *An Anthropological Approach to
   the Afro-American Past: A Caribbean Perspective.* Philadelphia: Institute for the
   Study of Human Issues.
Morgan, Philip D. 1998. *Slave Counterpoint: Black Culture in the Eighteenth-
   Century Chesapeake and Lowcountry.* Chapel Hill: University of North
   Carolina Press.
Mudimbe, V.Y. 1988. *The Invention of Africa: Gnosis, Philosophy, and the
   Order of Knowledge, African Systems of Thought: African Systems of Thought.*
   Bloomington: Indiana University Press.
Mufwene, Salikoko S. 1998. *African-American English: Structure, History, and
   Use.* London: Routledge.
Nishida, Mieko. 2003. *Slavery and Identity: Ethnicity, Gender, and Race in
   Salvador, Brazil, 1808–1888, Blacks in the Diaspora.* Bloomington: Indiana
   University Press.
Ojo-Ade, Femi. 1999. "Black Brazil: African Notes on a New Negritude." In
   Black Brazil: Culture, Identity, and Social Mobilsation, edited by Larry Crook and
   Randal Johnson, 175–98. Los Angeles: UCLA Latin American Publications.
Olodum. 2008. *A Escola Mirim do Olodum.* Retrieved 12 March 2008 from
   http://www2.uol.com.br/olodum/escola.htm
Palmares, Funação Cultural. 2007. *Fundação Cultural Palmares 2007.* Retrieved
   5 September 2007 from http://www.palmares.gov.br/

Palmié, Stephan. 1995. "Against Syncretism: 'Africanizing' and 'Cubanizing' Discourses in North American Òrìsà Worship." In *Counterworks: Managing the Diversity of Knowledge*, edited by Richard Fardon, 73–104. London: Routledge. http://dx.doi.org/10.4324/9780203450994_chapter_4

Palmié, Stephan. 2006. "Creolization and Its Discontents." *Annual Review of Anthropology* 35 (1): 433–56.

Palmié, Stephan. 2007. "O Trabalho Cultural da Globalização Iorubá." *Religião & Sociedade* 27: 77–113.

Parés, Luis Nicolau. 2001. "The Jeje in the Tambor de Mina of Maranhão and in the Candomblé of Bahia." *Slavery and Abolition* 22 (1): 83–90.

Parés, Luis Nicolau. 2004. "The "Nagôization" Process in Bahian Candomblé." In *The Yoruba Diaspora in the Atlantic World*, edited by Toyin Falola and Matt D. Childs, 185–208. Bloomington: Indiana University Press.

Price, Richard. 1975. *Saramaka Social Structure: Analysis of a Maroon society in Surinam*. Río Piedras: Institute of Caribbean Studies, University of Puerto Rico.

Price, Richard. 1983. *First-Time: The Historical Vision of an African American People*. Chicago: University of Chicago Press.

Price, Richard. 1996. "Introduction." In *Maroon Societies: Rebel Slave Communities in the Americas*, edited by Richard Price, 1–30. Baltimore: Johns Hopkins University Press.

Price, Richard. 1999. "Reinventando a História dos Quilombos: Rasuras e Confabulações." *Afro-Ásia* 23: 239–65.

Price, Richard. 2006. "On the Miracle of Creolization." In *Afro-Atlantic Dialogues: Anthropology in the Diaspora*, edited by Kevin A. Yelvington, 115–48. Santa Fe: School of American Research Press.

Price, Richard. 2008. *Travels with Tooy: History, Memory, and the African American Imagination*. Chicago: University of Chicago Press.

Price, Richard, and Sally Price. 1997. "Shadowboxing in the Mangrove." *Cultural Anthropology* 12 (1): 3–36.

Price, Sally. 2006. "Seeming Connections: Artworlds of the African Diaspora." In *Afro-Atlantic Dialogues: Anthropology in the Diaspora*, edited by Kevin A. Yelvington, 83–114. Santa Fe: School of American Research Press.

Ramos, A. 1934. *O negro Brasileiro: Ethnographia, Religiosa e Psychanalyse*. Rio de Janeiro: Civilização Brasileira.

Rausch, Jane M. 2008. "Frontier Theory as an Explanatory Tool for Brazilian History: A Viable Construct?" *Latin American Research Review* 43 (1): 201–7.

Reis, João José. 2001. "Candomblé in Nineteenth Century Bahia: Priest, Followers, Clients." *Slavery and Abolition* 22 (1): 116–34.

Reis, João José. 2003. *Rebelião Escrava no Brasil: A Historia do Levante dos Malês Em 1835*. São Paulo: Companhia das Letras.

Rodrigues, Nina R. 1932. *Os Africanos no Brasil.* São Paulo: Companhia Editora Nacional.

Roosevelt, Theodore. 1914. *Through the Brazilian Wilderness.* New York: Charles Scribner's Sons.

Ross, Doran H. 1998. *Wrapped in Pride: Ghanaian Kente and African American Identity, Ucla Fowler Musuem of Cultural History Textile Series.* Los Angeles: UCLA Fowler Musuem of Cultural History.

Sansone, Livio. 2004. *Negritude Sem Etnicidade.* Salvador, Rio de Janeiro: EDUFBA/Pallas.

Schwartz, Stuart B. 1970. "The "Mocambo": Slave Resistance in Colonial Bahia." *Journal of Social History* 3 (4): 313–33.

Scolese, Eduardo. 2008. *Demarcações de Áreas de Quilombos São Suspensas.* Grupo Folha.Retrieved 10 March 2008 from http://www1.folha.uol.com. br/folha/brasil/ult96u380309.shtml

Scott, David. 1991. "That Event, This Memory: Notes on the Anthropology of African Diasporas in the New World." *Diaspora: A Journal of Transnational Studies* 1 (3): 261–84.

Scott, James C. 1985. *Weapons of the Weak: Everyday Forms of Peasant Resistance.* New Haven: Yale University Press.

Segato, R.L. 1998. "The Color-Blind Subject of Myth; Or, Where to Find Africa in the Nation." *Annual Review of Anthropology* 27 (1): 129–51. http://dx.doi .org/10.1146/annurev.anthro.27.1.129

Selka, Stephen. 2007. *Religion and the Politics of Ethnic Identity in Bahia, Brazil, New World Diasporas.* Gainesville: University Press of Florida. http://dx.doi.org/10.5744/florida/9780813031712.001.0001

Senna, Ronaldo Salles de. 1984. *Jarê: Manifestações Religiosas na Chapada Diamantina.* PhD dissertation, Letras e Ciências Humanas, Universidade de São Paulo, São Paulo.

Senna, Ronaldo Salles de. 2004. "Jarê, a Religião da Chapada Diamantina." In *Encantaria Brasileira,* edited by Reginaldo Prandi, 74–119. Rio de Janeiro: Pallas.

Sheller, Mimi. 2003. *Consuming the Caribbean: From Arawaks to Zombies, International Library of Sociology.* London: Routledge.

Sheriff, Robin E. 2001. *Dreaming Equality: Color, Race, and Racism in Urban Brazil.* New Brunswick, NJ: Rutgers University Press.

Singleton, Theresa A. 2006. "African Diaspora Archaeology in Dialogue." In *Afro-Atlantic Dialogues: Anthropology in the Diaspora,* edited by Kevin A. Yelvington, 249–88. Santa Fe: School of American Research Press.

Skidmore, Thomas E. 1993. *Black into White: Race and Nationality in Brazilian Thought.* Durham: Duke University Press. http://dx.doi.org/10.1215/ 9780822381761

Smith, M.G. 1957. "The African Heritage in the Caribbean." In *Caribbean Studies: A Symposium*, edited by Vera Rubin, 34–46. Seattle: University of Washington Press.

Stoller, Paul. 2002. *Money Has no Smell: The Africanization of New York City.* Chicago: University of Chicago Press. http://dx.doi.org/10.7208/chicago/9780226775265.001.0001

Stoller, Paul. 2003. "Marketing Afrocentricity: West African Trade Networks in North America." In *New African Diasporas*, edited by Khalid Koser, 71–94. London: Routledge.

Sylvanus, Nina. 2007. "The Fabric of Africanity: Tracing the Global Threads of Authenticity." *Anthropological Theory* 7 (2): 201–16. http://dx.doi.org/10.1177/1463499607077298

Tedlock, Dennis, and Bruce Mannheim. 1995. *The Dialogic Emergence of Culture.* Urbana: University of Illinois Press.

Thomas, Deborah A., Tina M. Campt, Maureen Mahon, and Lena Sawyer. 2006. "Diasporic Hegemonies: Slavery, Memory, and Geneologies of Diaspora." *Transforming Anthropology* 14 (2): 163–72.

Thomas, Deborah A., Tina M. Campt, Maureen Mahon, and Lena Sawyer. 2007. "Diasporic Hegemonies: Popular Culture and Transnational Blackness." *Transforming Anthropology* 15 (1): 50–62.

Thomason, Sarah Grey, and Terrence Kaufman. 1988. *Language Contact, Creolization, and Genetic Linguistics.* Berkeley: University of California Press.

Thompson, K. 2003. "Forms of Resistance: Foucault on Tactical Reversal and Self-formation." *Continental Philosophy Review* 36 (2): 113–38.

Trouillot, Michel-Rolph. 1991. "Anthropology and the Savage Slot." In *Recapturing Anthropology: Working in the Present*, edited by Richard G. Fox, 17–44. Santa Fe: School of American Research Press.

Trouillot, Michel-Rolph. 1998. "Cultures on the Edges: Caribbean Creolization in Historical Context." In *From the Margins: Historical Anthropology and Its Futures*, edited by Axel Brian Keityh, 189–210. Durham: Duke University Press.

Turner, Frederick Jackson. 1928. *The Frontier in American History.* New York: H. Holt and Company. Original edition, 1893.

UNESCO. 2008. *The Slave Route: Unesco Culture Sector.*Retrieved 13 May 2008 from http://www.unesco.org/new/en/culture/themes/dialogue/the-slave-route

Van De Port, Mattijs. 2005. "Circling around the Really Real: Spirit Possession Ceremonies and the Search for Authenticity in Bahian Candomblé." *Ethos* 33 (2): 149–79.

Véran, Jean François. 2000. "Rio das Rãs Memória de Uma 'Communidade Remanescente de Quilombo.'" *Afro-Ásia* 21–22: 295–323.

Véran, Jean François. 2002. "Quilombos and Land Rights in Contemprary Brazil." *Cultural Survival Quarterly* 25 (4): 20.

Verger, Fundação Pierre. 2007. *Fundação Pierre Verger 2007*. Retrieved 12 April 2014 from http://www.pierreverger.org/fpv/index.php/br/a-fundacao/quem-somos/objetivos-e-historicohttp://www.pierreverger.org/en/index.htm

Verger, Pierre. 2002. *Fluxo e Refluxo do Trafico de Escravos Entre o Golfo do Benin e a Bahia de Todos os Santos dos Séculos Xvii a Xix*. Translated by Tasso Ganzanis. Salvador: Corrupio. Original edition, 1968.

Vincent, Joan. 1991. "Engaging Historicism." In *Recapturing Anthropology: Working in the Present*, edited by Richard G. Fox, 45–58. Santa Fe: School of American Research Press.

Wade, Peter. 1986. "Patterns of Race in Colombia." *Bulletin of Latin American Research* 5 (2): 1–19.

Wade, Peter. 1993. "'Race,' Nature and Culture." *Man* 28 (1): 17–34.

Wade, Peter. 1995. "The Cultural Politics of Blackness in Colombia." *American Ethnologist* 22 (2): 341–57.

Wade, Peter. 1999. "Working Culture: Making Cultural Identities in Cali, Colombia." *Current Anthropology* 40 (4): 449–71.

Wade, Peter. 2006. "Understanding 'Africa' and 'Blackness' in Colombia: Music and the Politics of Culture." In *Afro-Atlantic Dialogues: Anthropology in the Diaspora*, edited by Kevin A. Yelvington, 351–78. Santa Fe: School of American Research Press.

Wafer, James William. 1991. *The Taste of Blood: Spirit Possession in Brazilian Candomblé*. Philadelphia: University of Pennsylvania Press.

Wainwright, Joel. 2010. "On Gramsci's 'Conceptions of the World.'" *Transactions of the Institute of British Geographers* 35 (4): 507–21.

Watson, Graham. 1987. "Make Me Reflexive, but Not Yet: Strategies for Managing Essential Reflexivity in Ethnographic Discourse." *Journal of Anthropological Research* 43 (1): 29–41.

Weber, Max. 1915. "Religious Rejections of the World and Their Directions." In *From Max Weber: Essays in Sociology*, edited by H.H. Gerth and C.W. Mills, 323–59. Oxford: Oxford University Press.

Wesolowski, Katya. 2006. "A Diasporic Practice Goes Back to Africa." *Anthropology News* 47 (5): 27–8.

West, Cornel. 1990. "The New Cultural Politics of Difference." *October* 53: 93–109.

Wyllie, Robert W. 1994. "Gods, Locals, and Strangers: The Effutu Aboakyer as Visitor Attraction." *Current Anthropology* 35 (1): 78–81.

Yelvington, Kevin A. 2001. "The Anthropology of Afro-Latin America and the Caribbean: Diasporic Dimensions." *Annual Review of Anthropology* 30 (1): 227–60. http://dx.doi.org/10.1146/annurev.anthro.30.1.227

Yelvington, Kevin A. 2006a. "Introduction." In *Afro-Atlantic Dialogues: Anthropology in the Diaspora*, edited by Kevin A. Yelvington, 3–32. Santa Fe: School of American Research Press.

Yelvington, Kevin A. 2006b. "The Invention of Africa in Latin America and the Caribbean: Political Discourse and the Anthropological Praxis, 1920–1940." In *Afro-Atlantic Dialogues: Anthropology in the Diaspora*, edited by Kevin A. Yelvington, 35–82. Santa Fe: School of American Research Press.

Index

ANTHROPOLOGICAL HORIZONS

Editor: Michael Lambek, University of Toronto

Published to date:

An Irish Working Class: Explorations in Political Economy and Hegemony, 1800–1950 / Marilyn Silverman (2001)

The Double Twist: From Ethnography to Morphodynamics / Edited by Pierre Maranda (2001)

The House of Difference: Cultural Politics and National Identity in Canada / Eva Mackey (2002)

Writing and Colonialism in Northern Ghana: The Encounter between the LoDagaa and the 'World on Paper,' 1892–1991 / Sean Hawkins (2002)

Guardians of the Transcendent: An Ethnography of a Jain Ascetic Community / Anne Vallely (2002)

The Hot and the Cold: Ills of Humans and Maize in Native Mexico / Jacques M. Chevalier and Andrés Sánchez Bain (2003)

Figured Worlds: Ontological Obstacles in Intercultural Relations / Edited by John Clammer, Sylvie Poirier, and Eric Schwimmer (2004)

Revenge of the Windigo: The Construction of the Mind and Mental Health of North American Aboriginal Peoples / James B. Waldram (2004)

The Cultural Politics of Markets: Economic Liberalization and Social Change in Nepal / Katherine Neilson Rankin (2004)

A World of Relationships: Itineraries, Dreams, and Events in the Australian Western Desert / Sylvie Poirier (2005)

The Politics of the Past in an Argentine Working-Class Neighbourhood / Lindsay DuBois (2005)

Youth and Identity Politics in South Africa, 1990–1994 / Sibusisiwe Nombuso Dlamini (2005)

Maps of Experience: The Anchoring of Land to Story in Secwepemc Discourse / Andie Diane Palmer (2005)

Beyond Bodies: Rain-Making and Sense-Making in Tanzania / Todd Sanders (2008)

We Are Now a Nation: Croats between 'Home' and 'Homeland' / Daphne N. Winland (2008)

Kaleidoscopic Odessa: History and Place in Post-Soviet Ukraine / Tanya Richardson (2008)

Invaders as Ancestors: On the Intercultural Making and Unmaking of Spanish Colonialism in the Andes / Peter Gose (2008)

From Equality to Inequality: Social Change among Newly Sedentary Lanoh Hunter-Gatherer Traders of Peninsular Malaysia / Csilla Dallos (2011)

Rural Nostalgias and Transnational Dreams: Identity and Modernity among Jat Sikhs / Nicola Mooney (2011)

Dimensions of Development: History, Community, and Change in Allpachico, Peru / Susan Vincent (2012)